IMPUNITY
BERLUSCONI'S GOAL AND ITS CONSEQUENCES

SECOND EDITION

CHARLES YOUNG

THE HEADINGTON PRESS
www.headingtonpress.com

Published by The Headington Press, 2011
www.headingtonpress.com

© Charles Young 2011
The moral rights of the author have been asserted.

ISBN 978-0-9565461-1-1

Cover photo by Jewel Samad
The author and publisher would like to thank Getty Images, ANSA and Il Vernacoliere for permission to reproduce photographs, Faber and Faber for permission to reproduce a short poem by John Betjeman, and Oxford Economics for the data used in Chapter 5 and the chart opposite.

Designed by Andrew Magee Design, Banbury
Printed by SRP, Exeter

Growth in GDP per Head
■ Berlusconi Years ● Pre-Berlusconi Years

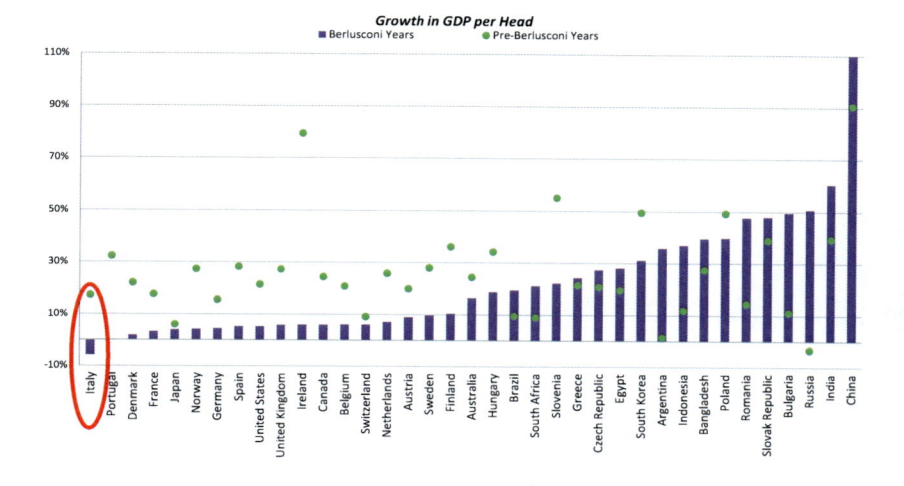

Source: Oxford Economics

"Charles Young's *Impunity* is an important contribution to the literature on Berlusconi – and not only that which is available in English. As an economist, Young has focused on an aspect which is as important as it is under-reported: the genuinely disastrous performance of the Italian economy during Berlusconi's long reign. Elected as an economic miracle-worker, Berlusconi promised to bring the rest of the country the kind of prosperity he himself has enjoyed. Young shows very clearly that in this area – more importantly than in the many recent sex scandals that dog Berlusconi – the Emperor has no clothes."

Alexander Stille, author of *The Sack of Rome*.

TABLE OF CONTENTS

CAST LIST 7
PREFACE TO SECOND EDITION 11
INTRODUCTION 13

PART I:
HOW SILVIO BERLUSCONI ACHIEVED POWER – AND WHY 28

CHAPTER 1: ECONOMIC POWER 29
    The Banca Rasini 29
    The Building Tycoon 32
    The Landed Gentleman 35
    The Return of Dell'Utri 37
    From Edilnord to Fininvest 38
    The Media Tycoon 42
    From Competitor to Monopolist 44
    Other business interests 48
    A Second Household 49

CHAPTER 2: POLITICAL COLLAPSE 51
    Tangentopoli 51
    Organisations in search of new political patrons 55
    Berlusconi enters politics 55
    The first Berlusconi government 64

CHAPTER 3: THE SCENT OF MAFIA 67
    The Mangano Relationship 67
    The Bontate Years 71
    The Riina Years 74
    Paolo Borsellino's Last Interview 76
    New Political Horizons 77
    A Verdict on the Verdict 82
    Scraps of Letters 83
    Marcello's Strange Behaviour 84

PART II:
WHAT SILVIO BERLUSCONI DID WITH POWER – AND WHAT IT DID TO HIM 87

CHAPTER 4: BERLUSCONI'S LEGAL PROBLEMS 89
- Outline of the Cases 90
- Some Peculiarities of Italian Criminal Law 91
- Early cases 92
- The P2 Libel Case 93
- Investigations during Tangentopoli 95
- The Mondadori Affair 96
- The Lentini Case 98
- Cases Connected with the Offshore Empire 99
- All Iberian 103
- The SME Affair 107
- Mediaset Film Rights 107
- The Mills Affair 109
- Outstanding cases 112
- Berlusconi's Search for Impunity 112
- Reform of Corporate Law 113
- Reform of Law on Foreign Documents 114
- The "ex-Cirielli" Law 114
- The Cirami Law 115
- The Pecorella Law 117
- Brief Trials 117
- Legitimate Impediment 118
- Stop the Telephone Interceptions 119
- Questions of Competence 120

CHAPTER 5: THE ECONOMY UNDER BERLUSCONI 121
- The Pledge to the Electors 121
- The Berlusconi Effect: *Più Stato, Meno Privato* 122
- Cutting Crime, Cutting Unemployment 126
- The Macro-economic Disaster 128
- Alitalia 132
- Tax Evasion and Tax Havens 137
- Berlusconi and the Market 143

CHAPTER 6: TELEVISION AND GOVERNMENT 145
- LA 7 – the competitor that might have been 145
- Squatter's Rights - Rete 4 147
- Mediaset – A mediocre stock 148
- Who provides Mediaset's cash? 150
- The Government's Publicity Budget 151

| **V**

The relationship with Sky TV 152
Spectrum Auctions; The Taxpayers' Gift to the Prime Minister 155
Control of RAI 156
The second attempt on Santoro 158
Summary 159

CHAPTER 7: SEX SCANDALS 161
Berlusconi's Degeneration 161
Do They Matter? 162
The Spy's ex-wife 163
Jobs for the Girls 164
The Bimbo Candidates 166
The Under-Age Girl 172
The attack on Veronica 184
The photos of Villa Certosa 186
Escorts and Recordings 187
The Hearstealer 195
The Meaning of Bunga-Bunga 197
Indictment for Abuse of Office and Juvenile Prostitution 200
Postscript: The Honest Clerk of Fkih ben Salah 201

CHAPTER 8: IMAGE AND REALITY IN BERLUSCONI'S ITALY 203
The Dear Leader 203
All those Mirrors are Ugly 207
The Image of the Sex Scandals on TG1 213
Another sex scandal 216
The Corruption of Others 218
The Party of Love 219
The Internet 220

CHAPTER 9: DEMOCRACY OR THE RULE OF LAW 223
Italy's Electoral System 224
The Fundamental Issue: Will of People versus Rule of Law 227
The President's Tough Decision 230
Foreign Policy 233
The deal with the Vatican 236
A Not-so-Glaring Absence 238
Farewell, Silvio 242

INDEX 244
ACKNOWLEDGMENTS 248
ABOUT THE AUTHOR 248
NOTES 249

CAST LIST

Accardi, Salvatore	Sicilian local government clerk, apparent co-founder of *Rete Sicilia*
Agrama, Frank	Trader in film rights and director of *Dawn of the Mummy* and *Queen Kong*
Alfano, Angelino	Minister of Justice in the 2008 Berlusconi government
Alleanza Nazionale	Political party, previously named MSI, now part of the *Popolo della Libertà*
Almirante, Giorgio	Member of National Fascist Party, later leader of the MSI, succeeded by Fini in 1987
Amato, Giuliano	Socialist politician, Prime Minister in 1993
Ambrosoli, Giorgio	Accountant, murdered while investigating the Banco Ambrosiano
Andreotti, Giulio	Christian Democrat politician
Ariosto, Stefania	Milanese antique dealer who reported on the possible corruption of judges
Armati, Federico	Spy, ex-husband of Virginia Sanjust
Attanasio, Diego	Neapolitan businessman cited by David Mills as source of some money
Azzaretto family	Owners of Banca Rasini after its sale by Count Rasini
Bacigalupo	Sicilian sports club where Dell'Utri first met Mangano and Cinà
Batliner, Herbert	Expert on tax avoidance, involved with Banca Rasini
Ben Ammar, Tariq	Franco-Tunisian media magnate
Berlusconi, Luigi	Father to Silvio and senior official at Banca Rasini
Berlusconi, Paolo	Younger brother to Silvio and owner of *Il Giornale*
Bernasconi, Carlo	Fininvest official and friend of David Mills
Berruti, Massimo Maria	Tax inspector, subsequently employed by Fininvest, now politician, convicted of money-laundering.
Biagi, Marco	Expert on labour economics, murdered by Red Brigades
Boffo, Dino	Ex-editor of Catholic newspaper, attacked by *Il Giornale* after criticising Berlusconi

Bontate, Stefano	Mafia boss before Riina
Borsellino, Paolo	Anti-Mafia magistrate, murdered in 1993
Bossi, Umberto	Leader of Northern League
Brancher, Aldo	Fininvest official, now politician, convicted of false accounting, on trial for embezzlement
Brunetta, Renato	PDL politician
Buscetta, Tommaso	Mafioso turned informer
Calderoli, Roberto	Northern League politician, deviser of current voting system
Calvi, Roberto	Banker, member of P2, found murdered under Blackfriars Bridge
Cancemi, Salvatore	Mafioso turned informer
Carfagna, Mara	TV presenter turned Minister for Equal Opportunities
Cartotto, Ezio	Politician who played a leading role in founding *Forza Italia*
Casati Stampa, Annamaria	Aristocrat who employed Previti as a lawyer and sold Arcore estate to Berlusconi
Ciampi, Carlo Azeglio	President of Italy from 1999 to 2006
Ciancimino, Massimo	Son of Vito and maker of allegations about Mafia links to politicians
Ciancimino, Vito	Mayor of Palermo, convicted of Mafia association
Cinà, Gaetano	Sicilian businessman, co-accused and convicted of Mafia association with Dell'Utri
Cirami Law	Law seeking to facilitate the transfer of cases to another regional jurisdiction
Cito, Ferdinando	Tutor to Berlusconi's children
Colannino, Roberto	Businessman, head of the new Alitalia
Confalonieri, Fedele	Head of Fininvest, talented pianist and schoolfriend of Berlusconi
Cozzolino, Domenico	TV personality who briefly claimed to be Noemi Letizia's fiancé
Craxi, Bettino	Socialist Prime Minister, fugitive from justice
D'Addario, Patrizia	Escort and authoress
D'Alema, Massimo	Prime Minister 2005-6, negotiator with Berlusconi on constitutional reform
De Benedetti, Carlo	Businessman, owner of *Repubblica* and *Espresso*, would-be owner of Mondadori
Dell'Oglio, Carla	Berlusconi's first wife
Dell'Utri, Marcello	University friend of Berlusconi, erstwhile head of Publitalia, creator of *Forza Italia*, convicted of Mafia association in first hearing and in appeal
Di Carlo, Francesco	Mafioso turned informer
Di Pietro, Antonio	Anti-corruption magistrate, now head of IDV party
Doris, Ennio	Founder of Mediolanum and business associate of

Edilnord	Berlusconi Name of various real estate companies managed, and possibly owned, by Berlusconi
El-Mahroug, Karima	Moroccan girl known as "Ruby Rubacuori", reason for Berlusconi's indictment in early 2011
Elio Letizia	Father to Noemi
Falcone, Giovanni	Anti-Mafia magistrate, murdered in 1993
Fauci, Jimmy	Mafioso whose wedding in London was attended by Dell'Utri
Fede, Emilio	Broadcaster
Feltri, Vittorio	Journalist, until recently editor of *Il Giornale*
Fini, Gianfranco	President of Chamber of Deputies, formerly leader of Alleanza Nazionale
Flaminio, Gino	Ex-fiancé of Noemi Letizia
Forlani, Arnaldo	Christian Democrat politician
Forza Italia	Political party, founded by Dell'Utri and Berlusconi, now *Popolo della Libertà*
Foscale, Giancarlo	Berlusconi's cousin, associated with some of his companies
Gasparri, Maurizio	Alleanza Nazionale politician and promoter of law regulating media plurality
Gelli, Licio	Head of P2 masonic lodge
Ghedini, Niccolò	One of Berlusconi's lawyers, also a politician
Giuffrè, Antonio	Mafioso turned informer
Giuffrida, Francesco	Official of Bank of Italy who studied Berlusconi's business career
Graviano brothers	Mafiosi involved in mainland terror attacks in 1993
Lario, Veronica	Berlusconi's second wife, currently divorcing him
Lentini, Gianluigi	Footballer whose transfer led to investigation of Berlusconi's offshore companies
Letizia, Noemi	Young friend of Berlusconi and aspiring politician
Mammì law	Law regulating media plurality passed at Craxi's instigation
Mangano, Vittorio	Mafioso employed by Berlusconi at Arcore estate
Mani Pulite	Investigations into illicit funding of politicians and parties in 1992-4
Marrazzo, Piero	Democratic Party politician who resigned after sex scandal
Mesiano, Raimondo	Judge who ruled on Mondadori civil damages suit
Metta, Vittorio	Judge convicted of having been bribed by Cesare Previti and others
Mills, David	British lawyer convicted of receiving bribes in exchange for misleading testimony
Minetti, Nicole	Showgirl, dental hygienist, regional politician and organizer of female guests at Arcore parties

Minzolini, Augusto	Journalist, currently head of TG1 news
Montanelli, Indro	Journalist and founder of *Il Giornale*
Montereale, Barbara	Image girl and friend of Patrizia D'Addario
P2	Masonic lodge, disowned by Freemasons, involved with subversive plots
Popolo della Libertà	Political party formed from merger of Forza Italia, Alleanza Nazionale and some minor parties
Previti, Cesare	Lawyer and friend of Berlusconi, convicted of corrupting judges
Prodi, Romano	Prime Minister 1996-8 and 2006-8
Provenzano, Bernardo	Successor to Riina as head of Mafia, captured in 2006
Publitalia	Division of Fininvest responsible for advertising sales, once headed by Dell'Utri
Rapisarda, Filippo Alberto	Sicilian businessman
Riina, Totò	Succeeded Bontate and preceded Provenzano as head of Mafia
Ruggeri, Giovanni	Author and investigative journalist
Saccà, Agostino	RAI employee and friend of Berlusconi
Salvo, Ignazio	Sicilian businessman murdered by Mafia
Sanjust, Virginia	Broadcaster and friend of Berlusconi
Santapaola, Nitto	Mafioso
Scapagnini, Mario	Sicilian politician and doctor, purveyor of elixirs to Berlusconi
Sciascia, Salvatore	Fininvest employee, now politician, convicted for bribing tax inspectors
Segni, Mario	Christian Democrat politician and reformer of voting system in 1993
Sindona, Michele	Banker and felon, connected to the Mafia
Spatuzza, Gaspare	Mafioso turned informer
Squillante, Renato	Judge accused, but not convicted, of taking bribes
Sucato, Vicenzo	Sicilian chicken salesman and apparent co-founder of *Rete Sicilia*
Sylos Labini, Paolo	Economist
Tangentopoli	Corruption scandal in early 1990s related to funding of political parties
Tarantini, Gianpaolo	Manufacturer of prosthetic limbs, friend of D'Addario and Berlusconi
Teresi, Mimmo	Leading Mafia figure associated with Bontate
Travaglio, Marco	Journalist
Tremonti, Giulio	Minister of Finance in current and previous Berlusconi government
Verzé, Don Luigi	Priest and health-sector entrepreneur
Zappadu, Antonio	Sardinian photographer

PREFACE TO SECOND EDITION

One of Giuseppe Verdi's best-loved operas – Rigoletto – concerns a ruler, the Duke of Mantua, whose private life is as dissolute as his power is absolute. Orgiastic parties are held at his palace, and among the many women he beds is the under-age daughter of his jester. The jester seeks his revenge by paying an assassin to deliver the Duke's dead body to him in a sack, and, in the final scene, he is just about to hurl this sack into the river when he hears the Duke in the distance crowing his famous cockerel-song "*La donna è mobile*" (woman is fickle). Once again, the Duke has got off scot-free. (The sack contains the jester's daughter instead).

During the year since the first edition of this book, Silvio Berlusconi has exposed himself to humiliations so embarrassing as to consign any other political career to the decent obscurity of the sack. Yet at the time of writing he still occupies the office of Prime Minister, and can still be heard intoning his favourite theme-songs ("Judges are Communists", for example).

Until recently, Berlusconi's humiliations came in at least two separate flavours – legal and sexual. On the one hand, he has been indicted on charges of tax fraud, corruption and misappropriation of funds, and, as this book will show, most of his political energies have been devoted to the attempt to fight off these legal challenges. On the other hand, his private life has been characterised by a series of sex scandals which have become increasingly bizarre since he took power in 2001. In themselves these need be of no political concern (though, human nature being what it is, they are certainly of interest) as long as they do not threaten his ability to govern – but they have begun to throw an alarming light both on his idiosyncratic relationship with the truth, and on his vulnerability to blackmail.

By the start of 2011, these two strands had become fused into one. For the first time, his legal woes relate specifically to his sex-life. He complains about intrusions into his privacy, but the right to privacy does not include the right to commit crimes in private. Paying for sex with a woman under 18 years of age is a crime under Italian law, and Silvio Berlusconi is suspected of having committed it – and, still more seriously, of having abused his office in the attempt to cover up this deed.

| 11

Whether his survival skills are equal to this new challenge is uncertain at the time of writing, though probably not at the time of reading. But whichever way it goes, the episode has sharpened still further the issue that lies at the heart of this book: the potential conflict between the will of the people and the rule of law. Berlusconi himself highlighted the issue in February 2011 when he said, of the "subversive" judges: "They will not be able to carry out their coup, because in a democracy, the final judge, when it comes to deciding who governs, is the electorate and parliament, who are the repository of political sovereignty". The implication is clear: in his view, winning a free and fair election (as Berlusconi has done) puts the ruler above the law.

Apart from studying this latest, and acutest, test of Berlusconi's ability to withstand scandal and put himself beyond punishment, the second edition of this book contains other important changes. During 2010, Marcello Dell'Utri, Silvio Berlusconi's long-time colleague and the founder of the political party that brought him to power, lost an appeal against his conviction in 2004 for aiding and abetting the Mafia. The conviction was upheld, but his sentence was reduced from nine to seven years, since the Court considered that there was inadequate evidence that he had continued to collude with the Mafia after the early 1990s. In Italy, after delivering their sentence, judges also deliver a document called the *motivazioni*, which sets out the reasoning behind the sentence. This document, 641 pages long, appeared in November 2010, and provides a fascinating, and sometimes surprising, summary of what is known, and what is not known, about Berlusconi's relations with Cosa Nostra. Chapter 3 of the book, which in the first edition had to be rather provisional because so much was at the time still *sub judice*, has been substantially rewritten in the light of this account. An English translation of the full document has been made available on the Headington Press website.

All of the other chapters have been updated. Chapter 7, which deals with sex scandals, has become disproportionately long, compared to the space it occupied in the first edition. The blame for this belongs, I feel, to the protagonist rather than to the author. Chapter 5, which covers the performance of the Italian economy (certainly the most important, if the least commented, failure of Berlusconi's political career), contains new material, as does Chapter 6, which covers the TV industry. The last chapter has been revised in detail. As in the previous edition, it is too soon to write a final assessment of his career – but more urgent than ever to understand the issues that it raises.

INTRODUCTION

"If by momentary discouragement, or temporary panic, or a fit of enthusiasm for an individual, [a people] can be induced to lay their liberties at the feet of even a great man, or trust him with powers which enable him to subvert their institutions...they are more or less unfit for liberty...and are unlikely long to enjoy it."[1]

The words are those of John Stuart Mill, at the beginning of his essay on representative government. This book examines how a majority of the Italian people came to be willing to trust Silvio Berlusconi with the addition of great political power to his pre-existing economic power, and why he now plans to use that power to subvert their institutions by changing the constitution. His career poses a fundamental, and recurring, political problem: does the will of the people over-ride the rule of law?

Previously this problem has been posed by leaders wishing to take charge of the judicial process in the name of some ideology, or in the name of national survival. Silvio Berlusconi is pursuing a more modest goal: his impunity in the face of allegations that include tax evasion, corruption and, more recently, juvenile prostitution, along with abuse of office in seeking to cover up the alleged offence. Because the goal is more modest, the risk seems more modest also. This is not a leader who wishes to use his power for national aggrandisement, for the systematic persecution of minorities, or for the expropriation of private property. To many Italians, especially those for whom his television stations are a window on the world, he appears charming, dynamic and well-intentioned. This perception, as far as it goes, is largely correct. Since the alternatives are uninspiring, they have been willing so far to take the risk.

What that risk involves is now becoming clearer. On the one hand, Berlusconi has repeatedly attempted to bring in laws which have subsequently been found unconstitutional, and has often proposed changes to the Constitution, though so far he has not succeeded in meeting the stiff requirements for such changes to occur. On the other hand, and more insidiously, his pervasive economic and political power has eaten away at the Constitution from inside, gradually removing checks and balances to the power of the executive – killing off what the economist Paolo Sylos Labini called "the antibodies of democracy". The critical power of the media has gradually eroded, while parliament has degenerated into little more than a mere voting machine.

IMPUNITY   BERLUSCONI'S GOAL AND ITS CONSEQUENCES

Silvio Berlusconi's rhetoric has always been that of liberty and democracy. But it is becoming clear that, in their name, he will – unless stopped – saw down the only trees capable of bearing such fruit: the rule of law and freedom of information.

He is an outspoken anti-Communist. One of the secrets of his political success has been his ability to portray all his opponents as "reds", and all his allies as "moderates". Yet, if one considers the changes that have occurred since he was elected in 2001, it is the increased *Sovietisation* of Italy that stands out. This may seem a surprising, or even an outrageous statement, but I believe it can be justified.

There were three features of life in Eastern Europe before 1989 which those of us who have lived in Western Europe or North America would have found objectionable. In two of these respects Italy remains very different from a Soviet state, but is clearly moving in that direction. In the third, it has already come to resemble a Soviet state quite closely.

The first of these is the absence of the rule of law. Under Stalin and his successors, it was the politicians, and not an independent judiciary, who decided which citizens should be punished and which should go free. For citizens to be free from the fear of arbitrary arrest and punishment, it is necessary that the exercise of power should be regulated by abstract general laws, interpreted by independent judges, and not by those wielding political power. Only the rule of law, as an institution higher and more lasting than any head of state or of government, can provide that freedom. Italy is still very far from resembling a Communist state in that respect, but since 2001 there can be no doubt that it is moving in that direction. In Berlusconi's Italy, the independence of the judiciary and the principle of equality before the law are increasingly under threat. So far the threats have been valiantly resisted – though those doing the resisting have been stigmatised as "subversives" and "reds". But the more Silvio Berlusconi runs into problems with the law, the more intense the threats become.

Free access to a plurality of information sources was also lacking in the Communist world, where the press and other media were dominated by the government. A political leader had only to pick up the telephone to ensure that a programme that displeased him should be banned from the airwaves. In the absence of a plurality of information sources democracy, if practiced at all, is a sham, since the information on which the electorate can base its decisions is lacking or distorted. Here too, Italy is still very different from a Soviet state, but here too there can be no absolutely no

INTRODUCTION

doubt about the direction of change. In a country that relies above all on television as an information source, the dominance of Berlusconi's own television channels, and the control he exercises over the state broadcasting company RAI, preclude the true plurality of information sources that democracy requires.

The third striking feature of life under Soviet Communism, and the one which perhaps did the most to undermine its popular support, was economic stagnation. In this respect, Italy's economic record under Berlusconi already fully matches the Soviet example – indeed stagnation would be a marked improvement, given the decline in Italian living standards that has occurred since 2001, the year in which Berlusconi began his first prolonged period in power. As Chapter 5 will show, out of the 120 countries in the world with populations of more than 4 million, there were only two – Zimbabwe and Italy – whose economy was smaller in 2009 than it had been in 2001. Of the major countries, none has come close to the 6% fall in GDP per head experienced in Italy over this period. The next worst performer was France, part of a large cluster of countries in which GDP per head was about 4% higher in 2009 than in 2001. It is rare that a country should fall behind by so much within such a short span of years as Italy has under the Berlusconi/Northern League governments.

Economic power, under Communism, was dominated by state monopolies. The dominance of monopolies controlled by the Prime Minister and his allies in Italy, and the use of state power to protect them, mean that despite his overt support for liberal principles, Berlusconi's Italy bears an uncanny resemblance to Communism in this respect too. Certainly the initial promise of a liberal economic revolution was never met. The liberal vision is of a small state holding the ring and enforcing contracts, while economic power is in the hands of households and competing businesses. The reality of Italy under Berlusconi is that business and politics have never been more closely intertwined.

Moreover, in contrast to Berlusconi's promise of a smaller state, the proportion of national income spent by the state has steadily risen while he has been in power, as we shall see in Chapter 5. In this context, it is no surprise that corruption, the mortal enemy of prosperity, has spread.

As Italy has drifted away from the other liberal democracies, its international relations have changed. The closest relations have recently been with states like Russia and Libya, where leaders enjoy equally unfettered power – until, in Libya's case, the people suddenly sought to undermine that power in early 2011. In October 2009, Silvio Berlusconi visited Russia to hold private talks with Vladimir Putin in the presence of Angelo Codignoni, a senior Fininvest executive who had been responsible for the (failed) attempt to run a Berlusconi-owned TV channel in France[2]. Putin wanted to draw on Berlusconi's experience of building a media monopoly, to reinforce his grip on Russia's politics. Berlusconi had come to politics via television; Putin had come to television via politics. Putin seeks to build a television channel, run by a group close to him, which will reinforce and maintain his popularity. Both leaders have personal knowledge of how media power and political power can reinforce each other. In a Russia where Stalin is being rehabilitated, where both the rule of law and press freedom remain hopes rather than realities, and where the economy is dominated by monopolies friendly to the government, Italy's current leader has found his closest natural ally.

Communism as practised in Eastern Europe before 1990 is now a thing of the past, but the politics of Silvio Berlusconi may be the politics of the future. He has been voted into power three times with increasing majorities, and remains popular among many different social and economic groupings. Perhaps his greatest success has been to mobilise that important part of the electorate which is profoundly cynical about politics.

In Britain, this demographic takes the view that them politicians is all the same, only out for themselves. Consequently they don't bother to vote. In Italy, they take the same view, but Berlusconi has achieved what other politicians can only envy – he has persuaded them that he is an anti-politician, and that they should therefore vote for him.

The model that Berlusconi presents is studied by aspiring politicians in other countries, particularly those which lack the checks and balances which are gradually being dismantled in Italy. His political experiment has, from one point of view – his own – been a striking success. But from another point of view – that of the Italian people – it has, as this book will show, been profoundly damaging.

The protagonist of this book, Silvio Berlusconi, is a man of exceptional energy, charm and generosity, with an outstanding grasp of detail and a unique talent for salesmanship. One of his friends[i] said of him that "he not only sees every tree in the forest, but every leaf on the trees". He has a prickly pride – when his father asked the 15-year-old Silvio what he spent his pocket money on, he preferred to forego any future pocket money than to answer. That thin skin is one of the characteristics that dif-

---

i Ezio Cartotto, who played a leading role in establishing Berlusconi's political party Forza Italia.

INTRODUCTION

ferentiate him from many politicians. He cannot bear to lose: Ferdinando Cito, who was the tutor to his children, tells that when Berlusconi's son, Pier Silvio, suggested that Cito and Berlusconi should have a race in the swimming pool at his home in Arcore[ii], Berlusconi whispered to the tutor to let him win.[3] In Cito's view, what he wanted from his children, and from everyone else, was to be admired. Everything was subordinated to the goal of winning: "It's not just that he doesn't respect the law, but he considers himself so close to God that nowadays his self-esteem has no limits. And he is totally convinced that the end justifies the means". His oldest friend, now head of his company Fininvest, Fedele Confalonieri, also alludes to this characteristic, saying "he wouldn't have achieved what he has achieved without a touch of megalomania".[4]

Connected to his self-esteem and to his boundless energy is an appealing optimism. It was one of his precepts for his sales force that they should carry "the sun in their pockets", and convey this optimism to others. The psychologist Cordelia Fine has written that "there is in fact a category of people who get unusually close to the truth about themselves and their world. Their self-perceptions are more balanced, they assign responsibility for success and failure more even-handedly, and their predictions for the future are more realistic. These people are living testimony to the dangers of self-knowledge. They are the clinically depressed."[5] Silvio Berlusconi is emphatically not a member of this group.

Indeed, he is so far at the other extreme that one of his most striking characteristics is a belief that the truth is whatever he would like it to be at the time. Many examples of his extraordinary mendacity will be found throughout the book, and particularly in the accounts he gave during the sex scandals that dogged his premiership from 2009 onwards. His ability to speak blatant lies with patent sincerity is part of his egocentric relativism. Almost by instinct he holds the belief that justice and truth have no objective status, but are merely praise-words for whatever opinions it is convenient to hold at the time.

Silvio Berlusconi is also a great communicator, with an instinctive knowledge, further honed by his experience in television, of what messages people want to hear and how they should be expressed. He may often lie, but he does so in clear, simple and accessible language, and that is a great virtue in Italy. Italian politicians – but not Berlusconi – often speak a language different from the man in the street. Pedants often criticise him for not using the subjunctive tense where it would in their view be

---

ii   The accent is on the A

appropriate, but this is just another aspect of the directness that is part of his appeal. Italian journalism, in contrast, is allusive and often pretentious, making it seem that the journalist cares more about conveying the impression that he is knowledgeable and cultured than about conveying the facts.

This is probably the reason why few Italians (about 5 million of them) read newspapers and most depend on the television for their information. It is Berlusconi's company that puts on air the immensely popular Italian version of Big Brother, and Berlusconi has understood that 21st century politics is a similar undertaking to winning reality TV shows. He knows that people want simple answers, and understands that the politician who is the last to be "voted out" will be the one who he is not afraid to pretend to have them.

Even his "gaffes" (describing Obama as "tanned", comparing a German politician to a concentration camp guard, making Angela Merkel wait while he finished a conversation on his mobile phone, to cite a small number) endear him to more Italians than they offend. Like many very wealthy politicians, he has understood that there is a group of people whom the public resent even more than they resent the wealthy. These are the intellectuals – after all, you never know when chance might put a bit of money your way. By sharply distancing himself from them, and even allowing them to mock him, he can count on public sympathy. His gaffes of course convey a different impression to foreigners, most of whom would agree with Slavoj Žižek: "The man may look like a corrupt idiot, and act like a corrupt idiot, but don't let that deceive you: he really *is* a corrupt idiot."[6]

There was an episode of the British reality TV show "Strictly Come Dancing" in which the contestants included the talented and amusing political commentator John Sargent – who is a much less talented (but still amusing) ballroom dancer. To the consternation of the experts on the panel, he kept being favoured by the voting public over more skilful dancers, and eventually graciously resigned when it became clear that a victory by him would make the programme something different from what had been intended. Berlusconi's skills in solving Italy's problems are as dubious as John Sargent's skills in dancing, but both know how to make the public like them. (Unfortunately, there is little prospect that Berlusconi, like Sargent, will step down).

Most of those who have met him are convinced of Berlusconi's underlying good intentions. The tutor Cito says: "He wanted people to recognise

INTRODUCTION

that he is the best, that he works more than anyone else. And he really does work more than those around him...He works on the principle that 'I'll look after you as long as you are loyal to me'. But when he gets angry, he isn't vindictive, and he didn't abuse his power. ..He is not a bad person...he has an incredible capacity to listen, is very quick to understand what you want, and has an incredible ability to say 'how can I help you?'"[7] David Gilmour's concise summing up of his personality is less flattering: "Sleek and smarmy, smiley and jokey, a self-assured entertainer who wants everyone to love him as much as he loves himself".[8]

He has a talent for friendship, and an endearing loyalty to his friends even when the latter occasionally fail to reciprocate it. In the mausoleum that he has constructed for himself at his home of Arcore, near Milan, he has provided space to accommodate the bodies of two of his life-long associates, Fedele Confalonieri, the school friend who now runs his business empire, and Marcello Dell'Utri, the university friend who now faces a seven-year sentence for association with Cosa Nostra. Dell'Utri, in particular, has on a couple of occasions behaved in ways damaging to Berlusconi, but has always been forgiven. A business associate, Ennio Doris, has said that "Berlusconi is absolutely incapable of hating".

While most fall under the influence of Silvio Berlusconi's charm, some remain impervious or can even find it irritating: Queen Elizabeth II, for example, was heard to mutter "Does he have to shout!" while Berlusconi, at a recent summit, was noisily manoeuvring for a photo opportunity in which he could interpose himself between Barack Obama and Dmitri Medvedev. (Chapter 8 shows that Berlusconi holds himself responsible for the recent improvement in Russo-American relations, and that his fans want him to get the Nobel Peace Prize as a result). Barack Obama also seems a little impervious to his charm – when Berlusconi addressed the US Senate in 2005 and was given a standing ovation, Senator Obama was one of the few to remain in his seat with his hands folded[9].

Silvio Berlusconi is certainly generous, but like most of us he is often more generous in the impulse than in the follow-through – for example, following the 2009 earthquake in Abruzzo, he said that he would provide accommodation for some of the homeless in his own properties, but no earthquake victim ever did move in to any of them; and Chapter 7 shows how he got into some trouble later that year by failing to follow up an undertaking to help a young lady get planning permission to build a bed-and-breakfast. There are, though, no qualifications concerning his salesmanship. If he were to try to sell you a second-hand car, you would find it difficult to restrain yourself from buying it.

But you would be well advised to try. I shall show that his success in convincing his compatriots to do what he would like them to do has had a powerfully damaging effect on his country. This is not because of any vicious intent – there is no doubting his love of his country. Nor is it because he, like many who have previously held such all-encompassing power, is in thrall to an all-consuming ideology. It is simply that, like all of us, but to a greater extent than most, he is in the grip of an egotism that causes him to confuse his own interests with those of the community as a whole, and creates in him the sincere belief that he is pursuing the latter when in reality his actions only promote the former. The defence of his interests has led him to a position where he has added great political power to his economic power, and he has convinced himself that actions which defend his personal economic power and his personal freedom ought to be taken because they benefit a country to which, in his perception, he has become indispensable.

Those of us who live in Western Europe and North America tend to take the rule of law, and our democratic rights, for granted. We nod assent to the idea that the price of liberty is eternal vigilance, but we don't believe that the loss of our liberty is in practice very likely, even if we should take our eye off the ball for a bit. What is happening in Italy is therefore a useful reminder of how a country can start down a slippery slope that really does threaten these values. Certainly some of the factors that contributed to the resistible rise of Silvio Berlusconi were highly specific to Italy – but others are clearly visible in other countries. For example, the mordant cynicism about all political parties and all politicians that was rife in Italy at the time of the *Mani Pulite* (Clean Hands) corruption scandals of the early 1990s was a necessary condition for the rise of Berlusconi. And a similar cynicism is clearly apparent in many other countries – for example in Britain following the MPs' expenses scandal in 2009.

Much of what the book has to tell is simply ridiculous. Silvio Berlusconi rivals Benny Hill in his ability to keep the world constantly amused by his antics in pursuit of attractive young women, though, as he ages, he increasingly resembles another person once familiar on British TV: the elder Steptoe in *Steptoe and Son* – the shabby, wily figure whose son used to upbraid him with the words "You. Dirty. Old. Man." But it is not just his sex life that is a cause for merriment – nobody can have an ego the size of Berlusconi's and not lay himself open to any amount of ridicule. Berlusconi's business dealings also conjure up images familiar from British television: while his business success has far surpassed anything achieved by the fictional characters Arthur Daley and Del Trotter, his business methods and ethics will be seen to be in the same mould, and give

INTRODUCTION

the same impression of fairly benign shiftiness. (He himself, however, has a much higher opinion of his ethics. He has said "I am a good chap, a gentleman of the highest moral standards"[10], and "I can demonstrate in black and white that I am ethically superior to other European politicians"[11].) In addition to providing occasional amusement, my hope is that the facts recounted in this book will not only help you to understand what is happening in Italy, but also to understand under what circumstances it might occur in your own country also.

It is commonplace for both foreigners and Italians to classify the Berlusconi phenomenon as one that is "typically Italian".[12] But national characteristics are mutable: Paolo Sylos Labini notes that England was one of the most corrupt societies in Europe at the start of the eighteenth century, and one of the least corrupt at the start of the nineteenth[13]. The revolution against corruption that started in Italy in the 1990s, and was aborted after it brought Berlusconi to power, was not immutably destined to fail. There may be some characteristics of the Berlusconi phenomenon that are indeed "typically Italian" – whatever that means: anyone who reads the newspapers of more than one country will be struck by how often the same phenomenon is described as "typically British" in the British newspapers, and "typically German" (or French or Italian) in the newspapers of another country. But the emphasis in this book is not on those aspects.

During the early part of his career, Berlusconi achieved wealth by accurately identifying what people wanted and were willing to pay for, and making sure that they got it. There were some questionable sides to his activity (the odd lack of transparency in the financing of his businesses, the bending of rules and, increasingly, the reliance on political favours), but as a property magnate his dealings helped to increase, not just his wealth, but also general welfare. When he entered the television industry, his breaking up of what had been a state monopoly of television advertising also contributed to economic welfare.

He has continued to preach the principles of economic liberalism, but once he absorbed the last major competing free-to-air private television company, and himself became a monopolist, his actions ceased to be in the public interest. Just as Communist governments operated in order to secure and maintain state monopolies, so Berlusconi's governments have been preoccupied, not just with maintaining Berlusconi's personal impunity, but also with the protection of his own private monopolies and those of his allies. "The Member of Parliament who supports any proposal for strengthening this Monopoly is seen to acquire not only the reputation for understanding trade, but great popularity and influence with an order of men whose members and wealth render them of great importance. If he opposes them, on the contrary, and still more, if he has authority enough to be able to thwart them, neither the most acknowledged probity, nor the highest rank, nor the greatest public services, can protect him from the most infamous abuse and detraction, from personal insults, nor sometimes from real danger, arising from the insolent outrage of furious and disappointed monopolists."[14] The words accurately describe the proceedings of any recent session of the Italian parliament at which broadcasting is discussed, though they were in fact penned a quarter of a millennium ago by Adam Smith, the father of economics.

The raft of government actions aimed against Sky television in Italy during the last two years is one example of this. Another is the use of the state publicity budget to give support to the prime minister's companies, or the donation of public goods such as radio frequencies to them, as documented in Chapter 6. Those who expected Berlusconi to bring about, as he promised to do, a liberalising revolution in the management of the Italian economy, have been disappointed. Indeed, to entrust to a monopolist the task of liberalising the economy is as misguided as it would be, for example, to entrust to a criminal the task of reforming the system of justice.

The topic of justice will be an important one in this book, since so much of Berlusconi's time as a politician has been devoted to attempts to make sure that he remains unconvicted of any of the crimes of which he has been accused. In examining these issues, it is very important to bear in mind two very different principles concerning the burden of proof.

In any civilised society, an individual is judged to be innocent of a crime until such time as he has been proven guilty, according to some process that is as impartial as practicable. However, it is fallacious to argue, as Berlusconi's supporters do, that the same principle should be applied in the choice of political leaders. If a man is accused in court of collaborating with the Mafia – to take an example which we shall discuss in Chapter 3 – then he should be acquitted if, in the light of less-than-conclusive evidence, the chance of his being guilty amounts to, say, a 60% probability. But if that man is – as in this case – the founder of a political party, then even if the evidence points to only a 20% probability that he has been colluding with the Mafia, red lights should flash and voters ought to seek their leaders elsewhere. Different levels of evidence are needed for different purposes.

INTRODUCTION

This analogy shows that there are good reasons why, in most democratic societies, politicians feel obliged to resign if there is a plausible stain on their reputation. Often they say that their reason for resigning is that they are going to devote their time to clearing their names of the allegations, and in a small minority of cases, they succeed in doing this. But it is unacceptable in a functioning democracy for a politician to continue in office when there are good reasons for suspecting that he may have been involved in corrupt or illegal practices, even if these reasons fall short of the kind of proof that would be required by a court of law. And it is unlikely that any politician except Berlusconi could have made the declaration that he made after the failure of his attempt in 2009 to secure immunity from prosecution by virtue of his office: that he would continue in office even if convicted.

The great journalist and historian Indro Montanelli said in 2001 that "the discovery that there is a Berlusconian Italy has made a deep impression on me: it's the worst of the Italies that I have known, and in my long life [he was then in his 90s and was to die later that year] I have known some ugly ones. But I've never experienced the vulgarity, the baseness of this Italy. *Berlusconismo* is really the sludge rising to the top of the [septic] tank."

Let's not exaggerate: Italy is still only on the upper reaches of the slippery slope, and is very far from being a police state – though if you are an immigrant to Italy from the third world or Eastern Europe, you may find the difference increasingly elusive at times. But, once the checks that limit power are removed, society remains vulnerable. And the ones that still remain will be removed, if he has his way. He has made it clear that he wants both to reform the justice system, and to have direct elections for the President. An astute comment has come from his ex-wife, Veronica Lario, who has said that she fears, not what Berlusconi himself may do with his unchecked power, but what his successors may do.

The first part of this book tells how Silvio Berlusconi rose to economic power, and how and why he then went on to acquire political power. This story has been particularly well told by Alexander Stille in "The Sack of Rome". Anybody wanting further information would do well to start there. David Lane's book "Berlusconi's Shadow" is also useful, though Stille's is more recent and therefore more comprehensive. Paul Ginsborg's book also tells the story of his rise, from the point of view of a leading political scientist. But these accounts stop before his return to power in 2008.

There are three reasons for including this background story, although it has been told before. The first is that many readers may not yet know it, and it is more convenient to summarise it here than to send them off in pursuit of other books. I have also tried to mine the Italian sources for material not previously available in English.

The second is this: each time a particular scandal threatens to sink Berlusconi, that scandal tends to obscure all previous scandals. Instead of accumulating, the scandals seem to substitute for each other, as previous scandals seem to be taken for granted, to lose their power to shock, and to disappear from view. Attention has long been distracted from the massive conflicts of interest that would alone require him to stand down in most countries. The recent scandals concerning his private life have led to a debate about whether a politician's private life is relevant to his political career. This debate has tended to distract attention from the shady financial dealings which stand at the origins of his business empire, and the suggestions that he may have engaged in criminal activity such as perjury or corrupting judges. His significance can only be properly appreciated when his career is seen as a whole.

The third reason is that information is still coming to light about many parts of this story – for example, within the last year, much has become clearer about the attempts by the Mafia to negotiate with the state during the early 1990s and thereafter, and to find new political points of reference when their previous ones had been overwhelmed by the corruption scandals of that period. After recounting, in Chapter 1, his business career and, in Chapter 2, the sequence of events that led him to enter politics and win the 1994 election we review, in Chapter 3, the issue of his links with organised crime, basing the account primarily on the detailed document issued by the judges who recently convicted Marcello Dell'Utri of colluding with the Mafia until the early 1990s, while finding the evidence of collusion after that date inadequate for a conviction.

The second part of the book reviews what Berlusconi has done with political power – and what it has done to him. He embarked in 2008 on his second prolonged spell in office, having been in power from 2001 to 2006. The struggle to achieve immunity from prosecution and impunity for any misdeeds for which he may be convicted has absorbed an overwhelmingly large proportion of the time and energy that he has devoted to politics. In order to put this into perspective, Chapter 4 reviews his past and continuing brushes with the law, the outcome of the cases in which he has been involved, and the ones that are still outstanding. (This section straddles the two parts of the book, since many, but by no means

INTRODUCTION

all, of the actions for which he is under investigation come before his accession to political power, while his actions to achieve impunity come after). We consider what action one might expect a criminal to take were he to achieve high office, and, while Berlusconi himself has – at the time of writing – yet to be convicted of any crime, we shall consider in what way his own actions differ from these.

This book is the first in English to review the economic record of his period in office, and to highlight the truly shocking, and still not widely appreciated, deterioration in Italy's economy to which it contributed. This forms the subject of Chapter 5, which also reveals that his rhetoric about cutting the role of government and promoting the market does not correspond to any real commitment, let alone to any achievement in these areas. While it is crucial to his political success that he conveys the impression of being in favour of small government and the market, and while many who ought to know better believe this, it is important to understand that the facts belie this contention.

In Chapter 6 we look at his businesses, and show how poorly they, like the Italian economy, have fared in recent years. We identify the outside businesses that are crucial in providing revenue to Berlusconi's empire, and also review the mass of government legislation aimed at propping up his businesses and securing their immunity from the anti-trust legislation and the concerns about plurality of information sources which would make their dominance illegal in most other countries. This Chapter also considers whether the internet is reducing the power of television to influence public perception, and reviews the attempts made by the Berlusconi government to limit the spread of the internet (in which Italy lags far behind other West European countries) as a news source.

Chapter 7 reviews the sex scandals that exploded during the term of office that began in 2008. It is sometimes argued that politician's private lives are irrelevant; still, they are often interesting, and perhaps more so in Silvio Berlusconi's case than in most others. One theme of the second section of the book is what power has done to him, and its corrosive impact is nowhere more obvious than here. What his second wife, when divorcing him, described as his "sickness" has led him to forsake the companionship of a wife for the adulation, or at least the company, of young women dazzled by his celebrity. Chapter 8 looks at the relation of image to reality in an Italy where Berlusconi's media are dominant, showing how the sex scandals and other matters are presented to the public, and how the media are used to attack political enemies.

Finally, in Chapter 9 we look at the constitutional issues that are raised by his invocation of the will of the people as justifying his immunity from justice. We also take a look at his foreign policies, and consider to what extent they are the result of the fact that other countries consider him mainly a figure of fun, to be seen in whose company is a vote-loser; how far they result from a conscious decision to promote energy security; and how far they are the expression of a natural affinity with other countries in which politics are dominated by a leader who controls the system of justice, and economics by monopolies that are allied to the leader.

PART I:

HOW SILVIO BERLUSCONI ACHIEVED POWER – AND WHY

"The truth is that if Silvio Berlusconi had not entered politics, if he had not founded Forza italia, today we would be under a bridge or in prison accused of being Mafiosi." Fedele Confalonieri.

CHAPTER 1:
ECONOMIC POWER

The Banca Rasini

Silvio Berlusconi was born the son of a Milanese bank official in 1936. His father, Luigi Berlusconi, spent most of his working life as an employee of the Banca Rasini, a small bank with only one branch, on Piazza Mercanti in Milan. Luigi Berlusconi retired in 1973, by which time he had become general manager (*Direttore*).

Before we turn to Berlusconi's own career, it is worth spending some time on the Banca Rasini. Like the overture to an opera, the story of this bank – which gave Silvio Berlusconi a helping hand in the early days of his business – brings out many of the themes that will recur during that career. The themes were to be amplified by the enormous successes that Berlusconi was to achieve in both his business and his political careers, but many of the leitmotivs are already there in the small bank for which his father worked.

The first of these themes is the relationship with the church. The support of the Catholic church has always been central to Berlusconi's political success. The voters that are most likely to vote for him are those who go to church, but not very often. In 2008, 44% of those who went to mass every Sunday voted for his party, and 35% for the opposition Democratic party; for those who go a few times a month, the proportions were 50% against 28%.[15] The political party that he was to form after the implosion of the Christian Democrats was seen by catholic voters as the natural successor for the votes of the devout, and the spat with the Vatican following the disclosures in 2009 about his private life (discussed later) was a major threat. He has always been willing to exchange the political support of the Church for very tangible fiscal and legislative action to promote its interests.

IMPUNITY   BERLUSCONI'S GOAL AND ITS CONSEQUENCES

Giulio Andreotti was one of the first, and also the last, and hence the longest-lived of the Christian Democrat politicians, and he was close, not only to the Vatican, but also to the Banca Rasini. Count Rasini, whose family had founded the bank, ran it together with a wealthy Sicilian family, Giuseppe Azzaretto and his son Dario. The Azzarettos eventually took over control and ownership when Count Rasini, beginning to feel uncomfortable with the way the bank was changing, left in 1973 – the same year in which Luigi Berlusconi retired. Andreotti was very close to the Azzaretto family, with whom he regularly spent his summer holidays. Ezio Cartotto, an old friend of Berlusconi who was to play a leading role in founding his political party, said that "people used to jokingly say that Andreotti was the boss of a bank", and one of the bank's aristocratic clients, Baroness Cordopatri, said that "formally the bank belonged to the Azzaretto family, but in reality the bank was controlled by Giulio Andreotti".[16]

Another theme which was to play a large role in Berlusconi's career is that of financial opacity, usually associated with offshore finance. (We will talk in Chapter 4 about his relationship with David Mills, and in Chapter 5 about the generous immunities his government has given to those repatriating money illegally held abroad). This theme too appears in the story of the Banca Rasini, in counterpoint with the theme of its relationship with the church. The Bank was owned in part by three Liechtenstein groups, the Wootz Anstalt, the Brittener Anstalt, and Manlands Financière. All three were represented in the Bank by their legal representative, Herbert Batliner.

Mr Batliner was an expert in tax avoidance, and figured in the scandals surrounding illegal funding for the German Christian Democratic Party which put an end to Chancellor Helmut Kohl's political career (and gave a boost to that of Kohl's protégée Angela Merkel). By the end of his career Batliner was wanted by German police in connexion with tax evasion activities, though in 2007 he was to settle the matter to their satisfaction by paying €2 million. He was also very close to the Vatican: a special immunity from arrest was granted to him by the German government in 2002 so that he could present to the pope in person an organ which he had donated in Regensburg cathedral. In 1998 he was granted the status of a Gentleman of His Holiness[iii], a kind of Vatican Privy Councillor. In short, he was a man with a personal take on Jesus Christ's famous recommendation: he had made it his life's work to remove from Caesar the things that are Caesar's, and render some of them to God, or at least

---

iii Coincidentally, the same status was held by Angelo Balducci, who was implicated in a corruption scandal in Spring 2010 associated with contracts awarded by the Civil Protection Agency, and supplied with boyfriends by a Nigerian chorister at the Vatican.

to the Vatican (while trousering most of them, until Caesar finally caught up with him in 2007). This was the man who controlled around a third of the Banca Rasini's capital, and whose approval was necessary for any major decision.[17]

A third theme that was to recur in Berlusconi's life was the "odour of Mafia" that surrounded some of his acquaintances and some of his dealings, and was to lead Umberto Bossi, now one of his closest political allies, to describe him in 1995 as "that ugly Mafioso who earns his money with heroin and cocaine".[18] This theme, too, is to be found in the later history of the Banca Rasini (though only to a limited extent in the period during which Silvio Berlusconi's father worked there). One of its clients was Michele Sindona, nicknamed "the shark", who was linked to the financial affairs of both the Mafia and the Vatican, and died poisoned in prison while serving a life sentence for the murder of the lawyer Giorgio Ambrosoli, the liquidator of the bankrupt Banco Ambrosiano. In an interview shortly before his death, Sindona said that the Mafia used, "a small bank on the Piazza dei Mercanti", which can only have been the Rasini bank, to recycle its money. Suspicions of Mafia links were nurtured by the fact that the clients included many figures known to be involved in drugs and other Mafia activities, such as Vittorio Mangano[iv], (see Chapter 3).

In 1983 the Banca Rasini was raided, and several clients suspected of having links with organised crime were arrested. A large amount of money was also confiscated from the bank. The operation was, however, called off, all the money returned and all the suspects freed, after the intervention of Corrado Carnevale, a lawyer known as the "sentence-killer" because of the large number of Mafia convictions that he overturned, often on technicalities.

These three themes – the church, offshore finance and the Mafia – along with a further theme relating to the P2 Masonic Lodge, are all woven together in one particular transaction of the Banca Rasini. In 1970 Luigi Berlusconi ratified a deal that gave Banca Rasini a share in Cisalpina Overseas Nassau Bank, on whose board sat Roberto Calvi, Licio Gelli, Michele Sindona and Monsignor Paul Marcinkus – four characters who between them have given rise to more mysteries and conspiracy theories than any other four you could think of – Calvi, "God's banker", whose body was found hanging under Blackfriars Bridge, Gelli the head of the P2 Masonic Lodge, Sindona, and Marcinkus the American head of the Vatican bank who was under investigation for racketeering in the USA.

---

iv The accent is on the first a

So much for the Banca Rasini. It provided support and a modicum of finance to Silvio Berlusconi in his early business career, and was used by many of his companies, including the 38 obscure Holding Companies discussed below which provided capital to his business empire. It also acted a channel for funds coming from the mysterious Swiss groups that financed Berlusconi's building company Edilnord. But it did not, at least according to Dario Azzaretto, provide much of the finance that was needed for his property development.

The Building Tycoon

After a religious education under the guidance of the Salesian Fathers at a boarding school in Milan, Berlusconi went to the University of Milan, graduating with excellent marks for a thesis on advertising contracts. While he was at University, he met a young man who had come from Palermo to study. Marcello Dell'Utri was some four years younger than he, and the two men were to spend much of their careers collaborating. Another lasting friendship dates from even earlier – his schoolmate Fedele Confalonieri accompanied Berlusconi on the piano when Silvio was working as a crooner on cruise ships during his vacation, and the two were to remain inseparable. Confalonieri is now chief executive of Fininvest, Berlusconi's holding company.

Berlusconi began his business career in building and real estate in his home town. A not uncommon beginning: as Roberto Saviano says in *Gomorrah*, "Successful Italian businessmen come from cement. They're actually a part of the cement cycle. I know that before transforming themselves into fashion-models, managers, financial sharks, and owners of newspapers and yachts, before all this and under all this lies cement, subcontractors, sand, crushed stone, vans crammed with men who work all night and disappear in the morning, rotten scaffolding and bogus insurance. The driving force of the Italian economy rests on the thickness of the walls. The constitution should be amended to say that it is founded on cement[19]".

I don't mean to insinuate that his scaffolding was rotten or his insurance bogus, but cement was also the foundation of Berlusconi's business. After successfully buying some land and building a block of apartments in Milan, his second, and much more ambitious, project, started in 1963, was to develop an entire new residential area at Brugherio, north of the city. His friend Marcello Dell'Utri also worked with him at this time, acting as his personal secretary between 1964 and 1965 before returning to

CHAPTER 1: ECONOMIC POWER

Palermo. They also participated together in a football team, Torrescalla-Edilnord, with Dell'Utri as trainer, Berlusconi as chairman, and his younger brother Paolo as centre-forward.

That a 27-year old with only one, admittedly successful, project behind him was able to finance the development of housing for 4,000 people, says much for his drive, initiative and selling skills, but it has always been unclear if these alone can adequately account for the mystery surrounding the finances of the project. Some of the finance for the Brugherio project, as for the first project, was loaned by Carlo Rasini, the owner of the bank where his father worked. Some came from a Swiss company called *Finanzierungsgesellschaft für Residenzen* (housing finance company), whose ownership and control have never been clarified. This is the first point at which the financing of Berlusconi's empire becomes opaque. It was to become impenetrably obscure in the years that followed.

One secret of Brugherio's financial success was that it was simply much larger than the authorities had intended. Planning permission had been granted to build the blocks of flats five stories high; they were in fact built eight stories high. Berlusconi offered a job to the urban planner who had imposed these restrictions – on various subsequent occasions he was again to make use of this technique of offering a better-paid job to the official who might cause problems – and the planner was later to refer to the unauthorised construction of these three additional floors as a "misunderstanding", which was subsequently settled by a €100,000 fine and the construction of a nursery school.

Brugherio required all of Berlusconi's salesmanship skills. His authorised biography contains an oft-told tale, of which he is proud, and which brings out the saloon-bar nature of his charm. It seems to date to 1965 – incidentally, and not irrelevantly to the story, the year of his first marriage, to Carla Dell'Oglio (whom he met when he offered her a lift at a bus stop)[20]. By this time the property market was wilting, and, since it was hard to find private buyers, he planned to get a pension fund to invest in the flats. He managed to get the fund's vice-president responsible for acquisitions to visit the development, and arranged to have many of his relatives also visit at the same time and pretend to be interested in buying flats. However, while the prospective client was there, a rather dotty cousin arrived and started embracing all her relatives. This infuriated the potential client who realised he had been deceived. In an attempt to retrieve the situation, Berlusconi recounts, "I rushed down to Rome and got myself introduced to the secretary to the vice-president, a very pretty girl. I didn't have to work very hard to start what we might call an intimate relationship with her, and when the vice-president next took a train to Milan, she alerted me. I paid my 'penalty' to the secretary, which wasn't really a penalty, since it was a nice relationship. ..When I got onto the train and sat opposite him he said 'Now I have to travel with my enemy'. These words, rather than depressing me, gave me great courage. I put all my charm to work, and by the time we arrived in Milan we were both at the bar half drunk, with him telling me how extraordinary the private parts of Circassian women were, with a thing that starts here and goes to here. I haven't had a chance to make a close study of the sexual organs of Circassian women, but I had no trouble in agreeing with him. We established a friendship based on what we might call these common cultural elements. He became my biggest supporter, my best friend, and I managed it all without having to pay a cent."

Thanks to the talents illustrated in this yarn, the properties were eventually sold, though the project doesn't seem to have been vastly profitable. He then moved on to a still more ambitious project known as Milan 2 at Segrate. A new company called Edilnord Centri Residenziali was founded to undertake the development, and its managing partners were Berlusconi's aunt and her daughter (his cousin), along with Umberto Previti, the father of Berlusconi's long-time friend and lawyer Cesare Previti. The earlier Edilnord was liquidated in 1972.

Berlusconi appears nowhere as an owner of this new company, despite having provided personal guarantees, along with his father, to Banco Popolare di Navona in respect of a loan of about €3.5mn to the new Edilnord. The new company's capital came from a Swiss company called *Aktiengesellschaft für Immobilienanlagen* (property development company), which had been formed ten days before the formation of the new Edilnord, and whose ownership was as murky as for the similarly named *Finanzierungsgesellschaft für Residenzen*. Both of these companies had applied for permission to bring the money into Italy (in those days exchange controls were much tighter) and were granted it on condition that profits were remitted to them in Switzerland. As *The Economist* recounts, in its open letter to Berlusconi in July 2003, "an internal document from one of your lenders shows that the bank believed you to be the beneficial owner [of the Swiss company's shares]. This was hardly surprising. Otherwise the bank would have been light on security for its loan". The Swiss company had an account at Banca Rasini.

Milan 2 sold itself as "an oasis of peace on the edge of the city", but in reality the noise from overflying aircraft was a major problem. Near to the property development was a proposed clinic, called San Raffaele, which was being developed by a priest, Don Luigi Verzé, who had acquired 46,000 square metres of land adjacent to the 712,000 acquired by Berlusconi. Although Verzé initially took against Berlusconi, he changed his mind when Berlusconi suggested combining the drainage system for the two developments[21]. Both of them faced the task of persuading the authorities to change the flight path of planes on their way to Milan's airport at Linate.

Berlusconi set up a local noise abatement committee to lobby for changes to the air routes. He also produced a map in which the area of his development, as well as the neighbouring area of the clinic, was designated as a hospital. A lobbying campaign was initiated in Rome – decisions about flight paths were taken at a national level – which suggested that the reason for changing the flight path was to ease the suffering of patients.[22] The campaign was successful, and the flight paths were changed, to the fury of those who now found themselves living in areas, such as Berlusconi's previous development in Brugherio, which were to suffer the noise pollution that had previously affected the hitherto empty area around Segrate. (The price of the land bought by Berlusconi at Segrate had of course been low so as to reflect the noise pollution, while the price of the flats sold by him in Brugherio had reflected the short-lived absence of noise pollution). Berlusconi pointed to research carried out by experts in Milan which allegedly proved that the new routes were optimal. It subsequently turned out that this research had been paid for by his companies.[23]

This was the first occasion on which Berlusconi's financial success was to depend on decisions taken by politicians in Rome, and it was also one of the first occasions on which a relationship with the Church was to prove useful. Berlusconi's own account of the story[24] is that the air routes were changed soon after he had acquired the land, so that his campaign was simply to get them changed back. However, this version of the story is unique to him. In recounting the story of Milan 2, Berlusconi also sticks to the story that he was merely acting on behalf of the independent sources of capital provided by the mysterious Swiss company.

The Landed Gentleman

By the early 1970s Berlusconi was sufficiently wealthy to want to establish himself in style. The story of how he became the owner, not only of an exceptionally fine house, but also of a fine library and art collection, has often been told since it was first pieced together by Giovanni Ruggeri in

Gli Affari del Presidente. As is almost the norm in the case of books about Berlusconi, the author was duly sued, and duly won, which creates some confidence in the truth of the extraordinary story that he unearthed.

The Villa San Martino at Arcore is an 18th-century gem of some 3,500 square metres set in about a hundred hectares of park. It contained valuable pictures from the 15th and 16th centuries along with a library of some 10,000 books. It had belonged to an aristocratic family named Casati Stampa. In 1970 Count Camillo Casati Stampa found his second wife Anna in bed with a young student. He shot them both, and then shot himself. His will left everything to his wife. After the murder, the wife's relations, claiming that the property would revert to them, hired a lawyer named Cesare Previti to represent their interests. (The accent is on the e, hence the well-known rhyme about Cesare Previti: *Se lo conosci lo eviti* – if you know him you avoid him). However, medical evidence established that the Count had lived a few minutes after the death of his wife, so the property reverted to his daughter by his first marriage, Annamaria Casati Stampa, who was at that time nineteen years old. At this point, Cesare Previti, despite having represented the family who had wished to deprive Annamaria of her inheritance, offered his help to her. The young girl accepted.

Her only surviving relative, an aunt, sought approval from magistrates in Rome that she should become her niece's warden. Annamaria, however, came to the court together with Previti and an elderly senator, Giorgio Bergamasco, who had been a friend of her father, and said that she wanted Bergamasco, rather than her aunt, to be in charge of her affairs. This was done, and Previti was appointed as her legal counsel and also her *protutore*, or deputy warden, whose job it was to adjudicate should there be any conflict of interest between Annamaria and her warden. (Conflicts of interest, as is already becoming apparent, are something of a specialty for Cesare Previti).

Annamaria soon left Italy, first for the Seychelles, and then for Brazil, where she married. On coming of age, she gave Bergamasco full power of attorney to deal with her financial affairs. In 1973, pressed by inheritance taxes, she asked Previti to arrange the sale of the villa at Arcore, expressly excluding the furniture, pictures, library and adjoining lands. In spring 1974 Previti rang her up in Brazil and announced that he had managed to sell Arcore, *including* its pictures, library and lands, for €250,000, presenting this as a great triumph. The fortunate buyer was Silvio Berlusconi, who appears to have been a friend of the Previti family prior to this, and was to be a much closer friend afterwards.

Berlusconi moved in during the spring of 1974, but he did not pay the €250,000 in cash – the agreement that Previti had negotiated allowed him to pay it in instalments that would come due at the same time as Annamaria's tax liabilities. Previti advised her that it would not be a good idea to insist on the formal handover of the property at once, but that she should instead nominate him and Berlusconi as administrators of it until the deal was done. Consequently Annamaria continued to be liable for all the property taxes associated with Arcore. However, she increasingly began to lose her faith in Cesare Previti – a man whose patent shiftiness caused Indro Montanelli to say that "as soon as you see him, you want him in handcuffs, without even asking who he is or what he has done", and the economist Paolo Sylos Labini to say "When I look at Previti's face, I am almost inclined to think that physiognomy is an exact science".

Only in 1980 was the final transfer of the property done, not to Berlusconi in person, but to a company called Immobiliare Idra, on whose board sat not only Berlusconi, but both Cesare Previti and his father Umberto.

In 1979, a deal was done to purchase a further 250 hectares of land from Annamaria. In this case, there was to be no cash payment at all: the land was exchanged for 800,000 shares in an unquoted company called Cantieri Riuniti Milanesi.

The Return of Dell'Utri

The career of Marcello Dell'Utri is closely intertwined with that of Silvio Berlusconi. Soon after Berlusconi had acquired his property at Arcore, Dell'Utri came back into his employment, initially with the task of helping to establish, renovate and run the new property. In the interim period, he had spent a couple of years in Rome working at a sports centre, before returning to Palermo, where he worked for the Bacigalupo Athletic Club. It was there that he made the acquaintance of Vittorio Mangano and Gaetano Cinà – two men who turned out to be Mafiosi, though Dell'Utri claimed not to be aware of this. Later he worked in a bank, before returning to Milan in 1974.

Dell'Utri is a man of taste, and an avid collector of books and watches. Berlusconi's children's tutor, Ferdinando Cito, recalls that "Berlusconi had with him a young man of great elegance and culture, who was charged with buying some important pictures, real works of art. Marcello Dell'Utri helped Berlusconi become more refined." Dell'Utri's activities at this time will be discussed in more detail in Chapter 3.

In 1977 the title of Cavaliere del Lavoro was conferred on Berlusconi (since then he is often referred to as *Il Cavaliere*, the knight), but by this time Marcello Dell'Utri had begun to feel underpaid and underutilised in his work, and he left to work for another property tycoon, Filippo Alberto Rapisarda, like him a Sicilian by birth, who also hired Marcello's twin brother Alberto. There is no doubt that the Rapisarda group had close links with the Mafia, and was involved in recycling Mafia money.[25] Rapisarda himself was linked to Vito Ciancimino, the Christian Democrat Mayor of Palermo who was later to be convicted of collusion with the Mafia. During the years that the Dell'Utri twins worked for it, the Rapisarda group encountered steadily growing financial problems. First the company headed by Alberto Dell'Utri failed, leading to his arrest on a charge of fraudulent bankruptcy. Later the rest of the company also collapsed, and in March 1982 Dell'Utri returned to work for Berlusconi. In October 1983[26] he took up the crucial job of directing Publitalia, the part of the group charged with selling advertising space in the television channels and other media outlets, and therefore the all-important source of revenue for the group as a whole. Hitherto his record of business success had been distinctly modest – although he claimed that the company that Rapisarda put him in charge of was already beyond salvation at the time he took it over. But his success in Publitalia was to be outstanding.

From Edilnord to Fininvest

While checking on Edilnord, the financial authorities found that it had failed to return to its anonymous Swiss shareholders about €1.2mn of profits, and called for an investigation of it, and of another similar company, SOGEAT, which was also involved in Milan 2. SOGEAT's ownership was equally obscure, but Berlusconi had guaranteed loans taken out by this company, as he had for Edilnord, without appearing to be the owner. To take up the story in the words of *The Economist*: "As a result, a posse of Guardia di Finanza officers came to your offices on November 13th 1979. Mr [Massimo Maria] Berruti, then a captain in the Guardia di Finanza, led the team. The previous day you had told Mr Berruti that you were merely a consultant to Edilnord and SOGEAT. Mr Berruti resigned from the Guardia di Finanza that month. Despite the strong evidence of exchange-control violations (i.e., your personal guarantees at BPN and another bank, and failure to repatriate post-tax profits), no legal action was taken against you."

Massimo Berruti went on to work for Berlusconi, looking after the foreign companies owned by Fininvest, Berlusconi's holding company. He was

CHAPTER 1: ECONOMIC POWER

arrested in 1994 and subsequently convicted of aiding and abetting (*favoreggiamento*), after promising his ex-colleagues in the financial police "tangible rewards" for leaving Berlusconi out of their enquiries. In February 2011 Berruti was sentenced to 2 years and 10 months detention for money-laundering in connection with offshore funds owned by Berlusconi's companies. He sits in Parliament as a member of Berlusconi's party, and is unlikely to be in any way inconvenienced by the sentence, since the statute of limitations will begin to apply before the sentence becomes definitive, and he will not be disqualified from continuing as a member of Parliament.

With the investigation of Edilnord having been staved off, these companies were subsequently wound up. Fininvest, which was founded in 1975, became and remains the main corporate centre of the Berlusconi family's wealth. Its financing is a matter of outstanding complexity, and was clearly designed to minimise transparency. A dizzying host of companies was set up, usually with frontmen or frontwomen as their nominal owners, and sometimes brought into being for the purpose of a single transaction. The one person who has tried hardest to understand this intricate web of companies is Francesco Giuffrida, a financial analyst based at the Bank of Italy who was seconded to Palermo magistrates following a request for an expert who would seek to investigate these matters in circumstances to be described later. His report is summarised in a book called *L'Odore dei Soldi* (the smell of money) by Elio Veltri and Marco Travaglio. Like many other books containing information about Berlusconi, and like *The Economist*'s letter to which we have referred, it became the subject of a libel action which Berlusconi lost. Giuffrida himself was also sued, and the dispute was settled only in 2007.

The proximate source of Fininvest's capital was, for the most part, 38 holding companies, unimaginatively called Holding Italiana 1, Holding Italiana 2 etc. When Giuffrida came to look up the records of these companies in the Banca Rasini's books, he found that all of them were officially, but erroneously, registered as ladies' hairdressers or beauty salons, though it is certain that none of them ever beautified anything more feminine than a balance sheet, or conceivably some money of doubtful origin. It is unclear why they were misclassified in this way – it could have been a simple mistake, or it may have been that it made them less likely to arouse the curiosity of the financial authorities than classifying them as what they really were, purely financial companies.

While investigating these holding companies twenty years after the events recounted in this chapter, Giuffrida, on behalf of the Palermo magistrates, asked Salvatore Sciascia, Fininvest's head of tax affairs, if he could see their books. Sciascia asked for a few days to look them out and get them ready. On the day when he had agreed to hand them over, however, he handed over instead a letter from a lawyer saying that Giuffrida's request was irregular. The magistrates responded with a formal note requiring confiscation of the documents, and the lawyers countered with a letter saying that this request violated the prerogatives accorded to Berlusconi in his capacity as a member of Parliament – as he then was – and couldn't be granted without the formal approval of Parliament. This was false – an Italian member of Parliament cannot personally be arrested without the approval of Parliament, but there is no law to prevent his or her documents being seized.[27] They acquired the documents, but the episode showed the extent of Berlusconi's fear of having light thrown on his business dealings.

Perhaps his fears were misplaced, because the transactions between these companies are truly baffling. One example may illustrate. A company called Palina was set up in 1979 by Enrico Porrà and Adriana Maranelli. The former was a 75-year-old retired accountant, confined to a wheelchair after a stroke; the latter seems to have worked as a carer or home helper. This company undertook essentially just one transaction: on Nov 28th 1979 it bought 800,000 shares in another Berlusconi company called Cantieri Milanesi Riuniti from Countess Annamaria Casati Stampa (who, as already noted, had acquired them in exchange for land). A few days later it bought a further 400,000 shares in the same company from Unione Fiduciaria at the same price, paying about €0.8mn to the Countess and €0.4mn to the trust company for a total of €1.2mn. Where it got this money from is not clear. Two weeks later, Palina sold these shares to another Berlusconi company, Milano 3, for €13.8mn. Doubtless, had this sale come to her attention, the Countess would have been surprised to find that someone else had paid ten times as much as she had received for the shares she had sold a few days earlier.

However, the €13.8mn paid by Milano 3 had a rather spectral character. Once received by Palina, it seems to have been used by Palina to finance the holding companies, which in turn subscribed an increase in capital to Fininvest, which in turn used the extra capital to finance Milano 3. The manager of the Banco Popolare di Abbiategrasso, where these companies held accounts, said when asked about these transactions: "I believe there was no effective movement of money. The operations reflected accounting transactions connected either with capital increases or the financing of associate companies. These operations, all transacted on the same day, represented a circulation of funds, leaving one company in the group, transiting via other companies, and ending up where they started from."[28] Accountants are always suspicious about these seemingly pointless circular flows of money between related companies. Nowadays they are most commonly found in the type of VAT fraud known as "carousel fraud", though there is of course no suggestion that that occurred in this case.

We have noted that in 1998 the Palermo anti-Mafia investigators had become interested in Banca Rasini, where some of the Holding Italiana companies also banked. Even before that, one of them, Paolo Borsellino, had been concerned about possible links between the Mafia, who had vast sums of money to invest, and businessmen whose legitimate businesses might provide possible outlets for laundering this money. Given the obscurity about the original sources of Fininvest's funds, and the extraordinary ingenuity invested in obscuring its financing, it was natural for the investigators to seek to probe, and then hopefully to be able to disprove and set aside, the hypothesis that this man, who was to govern Italy for longer than any leader except Benito Mussolini, had received funds from the Mafia.

Later, in November 2002, magistrates investigating the matter arranged an appointment with Berlusconi (who by then was Prime Minister) at which they would put to him various questions about the origins of Fininvest's funds. However, Berlusconi availed himself of his right to silence, and refused to answer any of the questions. Although he has often said that he has nothing to hide, he appears to have invested a great deal of effort and expended much political capital in his efforts to hide it. His refusal to collaborate with the authorities means that the hypothesis that some of the money used to finance Fininvest came from disreputable sources remains one that cannot be dismissed, though it cannot also be proved.

Most of the transactions by the numerous holding companies involved subscribing additional capital to fund Fininvest's expansion. Much of this capital was made available in cash. However, when in July 2007 the lawsuit between Fininvest and Giuffrida was settled out of court, with Fininvest abandoning any claim for damages, Giuffrida made a statement to the effect that the funds used to finance Fininvest's development may have come from its own retained profits. He did not produce any additional evidence to support this, and it is hard to reconcile the idea of organic growth via the re-investment of profits with the immensely complex transactions designed to fund Fininvest's capital increases. (Capital increases, for example by means such as rights issues or the issue of new shares, are designed precisely for cases in which a company cannot finance its growth by its own retained profits, or by bank borrowing). It is also hard to reconcile this with Berlusconi's own account that he was merely administering the finance for his property development on behalf of the Swiss providers of the capital. If this had been the case, then the reinvested profits would have accrued to them, and not to him.

During the 2004 Dell'Utri trial, the judges heard both from Giuffrida and from a consultant named Iovenitti who was called by the defense to contest Giuffrida's analysis. Their finding was that there was no clear proof that Mafia money had been recycled via Fininvest, but that "neither of the consultants could establish with absolute certainty and clarity the origin of the flows of money, whether illicit or legitimate, that had been invested in the creation of Fininvest's holding companies."[29]

The Media Tycoon

The idea of entering the television industry sprang up as a by-product of Berlusconi's property enterprises. Having built a large agglomeration of flats in a new residential area, he had the excellent idea of avoiding a proliferation of TV aerials by having only one, and supplying all of the properties with cables from it. The next step was to supply the captive audience with content: Berlusconi founded a company named Telemilano to broadcast within the region – at that time Italian law prohibited private broadcasters from operating on a national level. Later, Berlusconi sidestepped this law by buying a set of regional broadcasters, all of whom would broadcast identical content at the same time, thus in effect creating a national network. In order to do this, he needed to acquire a wide network of transmitting stations throughout the country. This was achieved by the same methods that we have seen in the case of the Holding Companies: a proliferation of companies set up by people acting as fronts, but controlled by Berlusconi.

One episode concerning a Sicilian company in the chain gives an insight into the role of the front men in these companies – or rather their lack of any role. It happened that Rete Sicilia had illegally constructed walled shelters for its transmitting equipment in areas classified as woodland. This led the authorities to seek out and question the two men listed as having started the company. The first, Salvatore Accardi, made his statement as follows:

> "I currently work for Enna District Council. In 1979 I was unemployed. At the end of the year, me and Vicenzo Sucato decided

to start a television company. We asked my uncle, the lawyer Giuseppe Bonincontro, how to go about it. In view of the precarious situation we were in, he advised us to go for it. We set up the company at the notary's and I subscribed €5,000 to the company. You have told me that Giovanni Del Santo [Giovanni Dal Santo was a Berlusconi employee often used in connection with companies set up by front-men] was named the sole signatory for the company. I have to say that I don't know anyone of this name, but I can't rule out the possibility that the man we named as sole signatory was called Del Santo. You tell me that the company's headquarters was 71, Corso Vittorio Emanuele, Palermo. If I remember rightly we chose that address because Sucato's fiancée lived there, and it seemed a good idea to have an address in Palermo. I don't think I've ever been there. I never got involved in the administration of the business. Since the business didn't get off the ground for a year, as we had intended, we decided to sell our shares, and I charged my lawyer, Mr Bonincontro, to do so. After a time he found a buyer, but I don't recall his name. You tell me that he was called Antonio Inzaranto. I don't know anyone of that name, but I can't rule out the possibility that it was the name of the man who bought my shares."

The authorities went on to question his colleague, Vincenzo Sucato, whose statement was as follows:

"I currently work for a wholesaler of chickens. I remember that in 1979 I was contacted by a lawyer whose name I can't remember who suggested to me that, along with a family friend, Salvatore Accardi, we should set up a private television company. Personally I've never been involved in anything of this nature. I just remember that we went, along with this lawyer, to the Palermo office of the Bank of Italy, where this lawyer made a payment on my behalf for setting up this TV business. I can't tell you anything more about this lawyer because I only saw him two or three times. I also can't remember whether I went to the notary to sign the document setting up the company. You tell me that one Giovanni Del Santo was nominated sole signatory of the company. Personally I don't know this man, and it definitely wasn't me who suggested that he be nominated. I can't tell you anything about this because it was the lawyer who did everything. He put up the money needed to set up the company. You tell me that on Nov 7th 1980 I sold my shares to Enrico Arnulfo and Antonio Inzaranto. I have to say that I don't know these individuals, and I didn't even know about the sale of the shares. The company's headquarters was where my girlfriend Maria Russotto lived, and maybe we said that was available as headquarters. I've never been to the company headquarters, and I would like to stress that personally I know nothing, because my participation in this company was a pure formality. I know nothing about how the company carried on its business."

Finally, they questioned Mr Bonincontro:

"Accardi is the son of my sister-in-law and Sucato is the son of my first cousin. The boys were unemployed, so we thought of setting up a company to transmit radio and TV, because at that time there was a boom in local transmission stations. They asked me if I could help with setting up the company. We went to the notary, who gave me the company statutes. I don't know any Del Santo, maybe he was there when we set up the company, but I'd like to stress that I don't personally know him. I played no part in selling the shares, and as far as I know I wasn't present when the relevant paperwork was signed. I don't know the purchasers. All I know is that the sale took place because the youngsters couldn't get the company off the ground, and meanwhile Accardi got a job with Enna District Council and Sucato got one as a chicken salesman. It's not true that I was charged with the sale of the company or that I tried to find a buyer. My young relatives just told me they couldn't get it going, and I advised them to sell their shares. I'm definitely not the lawyer Sucato refers to in his statement, because I didn't advance any money, nor did I suggest setting up any company, least of all did I make any payments at any bank."

Many Shakespearean tragedies have roles for characters like these. With their help, and that of many others like them, the network of transmitters was built up around the country, and, by sending tapes of all the programmes to each transmitter, viewers anywhere in the country had the impression that they were viewing a single nationwide network, which was exactly what the legislation was designed to exclude.

From Competitor to Monopolist

It is a very Mediterranean, even an operatic scene, and its consequences were to be deep and long-lasting: two men are in a room, and one has been trying to use his charm and bonhomie to persuade the other to do what he wants. Afraid that he is failing, he switches to a different tactic.

CHAPTER 1: ECONOMIC POWER

He drops to his knees, seizes the other man's hands and begins to kiss them, begging him not to ruin him and his two families (page 49 explains why there are two). This, according to Oscar Mammì, the Minister for Posts and Telecommunications in 1990 – the man whose hands are being kissed – is how Berlusconi pleaded with him for the legislation that would defy the constitutional requirement that there should be a plurality of sources of information in the television sector, and would create the near-monopoly of commercial television that Berlusconi has held ever since[30].

At the time he had set up his television business, there had been two other operators in the television industry: Rete 4 and Italia 1. The former was owned by Mondadori, the giant publishing group that, in addition to its book-publishing activities, owned the daily *La Repubblica* and the weekly *L'Espresso* and many other smaller magazines and newspapers. In 1982 Berlusconi bought Rete 4 and in 1984 he bought Italia 1, unimpeded by any anti-trust investigation. However, it remained unclear whether his way of sidestepping the law would be permitted. In late 1984 magistrates took the view that it should not be, and ordered the closure of his three channels.

The Socialist Prime Minister at the time, Bettino Craxi, also Milanese by birth, had always had good relations with Berlusconi, and he immediately passed a temporary decree legalising this method of transmitting. The lower house of parliament threw out the decree as unconstitutional. Craxi fought back and got it passed again by arduous arm-twisting, at which point the Constitutional Court also ruled that it was unconstitutional, and demanded permanent legislation to ensure adequate competition in the industry.

When the legislation came in 1990 – it was known as the Mammì law – it did exactly what Berlusconi wanted, and ratified his monopoly of commercial TV. It did this by announcing that there would be 12 TV channels, and that Berlusconi, with only 3 of them, would therefore not have an excessive share of the market. In reality, there were only six national stations – three held by RAI, three by Berlusconi – and there were never to be any more until Pay-TV came into being.

Getting this legislation through required all of the clout that Bettino Craxi could muster, and many of his partners in the ruling coalition put up strong resistance. By that time Craxi was no longer Prime Minister, but was a key part of a ruling triumvirate, together with the Christian Democrats Giulio Andreotti, who had taken over the premiership, and Arnaldo Forlani. There was more than a suspicion that bribery had eased the way for this law – which was to be the first of many laws that were drafted with the specific aim of helping Silvio Berlusconi – and the Milan magistrates were later to investigate these suspicions. However, the case was passed to the Rome magistrates, who have always given the political classes an easier ride, and came to nothing. Since then – surprisingly, given that Berlusconi's political opponents held office from 1995 to 2001 and from 2006 to 2008 – there has been no threat to the continuation of his near-monopoly of terrestrial private commercial television.

A key part of Berlusconi's television interests has been the purchase of films and programmes from foreign – mainly US – producers to show on his networks. These purchases were, until 1999, handled by a Maltese company called IMS, and since 1999 have been handled by a Mediaset company called Mediatrade. The financing of these film rights has been controversial. Financial investigators in Italy believe that, rather than simply purchasing the rights and declaring the price paid to the producer as a cost, Fininvest has channelled these purchases through a chain of offshore companies that it controls, swelling the price as the rights pass down the chain, so that most of the profit accrues in the tax havens where these companies are incorporated, and the tax revenues accruing to the government that Mr Berlusconi now directs are correspondingly reduced, as are the profits accruing to the shareholders of Mediaset.

One issue under investigation concerns an amount of some €100 mn which has been traced to a bank account in Hong Kong controlled by a Mr Frank Agrama, an Egyptian-American film director whose work includes "Dawn of the Mummy" and "Queen Kong", and who has produced the "Robotech" series of films. Initially he appeared to have misappropriated these funds from Berlusconi, but prosecutors have been working on the notion that he may in fact have been holding these funds on Berlusconi's account. An earlier case relating to these film rights resulted in Berlusconi and his co-defendants, including Mr Agrama, being charged with illicit appropriation of €276 mn and tax evasion of €60 mn in the period up to 1999. However, this case was eventually timed out under the statute of limitations – the period available before such cases get "timed-out" and the possible criminals become immune was reduced in Mr Berlusconi's second period in office. The funds accruing to these offshore Fininvest subsidiaries during this period appear to have been a source from which various covert, and some illicit, payments were made. When we review the law cases in which Silvio Berlusconi has been involved, we shall have more to say about these issues.

CHAPTER 1: ECONOMIC POWER

Berlusconi's media activities are not confined to television. In 1974, the great Italian journalist, Indro Montanelli, who had long worked with the *Corriere della Sera*, which is perhaps the Italian equivalent to *The Times*, found himself to the right of the prevailing current of opinion on that paper, and decided to found his own newspaper, *Il Giornale*. Montanelli had briefly flirted with fascism in his youth, but had quickly been disillusioned and became a critic of Mussolini, being subsequently imprisoned and condemned to death by his regime. He was strongly anti-Communist, and would probably have been at home as a member of the British Conservative Party. Three years after founding *Il Giornale*, he found himself in need of more working capital, and decided to accept funding from Silvio Berlusconi – as Montanelli put it, he decided to hire Berlusconi to be the paper's owner. For as long as Berlusconi's main interest lay in business rather than in politics, this collaboration worked well for both of them. However, the Mammì law specified that owners of television channels could not also own newspapers, so the nominal ownership of *Il Giornale* passed to Berlusconi's brother Paolo.

By the end of the 1980s the idea of a still more ambitious presence in the world of publishing began to interest Berlusconi. Having already bought Mondadori's television interests, he took a small stake in the remainder of the group, and began to contemplate the possibility of taking it over lock, stock and barrel. Mondadori's newspapers, particularly *La Repubblica* and *L'Espresso*, were strongly critical of the Craxi government, and Craxi therefore was attracted to the idea that his ally Berlusconi, who certainly owed him gratitude for the Mammì law (though he may well have expressed his gratitude in other ways), should take them over, along with the rest of the giant publishing group.

The difficulty was that the Mondadori Fermenton family, the heirs to Arnoldo Mondadori who had originally created the empire, had already made a written pledge to another entrepreneur, Carlo De Benedetti, to pass him a controlling stake by 1990. Undeterred, Berlusconi went to work with his persuasive skills, and finally induced them to pledge to him, also in writing, what they had already pledged to De Benedetti. This naturally led to a dispute between the two groups, Berlusconi's Fininvest and De Benedetti's CIR. It was agreed that it should be settled by arbitration, with each group nominating one arbiter and the third being supplied by the College of Arbitration. The arbiters came down in favour of De Benedetti. Berlusconi did not take this setback lightly, and took the matter to the Court of Appeal, which was called upon to confirm or refute the decision of the arbiters.

Once the case had been heard by the court of appeal, the judge, Vittorio Metta, retired to his chambers to write his decision. Within 24 hours, he produced that decision, a document some 169 pages in length. In the words of the journalist Marco Travaglio – on whose account of this episode I am drawing: "Either Metta could write faster than Balzac, or he had written the judgment before hearing the case, or someone had written it for him." The fact that, immediately after this judgment, Metta received about €200,000 in cash originating from Fininvest's undeclared Swiss accounts, apart from being improper in its own right, suggested that the judgment had been written for him by Fininvest's lawyers, one of whom was Cesare Previti. Berlusconi had succeeded in becoming owner of Mondadori, (though the affair was to have legal implications discussed in Chapter 4).

While this was just what Craxi wanted, it wasn't to the taste of the Christian Democrats, who already in passing the Mammì law had had to swallow many of their principles (such as they were – Margaret Thatcher famously said of their leader Giulio Andreotti that he seemed to have a positive aversion to principle). Andreotti therefore insisted that Berlusconi hand back to De Benedetti some parts of the Mondadori group, including principally the daily *La Repubblica* and the weekly *L'Espresso*, which to the present remain the main focus of opposition to Berlusconi in the mainstream press.

Other business interests

While the media empire forms the true heart of Berlusconi's power, he had also diversified into a couple of other areas: insurance and football. His holding company Fininvest has a 36% stake in the Mediolanum group, which is controlled by Ennio Doris who has a 40% stake. The insurance business that lies at the heart of Mediolanum has prospered and grown, and the group has also diversified into banking: its Banca Mediolanum now has about 800,000 account holders. The group was, however, heavily exposed to Lehman brothers, whose collapse in 2008 required large infusions of cash into the Mediolanum group from the two main shareholders, Fininvest and Mr Doris.

Much more important to Berlusconi's image is his ownership of the football club AC Milan. He saved the club from approaching bankruptcy in 1986, and in the ensuing years it has achieved enormous success in winning competitions. As owner of the team, Berlusconi's name is omnipresent in the sports pages, as well as the financial pages and the political pages of the newspapers, and the blokeish image that he is able to convey, as a soccer fan who has steered a team to success, is worth many votes.

A Second Household

While it is not relevant to his business interests, it is convenient to note here another important change that occurred in the years covered in this Chapter. In 1980 Berlusconi saw a play featuring young actress named Miriam Bartolini, acting under the stage name of Veronica Lario. He became infatuated, and set her up in a separate house in Milan, while continuing to remain married to his first wife for the next five years. In 1984, Veronica Lario gave birth to Berlusconi's daughter Barbara in Switzerland in great secrecy – Craxi was witness at the baptism – and in the following year, after divorcing his first wife, Berlusconi started a marriage which was to last for twenty-nine years.

CHAPTER 2:
POLITICAL COLLAPSE

Tangentopoli

During the late 1980s, magistrates in Milan began to investigate a number of white-collar crimes connected with the financing of large public sector contracts. The first investigation led to the arrest by Antonio Di Pietro – the magistrate whose name was to be associated with the ensuing assault on corruption – in early 1992 of a member of the Socialist Party, and aspirant to be mayor of Milan, Mario Chiesa. Chiesa was operating a scam involving large payments for the removal of corpses by undertakers from the hospital where he worked. Bettino Craxi, leader of the Socialist Party, described Chiesa as a "wild splinter" of a party that was otherwise uncorrupt, and "in fifty years of government in Milan, had never had a single politician under investigation for such crimes". The investigations continued, with no public announcements being made by the magistrates in order not to influence the elections that were held in April 1992. However, Craxi accused the magistrates of having a "well-defined political goal", while the Northern League, the party whose programme involved greater autonomy, and even a separate state, for the North, used the investigations to sow widespread disillusion about "thieving Rome" – *Roma ladrona* – whose corrupt ways were draining wealth from the hard-working Northern provinces.

The Northern League did well in the elections, while the Christian Democrats lost five percentage points, falling to just under 30% of the vote, and the Socialists lost one percentage point. Immediately following the elections, the investigations that had been under way since February and before led to the arrest of an increasing number of businessmen and politicians. The growing scandal, widely referred to as *Tangentopoli*, or Bribesville, brought to light the fact that political parties were increasingly relying on hand-outs from the up-and-coming businessmen in Lombardy and elsewhere, in return for which they would deliver favours. The investigation was known as *Mani Pulite*, or Clean Hands, and rapidly spread from Milan to other Italian cities. Both politicians and businessmen began to confess. One Socialist politician panicked when two policemen arrived at his residence, and immediately confessed to his misdemeanours, only to find subsequently that they had come to fine him for a traffic offence.

It was becoming clear that the costs of public works were being swollen, at massive cost of the taxpayer, not only to finance the costs of the political parties, but also to increase the private wealth of the politicians. A joke of the time expresses what was going on: three companies were asked to provide a quote for repainting a town hall. A German company quoted €150,000, a French company €300,000, and an Italian company €450,000. The town clerk asked each to explain their quote. The German company said the costs included €50,000 for materials, €50,000 for labour and €50,000 for their profit. The French company said their labour and material costs were much higher since they were employing only the most experienced painters and using the finest quality paint. The representative of the Italian company explained his bid to the town clerk in this way: "€150,000 for you, €150,000 for me, and €150,000 to pay the Germans".

As the investigations proceeded, public opinion was decisively on the side of the magistrates, and Di Pietro enjoyed immense popularity. Conversely, Craxi was becoming a figure of ridicule and contempt as it became clear that his Socialist Party had been leading the decline into an increasingly amoral political climate. Although he had hoped to resume as Prime Minister after the election, the President insisted that the job be held by someone not under investigation, and Giuliano Amato took over the reins of government. Public disenchantment with politicians was almost universal – an atmosphere strikingly similar to the one seen in Britain following the MPs' expenses scandal of 2009. However, if the public reaction was similar, the scale of the corruption was certainly significantly larger in Italy. In September 1992, a Socialist politician named Sergio Moroni committed suicide, leaving a letter saying that his crimes had been committed, not for personal enrichment, but for the benefit of his party, and denouncing the system by which political parties were funded. However, it was by no means the case that all of the bribes went straight to party funds; many politicians were found to have benefited privately.

Craxi tried to undermine Di Pietro and the other magistrates in the Milan Pool, saying "we shall soon find out that Di Pietro is anything but the

CHAPTER 2: POLITICAL COLLAPSE

hero that he is made out to be. There are many, too many, aspects of *Mani Pulite* that remain unclear". Craxi also tried to smear Di Pietro with various accusations of improper conduct – two of Di Pietro's friends were offered money to say that Di Pietro took drugs – though none of the investigations into these smears threw up any wrongdoing.

Chapter 8 will show that Berlusconi's supporters have followed essentially the same smear tactics that were then followed by Craxi, though their control of television has made them much more effective. A small town in Northern Tuscany, Aulla, has even erected a statue to the heroes of Tangentopoli – the heroes being considered to be, not the magistrates who brought the malpractices to light, but the businessmen and politicians who lost their careers and sometimes committed suicide when their misdeeds became known.

Initially Berlusconi was untouched by this scandal, though, given his close political alliance with Craxi and the extent to which he had benefited from the legislation that Craxi had pushed through, he could not remain indifferent. Craxi resigned as Secretary of the Socialist party in February 1993. In April he admitted having received illegal funding, defending this on the grounds that that was what everyone was doing. Although magistrates wanted to arrest him, parliament for the time being kept him immune. But his unpopularity was such that coins were flung at him, and banknotes waved at him, when he appeared in public. (The wavers of banknotes sang, to the tune of *"Guantanamera"*, the refrain *"Vuoi pure questo, Bettino vuoi pure questo?"* – do you want this too, Bettino?) In June, the investigations came a step nearer to Berlusconi when Aldo Brancher, a manager at Fininvest, was arrested for giving bribes. Berlusconi sent a fax to Montanelli, editor of *Il Giornale*, demanding that the newspaper attack the pool of magistrates, but Montanelli refused.

In May, De Benedetti, the industrialist with whom Berlusconi had contested the ownership of Mondadori, admitted that he had provided illicit funds to political parties. In July, another leading industrialist, Raul Gardini, committed suicide when his business crashed and he himself was about to be arrested. A few days earlier, the president of the state-owned oil company ENI, Gabriele Cagliari, had also committed suicide. These suicides were the precursors to a trial concerning a joint venture between ENI and Montedison, Gardini's group. The trial was broadcast live, and involved all of the main political parties. Although the Northern League had always supported the *Mani Pulite* investigations, and had claimed that the misdeeds that had come to light were characteristic of a political

IMPUNITY BERLUSCONI'S GOAL AND ITS CONSEQUENCES

system that it vigorously opposed, its leader, Umberto Bossi, was one of those convicted of having received large bribes.

From 1992 onwards, it was becoming clear that the Italian political system was sinking. Ever since the war, the Christian Democrats had been at or close to the centre of power, with changing coalition partners. Since the ending of Soviet Communism in 1989, the Communist party, which had until then been the major threat to the continuation of the status quo in Italy, had been trying to reform itself into a Social Democratic Party, but had been upstaged by Craxi's socialists who had been governing with the Christian Democrats since 1983. But the socialists were now even more discredited than the Christian Democrats. On the right was the Italian Social Movement, in direct line of descent from Mussolini's fascist party. It had been headed since 1991 by Gianfranco Fini. Fini's ultimate aim, still far from having been achieved at that point, was to convert the MSI into a respectable right-wing party and to gradually drop the association with fascism. On the right too was the Northern League, with a vague ideology comprising Celtic mysticism, xenophobia, resentment of the volume of taxes being spent and mis-spent in the South, and resentment of Roman bureaucracy. The first of these parties represented centralism, and drew its support mainly from the South, while the second aimed at decentralisation, if not outright secession, and drew its support from the North. They could scarcely ally with each other to create a coherent alternative to the parties of the left.

The mood of the public was above all one of disenchantment and cynicism. The middle-of-the-road voter – the kind of voter who would vote SPD or Christian Democrat in Germany, Labour, Liberal or Conservative in Britain – did not know where to turn. The only public figure they liked the look of was the magistrate Di Pietro who had helped to bring down this edifice of corruption, but he was not standing for office. By December 1993, Craxi himself was in court, and in May 1994 he fled to Tunisia in order to escape jail. By the time of his departure, he was the most thoroughly discredited politician in Italian history. At no point did his friend Berlusconi visit him in exile, nor did he publicly defend Craxi until after his death in 2000. Yet, sixteen years later, the Mayor of Milan was to name a street after him, and it was the magistrates, and not Craxi, who were portrayed by Berlusconi's government and his media as being the wrongdoers in the matter. What strange alchemy succeeded in bringing about a change which led to Craxi coming to be seen as the Father and Berlusconi as the Son, (while Corruption is the less-than-holy spirit)?

Organisations in search of new political patrons

Those who had looked to the Craxi-Andreotti-Forlani group for political assistance needed to find other sources of support. One such organisation was the Catholic Church. The Christian Democrats had, as their name implies, been the main reference point for the Vatican, whose interest in Italian politics has always been closer and more intense than in the politics of any other country. (Nietzsche's description of the Catholic Church as the last and greatest of the ruins left behind by the Roman Empire still strikes a chord). For the time being the Church continued to support the Christian Democrats, and when the party began to crumble, it transferred its support to some of the small successor parties that were set up in the hope of inheriting the mantle of the once dominant and now disgraced party. In particular, the PPI party of Rocco Buttiglione was close to the Vatican. But these parties were too fragmented and leaderless to succeed, creating an opportunity for any new party that could demonstrate itself as worthy to inherit the immensely valuable political support that the Vatican could provide.

Fininvest itself was also badly in need of a new political reference point. Berlusconi had seen many of his fellow-industrialists disgraced, imprisoned or even driven to suicide. It was clear that he himself would be investigated eventually. He said to Montanelli at this time that his only option for avoiding bankruptcy and jail was to go into politics himself. He had spotted a gap in the political market: someone who was rich enough not to need to take bribes from anyone, and thus might avoid the public's cynicism about existing politicians; someone who was able to provide continuity in the country's broad political and economic policies along with a change in its personalities; and someone who could present himself as a man of action with a proven record of getting things done. This gap he set out to fill.

There was one other important organisation which had lost its previous political reference point. Cosa Nostra had actively supported the Christian Democrats for most of the post-war period. In 2003 a court found that the Christian Democrat leader Giulio Andreotti had assisted the Mafia until, but not after, 1980, though the statute of limitations meant that he remained unpunished. In the early 1990s, finding that he had ceased to provide the support that they expected, Cosa Nostra switched its support to the Socialists, but when Craxi was discredited they again found themselves adrift. This part of the story will be taken up in the next Chapter.

Berlusconi enters politics

The story of Berlusconi's entry into politics has been well told both by David Lane and by Alexander Stille, and only the briefest summary is necessary here. As far as the general public was concerned, it began with a broadcast from his house at Arcore in January 1994, in which he began by saying that he did not wish to see the country governed by those who were inseparably linked to the economic and political failures of the past. This broadcast is always referred to, particularly by Berlusconi himself, as the day in which he "entered the field" (*la discesa in campo*), a phrase suggesting knights setting off to a tournament – though, as the comedian Roberto Benigni has pointed out, the phrase was often used with a different meaning in rural houses that lacked a toilet. He established a new political party, Forza Italia, which, in the April 1994 elections, became the largest in the country, in terms of votes cast.

How does one set about turning a business into a political force within a matter of months? The achievement was the greatest in Berlusconi's career, and provides ample testament to his organisational skills and his ability to seize opportunities.

Clearly the political framework was one which gave the best chances for a new political party. The public's disenchantment with what it saw as the corruption of the old political forces was manifest. But in addition, Berlusconi had at his command a business organisation which was uniquely well placed to diversify into politics, adding a new and different product line – Berlusconi's political leadership – to the existing range.

That range comprised not only television and printed media, but also financial services, building and, at that time, retail (Berlusconi had bought, though he was later to sell, the Standa retail chain). The retail and financial services activities, in particular, had a staff that was spread throughout the country. Moreover, as in many successful young businesses, the style of management was lean and informal, giving plenty of opportunity for able young employees to innovate and take risks. At the same time, it was highly centralised in the sense that there was no challenge to Berlusconi's authority – ultimately, he was the one to take decisions. The history of rapid growth in turnover, of the successful challenge to the existing RAI television network, of constantly moving into new areas, had built a high level of morale and a great belief in Berlusconi's leadership qualities. All of these factors were essential to the move into the political arena.

CHAPTER 2: POLITICAL COLLAPSE

The idea of moving into politics was first mooted in mid-1992, when Dell'Utri contacted a politician on the left of the Christian Democrats, Ezio Cartotto, and asked him to work on the possibility of Fininvest entering politics, given that the political forces which had been supporting Fininvest were under grave threat. Dell'Utri explained to Cartotto that there was great resistance within Fininvest to the idea of entering politics, and that he must therefore work in secrecy to draw up plans which could be taken out of the drawer if and when the time was ripe. Cartotto says that he is not sure when Berlusconi first came to know that he was there and what he was doing, but is sure that it was not later than September 1992. At that time Berlusconi gave a speech to his managers, saying that "the friends that are helping us count for less and less, our enemies for more and more, and we must prepare ourselves for any event in order to fight these enemies" [31].

In April 1993 Berlusconi called Cartotto to say that he couldn't decide between the views of Dell'Utri, who favoured entering politics, and his other old friend Fedele Confalonieri, who opposed it, and that he had never been uncertain about something for so long. He told Cartotto that he wanted to seek the advice of a friend whom he held in high esteem, namely Bettino Craxi, and to hold a meeting between the three of them, without Dell'Utri. In the meeting, Craxi supported the move into politics, though it was his understanding that Berlusconi would lend support to existing political figures, rather than create a new party with himself at the fore. This indeed was the assumption on which Cartotto had been working – that Fininvest would help to set up a party that would be a "container" for an alliance of those political groupings who on the one hand were not Communists, and who had also emerged relatively clean from the Tangentopoli scandals. It was not at this stage anticipated that Berlusconi himself would lead the new party.

Craxi was opposed to the idea of any alliance with the neo-fascist MSI, feeling that this would undermine the credibility of any new political party, and he was also dubious about whether an alliance with the Northern League could be made to work. Berlusconi, on the other hand, felt that it was necessary to bring all anti-left groupings into play, as far as possible.

At the end of the meeting, Berlusconi had decided that Dell'Utri's line was the right one. However, he had a specific and perhaps rather peculiar fear that he expressed to Cartotto: "Confalonieri and Letta tell me that it's crazy to go into politics – they [the politicians and the press, not Confalonieri and Letta] will destroy me. They'll do everything they can against me. They'll go ferreting around in my papers and say that I'm a Mafioso."

| 57

The first step was taken in July 1993, when two of the major daily papers, *Corriere* and *Repubblica*, carried articles stating the need for a new political grouping and a new political caste. The one in *Repubblica* was by Berlusconi, the one in *Corriere* by a political scientist called Giuliano Urbani. At first the two articles seemed quite independent, but Urbani had in fact been working with Berlusconi. The programme set out in the articles was essentially to extend the Thatcher-Reagan revolution to Italy: to reduce the size of the state and to give freer play to market forces.

Having set out the kernel of the political programme, the next step was to establish organs for monitoring and measuring public opinion, in effect carrying out the same type of market research for the new political product as one would do for a new commercial product. In October 1993 an organisation named Diakron was established, whose function was to carry out surveys and focus groups in order to establish the voting public's priorities and concerns, the style that would please them, the hopes and fears that would motivate them, and the type of advertising that would strike a chord. Even before July, Berlusconi had commissioned a survey from an external consulting arm, but the aim of Diakron was to bring this type of activity inside the company's framework.

The next, and perhaps the most important, step was to establish what were to be the local branches of the party. In November 1993 an organisation called the National Association of Forza Italia clubs was set up in Milan. At that point, there were no such clubs, but the intention was to set up one in each of 8,000 parishes in the country. The first was set up the following month in Brugherio, where, 30 years earlier, Berlusconi had built his first property development. The financial services division of Fininvest played an important role in getting local clubs off the ground, while ample television advertising helped to arouse interest throughout the country in this new political development (which was not yet a political party). The clubs financed themselves through a €12 membership fee, and did not get direct financial support from the centre. Having had their curiosity aroused by the TV coverage, many voters welcomed this novel alternative to the traditional political parties, and there was no shortage of volunteers to help. These clubs acted as shop windows in which the new political product could be displayed, and their rapid proliferation increased Berlusconi's bargaining power when it came to negotiating with political allies. Berlusconi was conscious that the very concept of a political party had been put into question by the corruption scandal, and has always been careful to avoid describing Forza Italia, or its successor the Popolo della Libertà (PDL), as a party, or of giving it a name that includes the word "party".

CHAPTER 2: POLITICAL COLLAPSE

After the decision to contest the election had been made, the next step was to select candidates. This was left to Publitalia, the branch of Fininvest whose responsibility it was to sell advertising space on the TV channels and other media owned by the group. This group, headed by Marcello Dell'Utri, had excellent contacts throughout Italy with industrialists, chambers of commerce, local authorities and other notables. It had always been the spearhead of the business, with its morale boosted by the knowledge that it was the sales that it brought home that were paying for just about everything else in the Fininvest empire. Candidates were chosen on very much the same criteria that were used to select sales representatives. The ideal candidate would be someone in their 40s, respected in the local community, without any previous experience in politics, but committed to the free-market creed that had been set out by Urbani. Prospective candidates undertook, at their own expense, an intensive course of training in how to put their message across and how to conduct themselves on television and in interviews. Those who did not perform well in the training course were dropped. Ezio Cartotto, who had played such an important role at the outset of Fininvest's diversification into politics, was not selected as a candidate since he was felt to be too much to the left of the Christian Democrats, and had opposed the idea of allying with the MSI (soon to be renamed Alleanza Nazionale).

By the end of November, Berlusconi had become convinced that he personally must lead the new party. The focus groups and market research that had been done by Diakron showed that he enjoyed a high level of public recognition and respect, as a man of action, and as someone seen as being outside the corrupt politics of the day.

The final, and crucial, step was to choose his political allies. Berlusconi was convinced of the need for all parties that were not of the left to join together in the alliance. Two of the largest parties of the right, however, were seen at the time as being beyond the pale. The first of these was the Movimento Sociale Italiano (MSI), which changed its name to Alleanza Nazionale (AN) in January 1994. The old name harked back to the party's origins: the Repubblica Sociale Italiano was the official name of the puppet state (usually known as the Repubblica di Salò) that was set up by Mussolini in the North of Italy, under German protection, after Mussolini's fall from power, imprisonment and subsequent release by German troops. The MSI was a direct successor to Mussolini's party. The post-war Italian state was founded explicitly upon the values of the Resistance that had fought against the Germans and the Fascists in the final year of the war, and the MSI was therefore a party that was in a sense in opposition not just to the post-war governments of Italy, but to the constitution itself.

Central to Berlusconi's decision to ally with AN was not only, as we have seen, his view that all forces opposed to the Communist party (or its successors) must combine, but also the new electoral system that had been brought into being by a referendum in 1991. This increased the number of single-member constituencies and reduced the role of proportional representation. Alliances in which a number of parties could agree to back a single candidate for a particular seat were necessary in order to win. It is to Berlusconi's credit that he quickly appreciated the new style of politics that this would bring, and in particular the greater importance of individual leaders of parties and of coalitions.

The leadership of the MSI had been taken over in 1991 by the 38-year old Gianfranco Fini, whose aim was to move it closer towards being a "respectable" party of the right, and gradually to drop the Fascist heritage. The change of name was part of this move, which had been tentatively begun by Fini's predecessor Giorgio Almirante. Old hands and hard-liners were reassured, though, when Fini described Mussolini as the "greatest statesman of the 20th century".

The other alliance was with the Northern League, the populist grouping under Umberto Bossi which represented the resentment of Northern Italy against the centralised state which was taking their taxes to pay for the backward and corrupt south, as well as for a large bureaucracy. The resentment was targeted above all at immigrants, at first from the south of Italy, and later, and much more strongly, against those coming into Italy from outside, and especially from outside Europe. If Berlusconi's personal style was that of the saloon bar, with its nudges, guffaws and risqué jokes, Bossi's style was that of the public bar, with outright verbal and even physical abuse never far from the foreground.

Though both of the right, the centralism of the AN was radically opposed to the federalism, or outright separatism, of the Northern League, and they could not ally with each other. However, each could ally with Berlusconi, the outsider whose massive wealth, strong personal image and burgeoning Forza Italia clubs promised new hope of power to parties that were widely regarded as being on the fringe. Berlusconi made one alliance with the AN in the South, called the "Pole of Good Government", and another with the League in the North, called the "Pole of Freedom". To secure their support, Berlusconi was initially generous with both partners in allocating them seats in the regions where they would stand together.

CHAPTER 2: POLITICAL COLLAPSE

However, the one factor that made this triumph possible was the one factor that also made it wholly undesirable: Berlusconi's business empire. In Wagner's Ring cycle, the deed that is essential in order to set up Wotan's palace at Valhalla – the theft of the Ring – is also the deed that condemns it to eventual doom. In exactly the same way, the association of business with politics, which was essential in order to realise Berlusconi's goal, was also to ensure that, whatever electoral successes might be achieved in the future, the whole enterprise was destined to be deeply prejudicial to the interests of the country which Berlusconi hoped to serve. (In this hope he was certainly completely sincere. One of the secrets of his salesmanship is his ability to persuade both himself and others that what is in his narrow personal interest is also in the broader interests of whoever he is currently seeking to persuade).

In his TV broadcast, he announced that he was setting aside all his managerial roles within the businesses that he had founded in order to devote himself to politics. Many of the listeners would have taken this as signalling an intention to deal with the conflicts of interest that, in all democratic countries, would preclude a businessman from entering politics while continuing to own large enterprises. In these early days in particular, Berlusconi made many statements, usually rather ambiguous in their phrasing, which indicated his intentions to deal with the problems of conflict of interest. One statement that was not at all ambiguous was made in November 1994. He said "Today I have decided to sell my businesses, because I believe that, when someone takes on a task, and certain conditions exist that could be prejudicial to his fulfilment of that task, he should have the courage to sacrifice himself".

This promise was never fulfilled, and he continues to this day to be the beneficiary owner of the same businesses that he owned at the time that he entered politics. Measures taken by the state that benefit Mediaset also benefit him personally, and Chapter 6 shows that, while he has been in charge of the government, the state has indeed taken many measures that specifically benefit Mediaset.

It may seem strange that it was left entirely to him to decide whether and when to try to resolve his conflicts of interest. Were there no laws or precedents which could have been used to prevent somebody in his position entering politics? Yes, there were. A law passed in 1957 laid down that those who had "significant licences (*concessioni*) granted by the state", along with their permanent advisors, were ineligible to hold public office. The licences to transmit television programmes, which Berlusconi held thanks to the actions of Craxi in his favour, were exactly the type of operation envisaged by this law (passed, of course, long before Berlusconi was on the political or even the business scene, and therefore in no way directed against him). However, it so happened that another, rather minor political figure, Mario Cecchi Gori, who was a senator for the party that had sought to replace the Christian Democrats, had some interests in the field of television, much smaller than those of Berlusconi (he had an interest in the pay television Telepiu, and in the *La 7* channel). Since Cecchi Gori had political allies on the other side of the spectrum from Berlusconi, parliament decided by a vote not to apply the law. The cavil that allowed them to do this was that the licences held by Berlusconi's company were actually in the name of his managing director, Fedele Confalonieri, and not in Berlusconi's own name. However, this was clearly exactly the kind of circumstance for which the law was designed.

Parliament's action in deciding to interpret the letter of this law in a way that totally negated its spirit was indefensible, and was to have dire consequences for many decades to come. It may have been taken on the basis that the strong popular vote for Berlusconi's party indicated that the voters wanted him personally to take power. There is some force in this argument, but it set the tone for many subsequent occasions when legality was to be opposed to the alleged will of the people.

In the event, the action that was supposed to regulate his conflict of interest was based on that of a "blind trust". But the analogy with a blind trust in the sense that it would be understood in other countries is wholly misleading. When a politician puts his wealth into a blind trust (in the usual sense of the term), the blind trust will then invest it in some mix of equities, property and bonds, and the politician in question will not know exactly which assets it has been invested in. Thus it might all be invested in an oil company, for example, but if the politician then takes steps that affect the taxation of oil companies, he will not be suspected of a conflict of interest because he will not know that that is where his money is invested. These principles do not apply in Berlusconi's case. Everybody knows that his wealth is tied up in Fininvest and its related companies, and that any action that helps these companies directly benefits him. The poisonous conflict of interest remains utterly unresolved, seventeen years after Berlusconi stepped into the political arena. What is still more worrying is that many Italians have begun to regard it as a normal and acceptable state of affairs. A law passed by the 2001 Berlusconi government declared, ridiculously, that "mere" ownership does not in itself give rise to a conflict of interest, provided that the owner has delegated others to look after his interests on his behalf.

CHAPTER 2: POLITICAL COLLAPSE

By the time of Berlusconi's broadcast, Fininvest, like most other groups of its size, was already being investigated by magistrates in Milan, Turin and Rome. It is one of the commonly repeated myths of Berlusconi and his supporters that magistrates only began to be interested in him once he had entered politics. This is quite false – indeed by the time of his broadcast four years had already elapsed since an amnesty had prevented him from paying the consequences of an act of perjury. Fininvest was in trouble both because of its debts and because of the suspicion that it had illicitly provided funds to Craxi's Socialist Party in exchange for the legislation needed by its TV interests. Marcello Dell'Utri himself, at the end of 2004, was to say that "Berlusconi entered politics in order to defend his companies". Towards the end of 2003, Berlusconi had told Montanelli, the editor of *Il Giornale* that "if I don't enter politics I will end up bankrupt and in jail".

This relationship with *Il Giornale* was one of the ones most directly affected by Berlusconi's entry into politics. As we noted, he had become the owner of this newspaper in order to provide the capital needed by its editor, Indro Montanelli. As long as Berlusconi remained an entrepreneur outside of politics, the relationship worked well. Montanelli had the editorial freedom that he expected – we have seen him decline Berlusconi's request to start attacking the Mani Pulite magistrates.

However, once Berlusconi had entered politics, the two men had drastically different visions of what the newspaper's role was to be. Montanelli had told Berlusconi, some time before the TV broadcast, that he was entirely opposed to the idea of Berlusconi entering politics. Silvio Berlusconi, remember, was not the owner of the newspaper. The Mammì laws laid down that the licence to broadcast on TV would be withdrawn from anyone who owned a newspaper. For that reason, the paper had been passed on to Berlusconi's younger brother Paolo (referred to by Montanelli as *Berluschino*). However, it became abundantly clear that this was a mere pro forma change, and that real control continued to lie, illegally, with Silvio, who presented himself at the offices of *Il Giornale*, soon after Montanelli had made clear his opposition to Berlusconi's political ambitions, and demanded that the paper take a line that would be strictly in accordance with the electoral needs of his new political party.

This was unacceptable to Montanelli, who resigned in short order, taking with him a large number of the best journalists on the paper (including Marco Travaglio, to this day the most trenchant and well-informed critic of Berlusconi, and a worthy successor to Montanelli). Montanelli was to start another newspaper, *La Voce*, despite being by then 85 years old, but it did not last long, and from 1995 to 2001 Montanelli was to continue his criticism of Berlusconi from the pages of the *Corriere della Sera*. Montanelli had a close knowledge of Berlusconi's personality, as a result of their years of collaboration before the break. We quoted in the Introduction his views on Berlusconian Italy ("the basest and most vulgar of all the Italies I have known in my long life"), and he was also a connoisseur of one of Berlusconi's most salient characteristics: "he lies as he eats", and again "Lying is to him what breathing is to you or me". "Berlusconi's ability to lie is almost touching. Because he is the first to believe in his lies. In 90 years I've seen many liars, but never one as 'sincere' as he is. I've even seen him weeping, like great actors do." And again, "Berlusconi is a man of unimaginable resources, who has a completely personal conception of the truth: for him, the truth is what he says."

The first Berlusconi government

While the achievement of the first election victory was astonishing, the success was to be short-lived. A foretaste of what was to come came when the government tried to bring in a law that would free from gaol many of those who had been convicted during the *Mani Pulite* trials, in which by this time Berlusconi's brother Paolo was also at risk. The other major piece of legislation was a law passed by Finance Minister Tremonti to encourage investment by allowing large tax immunities to companies undertaking such investment. One of the major beneficiaries of this law was Mediaset, which claimed large volumes of expenses associated with the purchase of film rights as investment, and duly got the tax benefits.

Berlusconi had sought to turn the great popularity of the *Mani Pulite* investigations to his advantage by offering a post in his government to Antonio Di Pietro. Di Pietro refused, knowing that the investigations would soon begin to involve Berlusconi's own company. Later, Berlusconi was to deny ever having made this offer. In 1997, Di Pietro entered politics, subsequently founding his own party, Italia dei Valori, which remains the most outspoken supporter of the rule of law, and consequently the most trenchant and consistent opposition to Berlusconi's party.

Berlusconi's first coalition was brought down by the defection of Bossi. The leader of the Northern League felt that Forza Italia was fishing in his pond and poaching the kind of elector to whom the League owed their support. Unable to command a majority, Berlusconi was replaced by a technical government headed by Lamberto Dini.

CHAPTER 2: POLITICAL COLLAPSE

In the months following the breakdown of the coalition, some of Bossi's fruitiest vituperation – and vituperation has always been the quality in which Bossi has excelled – was directed at his ex-ally. Even before the election he had declared that "a P2 businessman can't become Prime Minister". After the coalition broke up he called him "a little tyrant, a dictator", "an incompetent", "a Nazi", "an antidemocratic monster", "the great fascist from Arcore", "that ugly Mafioso who earns money from heroin and cocaine", and so on.

The whole episode of Berlusconi's first government had lasted only a few months, and the centre-left convincingly won the elections in 1996. Montanelli was to say, in 2001, that "Berlusconi is one of those diseases that get cured with a vaccine. To be cured of Berlusconi we need a good dose of the Berlusconi vaccine." The 1994 vaccine was not yet sufficient: even the almost lethal injection of the Berlusconi vaccine from 2001 to 2006 was to prove inadequate to cure the disease.

The period after the centre-left's election victory in 1996 should have provided an opportunity to pass legislation concerning matters such as conflicts of interest, media plurality and the eligibility of those under investigation to hold office. Had this been done, there would have been no need for the further painful vaccinations. But, in perhaps his greatest political coup to date, Berlusconi managed to sidetrack the government into a long-drawn out and ultimately fruitless negotiation about constitutional changes, which effectively distracted them from passing the much-needed legislation that would have prevented the anomalies that were to follow. Much of the blame for this fiasco must go to Massimo D'Alema, leader of the Left Democrats - the successor party to the Italian Communist Party. The centre-left were also riven by infighting within their coalition, just as Berlusconi's coalition had been. Though they managed to survive for longer, the price that they paid for this was a growing exasperation on the part of the electorate, who began once again to yearn for clear and decisive leadership.

Co-operation with the Northern League was eventually re-established in the late 1990s when it became clear that Forza Italia and the League needed each other if either were to have a chance of returning to power. Co-operation with Alleanza Nazionale continued, and culminated in the party's merger in 2009 with Forza Italia, now renamed the People of Liberty (PDL)[v]. The name is significant in that it continues to show Ber-

---

v   Gianfranco Fini was to leave the PDL little more than a year later, unwilling to abet Berlusconi's pursuit of impunity any longer. But most of the other politicians from AN remained in the PDL.

lusconi's wish to avoid anything that could be described as a traditional political party – hence the word "party" remains taboo. If the lightning success of Forza Italia in the 1994 elections, so soon after its founding, is one of Berlusconi's greatest achievements, the patient rebuilding of his political fortunes over the years from 1994 to 2001 must rank alongside it.

CHAPTER 3:
THE SCENT OF MAFIA

Even to include a chapter discussing the links between Silvio Berlusconi and organised crime will seem to Berlusconi's supporters to constitute proof of an irredeemable bias against the man. To many of his critics, the lack of any such discussion would mean omitting one of the most alarming features of current Italian politics. We must tread carefully, and will try to make it clear where there is doubt, and where the onus of proof lies. As in the discussion of Berlusconi's legal cases, it is important to bear in mind the notion of different levels of proof for different purposes. If an individual is to be publicly condemned and punished for a crime, a high degree of proof is essential. But if an individual stands for public office, the onus of proof must be on him or her to establish that any suspicions are unfounded. A 60% probability of guilt, for example, is inadequate for a criminal conviction, but massively excessive for a political leader.

One thing is certain: if there has been a relationship between Silvio Berlusconi and Cosa Nostra, then that relationship has been mediated through the person of Marcello Dell'Utri, his lifelong friend. Most of the relevant suspicions relating to the presence of links between Berlusconi and organised crime were discussed in the 2004 trial of Marcello Dell'Utri (together with Gaetano Cinà) for aiding the Mafia. Dell'Utri was convicted in that trial and sentenced to nine years' detention, but before the conviction is regarded as final, and the punishment imposed, two more stages had to be gone through. The first of these, the appeal, was concluded in June 2010 and resulted in a reduction in the sentence to seven years. It was held that, while there was proof of the assistance he provided to the Mafia until the early 1990s, the evidence thereafter was inadequate to justify the finding that he had continued to work with them later – including, crucially, the years when he was setting up the political party which was to propel Berlusconi to power. The final stage will be a hearing before the *Corte di Cassazione,* after which, if the sentence is confirmed, Marcello Dell'Utri will go to jail.

In Italy, as elsewhere, judges provide a full explanation of their reasons for reaching their conclusions, but in the Italian system these documents (known as *motivazioni*) are often much more detailed. This chapter draws heavily on the 641 pages of the document published in November 2010 in which the Palermo appeal court set out its reasons for a verdict which surprised many on both sides of the political divide. Other relevant matters are to be found in other court proceedings, in particular the investigations of magistrates in Caltanissetta and in Florence into the Mafia outrages of the early 1990s. These investigations were ultimately archived, but turned up some worthwhile facts.

The Mangano Relationship

The mid-1970s were years of violence and lawlessness, subsequently referred to by Italians as "the years of lead". Kidnappings were common, and no rich family could feel itself safe. It was natural that Berlusconi should take steps to safeguard himself and his family. The Dell'Utri appeal recounts how he reacted:

> Berlusconi had indeed received serious threats – it was not really important where they came from – which led him to use his recently recruited employee Marcello Dell'Utri who, thanks to his Sicilian origins, would find the right solution to guarantee his safety, thanks to his friendships with people who had links to the highest levels of the mafia.[32]

One of these people was Gaetano Cinà, the owner of a laundry in Palermo, but, more significantly, linked by close family ties to prominent Mafiosi. His sister was married to Benedetto Citarda, a member of the Malaspina mafia family, to which their son Giovanni also belonged. One of the daughters of this Cinà-Citarda couple married Girolamo ("Mimmo") Teresi, a Palermo businessman who was deputy to Stefano Bontate, then effectively the most prominent Mafioso. Another daughter married Stefano Bontate's brother Giovanni, and two other daughters also married Mafiosi. Gaetano Cinà was co-defendant with Marcello Dell'Utri in the trial and the appeal, but was dead by the time the appeal was heard.

Cinà's son had played in the Bacigalupo football club in Palermo when Dell'Utri worked there, and the two men became lifelong friends. The Bacigalupo football club attracted young men from the wealthier parts of Palermo, but when they played away games in less salubrious areas,

CHAPTER 3: THE SCENT OF MAFIA

there was often the threat of violence after the match, especially if the Bacigalupo boys won. For greater security, they found it helpful to be accompanied by a man named Vittorio Mangano, who Dell'Utri said belonged among the "less refined people", but because he was able to "respond physically at the skirmishes that often took place", his presence was found to be helpful. He was not a friend of Dell'Utri in the same way that Cinà was, but their careers were to be more closely linked than perhaps either would have wished.

The way in which Dell'Utri responded to the need to provide Berlusconi with security was recounted by Francesco Di Carlo, in an account which was considered truthful both in the original trial and in the appeal. Di Carlo was a leading Mafioso who became a *pentito* in 1996 – in other words he received protection in exchange for revealing what he knew.

Di Carlo recounts that in May 1974 the leading Mafia boss Stefano Bontate was due to visit Milan together with his sidekick Mimmo Teresi and Gaetano Cinà. Di Carlo met up with them, and it was suggested that he accompany them to a meeting that had been arranged with Silvio Berlusconi and Marcello Dell'Utri. The party was met by Dell'Utri, who exchanged kisses with all of them except Di Carlo. After about a quarter of an hour, they were joined by a young man informally dressed in jeans and roll-neck sweater. This was Berlusconi, and his informal dress slightly disconcerted the Mafiosi who were dressed to the nines. During the meeting Berlusconi, according to Di Carlo, said to Bontate "Marcello told me that you could guarantee my safety", and Bontate replied "You can relax – I'm telling you you can relax, you can sleep soundly, you will have people at your side who will do whatever you ask. And then you have Marcello here nearby, you can turn to him for anything you need, because Marcello is very close to us." It was after this meeting, according to Di Carlo, that Cinà suggested Vittorio Mangano as a suitable person to be sent to look after Berlusconi's safety. Di Carlo did not specify where the meeting took place – the first trial hypothesised that it might have been at Berlusconi's offices, but the appeal suggests that it may have been elsewhere.

Another Mafioso, Antonio Galliano, also reported that Cinà had told him of the meeting, saying that Berlusconi seemed to be fascinated by the personality of the Mafia boss Bontate. It was after this that Mangano was hired, apparently to look after the stables at Berlusconi's recently-acquired country estate at Arcore, but in reality in order to provide reassurance to Berlusconi. Or rather, to provide that mixture of threat and reassurance in which the Mafia specialise: in Di Carlo's words "We in Cosa Nostra

| 69

first threatened and then provided protection, that was the usual thing in Cosa Nostra, else why would anyone need to ask us [for protection]".[33]

Another version of the facts has occasionally been offered by Berlusconi, who claimed to Paolo Guzzanti[34] that Mangano was already in residence at Arcore at the time that Berlusconi took possession of the property. None of the other people involved confirm this. He also appears to have told this story to his mother, since that is the version that she recounted in an interview[35]. However, even Berlusconi himself, when asked by a judge, said that he himself had hired Mangano on Dell'Utri's recommendation.[36] The story about Mangano already being at Arcore when Berlusconi purchased the property should be taken merely as a further example of Berlusconi's idiosyncratic relationship to the truth – or, to say it in plain English, of his readiness to lie whenever he thinks he can get away with it, together with his tendency to overestimate how often he can get away with it.

Vittorio Mangano started to work for Berlusconi in the summer of 1974, and the kind of work he did was certainly unusual for someone nominally in charge of the stables. He accompanied Berlusconi's children to school, and Berlusconi's wife on her shopping trips to Milan. Moreover, the cost of his employment was higher than the going rate for stable hands. After the meeting with the Mafia bosses, Bontate told Cinà to demand €50,000 (100 mn lire). In Di Carlo's words:

> Tanino [Cinà] told me, he said, "I'm embarrassed". I asked "Why?" He says "they immediately asked me to ask for 100 million". So Tanino was...he says "It somehow doesn't seem right", and I said "so what, they're so rich, and they wanted us". So I encouraged Tanino... and later he told me "I got them this 100 million."[37]

Money had thus started to flow from Berlusconi into the coffers of Cosa Nostra. At this point, one can feel some sympathy for Berlusconi's position. At a time when kidnappings were frequent occurrences, he knew he was being targeted by criminals, and he took the view that the best guarantee of his security was for the criminal fraternity to know that he was being protected by someone in touch with the upper ranks of Cosa Nostra. That may well have reduced the risks to himself and his family more than relying on the police or a private security company would have done. Of course, once one starts making regular payments to organised crime, one would expect to have to renounce any hope of a political career. But that is just one of the many respects in which Silvio Berlusconi's career confounds expectations.

The disadvantage of this form of protection began to appear when, in December 1974, Mangano used his insider position at Arcore to attempt to kidnap a guest whom Berlusconi had invited to a dinner party – an initiative which perhaps was also aimed at making clear what might happen to Berlusconi himself should the protection money dry up. The attempt failed, and it had the effect of drawing the attention of the police towards Mangano, who soon after was briefly arrested and detained on a fraud charge. He seems to have left Arcore in January 1975, though his family stayed on, and it remained his official address until October 1976.

In May 1975 a bomb attack was made on another of Berlusconi's properties, at Villa Rovani. The appeal court explained its logic as "the logic which underlies all mafia activities, which are aimed at progressively increasing the pressure on the victim, after hooking him by using the appropriate channels and people, keeping the tension high so as to avoid any second thoughts or even an interruption of payments. The attack should be considered as a kind of warning, without causing any particular damage or alarm in a building that was undergoing reconstruction, and was therefore uninhabited when the bomb went off."[38]

At this point, Berlusconi began to use a private security firm, but his payments to Cosa Nostra continued. His business activities were then expanding throughout the country, and, in the appeal court's view, "could hardly have been safeguarded only by a legal security company". He "remained convinced that in those difficult years paying those who threatened or extorted, rather than reporting them to the authorities, was the best way of solving problems".[39]

The Bontate Years

For the next decade and more the relationship remained unchanged. Berlusconi continued to provide significant amounts of money to Cosa Nostra, who nominally provided protection, but also kept him on his toes by threats and extortion. Marcello Dell'Utri continued to mediate between Berlusconi and the mafia, remaining friendly with both. As the appeal court remarked: "the fact that Dell'Utri maintained for many years friendly relations with those who were tormenting his friend and employer, periodically meeting Cinà and Mangano, not disdaining to have lunch with them, and turning to them every time there were problems caused by criminal activities in which they had a proven ability to intervene – that fact is quite incompatible with the defence's notion that his sole aim was to seek a solution to Berlusconi's problems."[40]

Eleven years later, in 1986, a very similar attack to the one in 1975 was again made on the Villa Rovani property, and telephone interceptions picked up Berlusconi's reaction. It happened that, at this time, Vittorio Mangano was in jail, but Berlusconi had been misinformed by the police that he was out, and immediately leapt to the conclusion that he was responsible. Here he talks to Dell'Utri on the telephone – his usual recourse when there were matters of Mafia relations to be settled:

> "So it's Vittorio Mangano who put the bomb there...Well, a series of deductions, it's not rocket science...He's out...Yes, he's out... Unfortunately I was questioned by the Carabinieri, the ones from Monza, about Vittorio Mangano...and I had to say, well! The thing is, I had to say "Yes, it's true, he was there"...I told them the story which they already knew all too well...They got there before me... So...I...I think it was him" – "Well, I think it must be like that! So now we wait for...Ah, there's no other explanation!..It's the same Via Rovani as it was then..." – "And him out of jail" – "So it's a signal of extortion, think about it...that eleven years ago...No, when they later told me he had recently been released."

As the appeal court judges note, "it is noticeable that in the phone call, confirming once again that his relations with Mangano remained anything but hostile, Berlusconi calls the bomb a 'wake-up call' and expresses displeasure at the possibility that Mangano, who the investigators suspected of being the perpetrator, might even be arrested ('Now it's a pity, though if the Carabinieri...from this affair...he gives a wake-up call, and they deprive him of his personal liberty')". Berlusconi told his friend Dell'Utri that the attack had been carried out "with great respect, because they only damaged the lower part of the gate...a matter of 200,000 lire...so something that was respectful and affectionate".

It took only a short time for Dell'Utri to contact Cinà and find out that in fact Mangano had not carried out this respectful and affectionate attack, and was still in jail, and to provide reassurance to Berlusconi.

Throughout this period Dell'Utri remained in friendly contact, not only with Cinà and Mangano, but to some extent with other members of the mafia. One *pentito*, Antonino Calderone, speaks of a meal at a restaurant in 1976 with Mangano and various other Mafiosi at which Dell'Utri was present. Calderone said that his companion, one Nino Grado, also a Mafioso, already knew Dell'Utri and went and shook his hand. In addition, Dell'Utri was present at the wedding in London in 1980 of Jimmy Fauci, a Mafioso connected to drug dealing in London. The other guests included

CHAPTER 3: THE SCENT OF MAFIA

several well-known Mafiosi including Mimmo Teresi, who was best man (*testimone d'anello*) at the wedding. Dell'Utri says that he happened to be in London to attend an exhibition on the Vikings, and that his friend Cinà invited him along at the last moment, but that he did not know the other guests. He said that at the wedding there was an odd mixture of Sicilian faces and London high society (*buona società Londinese*). Francesco Di Carlo was also present, and spoke of a discussion at the wedding with Teresi and Dell'Utri, and also says that Teresi told him that he and Bontate were going to do business with Dell'Utri. Fauci says that he did not know, and did not invite Dell'Utri. Asked if he had photographs of the wedding, Fauci said he had torn them all up and destroyed the negatives in anger at the time of his subsequent divorce.

There is also no doubt about a telephone conversation that took place in 1980 between Dell'Utri and Vittorio Mangano, which was intercepted during a ten-day period in which police were monitoring Mangano's phone calls as part of an investigation into Mangano's activities. In it, the two talk about meeting someone called Tony Tarantino, and arrange to meet up later in the day at a place described by Dell'Utri as "the usual place in Via Moneta". Mangano talks of having set up some business with a horse, and, when Dell'Utri says that he has no money at present, Mangano suggests he goes to "your boss, Silvio" (although at that time Dell'Utri was not working for Berlusconi). Dell'Utri replies in Sicilian slang that he (Berlusconi) won't pay up. All these three episodes – the lunch, the wedding and the phone call – are in themselves without criminal significance, but show Dell'Utri's continuing closeness to leading Mafiosi.

These relationships appear to have been a source of pride to Dell'Utri. After he left Berlusconi's employment for a time in the late 1970s, he applied for employment with Filippo Alberto Rapisarda, who, Dell'Utri said was "impressed" when Dell'Utri appeared in the company of Cinà, a man whose mafia connections were well-known to Rapisarda. Rapisarda and Dell'Utri seem to have boasted to each other about their links to leading mafiosi. In Dell'Utri's words "Rapisarda said he knew important people in the criminal world, and I boasted that I knew even more important ones" – "he told me he knew big guns in the mafia in Palermo `I know Tom, Dick and Harry', and because he was boasting, in order not to seem less important than him I said `I know Tom, Dick and Harry too'. It's true I said that, but I repeat it was only for that reason". [41]

For their part, the mafia leaders of the time, Bontate and Teresi, were proud of their relationship with Berlusconi. Another *pentito*, Angelo Siino, said that "the relationship between Berlusconi and Bontate was waved about a bit...not so much by Bontate, who was a rather superior sort of bloke, but especially by Mimmo Teresi. Every three words he said 'Berlusconi is my friend'...he said he was on Christian name terms with [Berlusconi's brother] Paolo".[42]

Bontate was also keen to prevent any of Italy's other crime gangs from muscling in on this privileged relationship. In the late 1970s it was discovered that the Calabrian 'ndrangheta was planning to kidnap Berlusconi or one of his family. This greatly annoyed Bontate, who hurried to Milan to head off the possibility. As Siino reports "I must say that Bontate was particularly annoyed by the fact that these people, who he didn't think were up to it, could have done...could have taken an interest in somebody close to him, as he thought Silvio Berlusconi was." At that time two brothers, Giovanni and Ignazio Pullarà, were handling the relationship with Berlusconi on behalf of Cosa Nostra, and such was Bontate's concern that he even seems to have feared that too much money was being demanded. In Siino's words "he said that the Pullaràs had in general protected Berlusconi from interference by the Calabrians, from the annoyance these Calabrians were causing him, and that because of this they had had significant compensation, in cash, and he even used a particular phrase, "the Pullaràs are pulling up the roots", that is they were almost uprooting the relationship, because they were making him pay a high price for this protection".

The Riina Years

In 1981 a war for control of the Mafia was ended by the murder of Bontate and Teresi, and their replacement at the summit of Cosa Nostra by the Corleone family headed by Totò Riina. For some time this changed nothing in the relationship between the crime syndicate and the Berlusconi group. Shortly before Bontate's death, another layer had been added when the growing television business led to the acquisition of transmission stations in Sicily. This provided another opportunity for Cosa Nostra to extend its "protection".

A number of *pentiti* confirm that money continued to flow regularly from the Berlusconi group to Cosa Nostra, up to 1992, after which time the appeal court found that there is no evidence of further payments. One witness said that money continued to be paid until 1995, (by which time Berlusconi had already finished his first brief period as Prime Minister), but the appeal court found this inconclusive, in the absence of any external corroboration of the claim.

CHAPTER 3: THE SCENT OF MAFIA

During the 1980s Riina himself began to take a closer interest in the relationship. In 1986 Cinà began to complain that Dell'Utri's attitude had changed, and that he was beginning to treat Cinà in a stand-offish way. The "respectful and affectionate" attack on Berlusconi's property in Via Rovani seems to have been Riina's way of making sure that Dell'Utri did not forget where respect was due. Riina also decided to double the protection money that Cosa Nostra demanded from €50,000 to €100,000 per year in three or four instalments.

It is not clear whether these sums, which had their origin in 1974 when Gaetano Cinà was "embarrassed" to ask for €50,000, were the full amount that the Berlusconi group was contributing to Cosa Nostra. There appear to have been further "gifts". One such was recorded in a notebook in which the San Lorenzo mafia family recorded its receipts, which included a "gift" of €2,500 from "Channel 5", one of Berlusconi's television companies. It also appears that payments relating to television transmitters were separate from the core funding. After meeting Dell'Utri in 1986, Cinà reported back that "the protection money for the transmitters should be 'extracted from the people on the spot', that's to say those responsible for private broadcasting stations which were transmitting in accordance with contractual agreements with Berlusconi".

Naturally there was also heated debate within the various Mafia families about who was entitled to the Berlusconi booty. Thus the head of the Acquasanta family complained that "those people from Channel 5 pay millions and millions, and Shorty [Riina] gets them...and we don't get a penny". Equally Vittorio Mangano thought that some of the money that was going to the Pullarà brothers ought to have come to him.

The appeal court, reviewing all the episodes listed to date, had concluded that "the accused (Marcello Dell'Utri) represented a constant and indispensible point of reference, both for Berlusconi, who consulted him and involved him each time he had to deal with the threats, attacks and demands for money which systematically pursued him down the years, and especially for the mafia, who used his preferential and friendly relations with two of its members, Gaetano Cinà and Vittorio Mangano, so as to have at its disposal at all times, as has been shown, a channel which was always open and fruitful in that it allowed them to pursue their illegal goals in the knowledge that the victim would pay up without going to the police."[43]

In 1990, by which time Berlusconi had incorporated the Standa chain of stores into his business empire, the Catania mafia saw a further opportunity for extortion, and mounted a series of attacks on the stores. Given the background, one might guess that Berlusconi would respond in the same way to the attacks on the Standa as he had to previous episodes of this kind, and it is true that Marcello Dell'Utri flew to Catania on various occasions around this time. However, the accounts from those involved which suggested that he might have again played a mediating role in settling the matter, as found in the original trial, were found by the appeal court to have been inconsistent and inconclusive in determining exactly when and with whom he might have been involved, and the appeal court therefore concluded that there was insufficient evidence that he had played a role in settling this problem.

Paolo Borsellino's Last Interview

In March 1992, a journalist working for a French television company interviewed the Palermo anti-Mafia investigator Paolo Borsellino. The journalist's special interest was in the links between the Mafia and the Milan business world. He asked Borsellino about Vittorio Mangano, and Borsellino confirmed that when Mangano spoke about horses, this was often a coded way of speaking about drugs. Borsellino made it clear that he himself was not involved in, and had no special knowledge of, any investigation concerning Dell'Utri. The journalist asks:

> Q: Doesn't it seem strange to you that big industrialists like Berlusconi, Dell'Utri should be mixed up with "men of honour" like Vittorio Mangano?
> A: At the beginning of the 1970s, Cosa Nostra was itself starting to become a business enterprise – a business in the sense that, through its increasing involvement, which was to become a proper monopoly, in the drugs business, Cosa Nostra began to look after an enormous quantity of capital, for which of course it was looking for outlets, because this capital was partly exported or put on deposit abroad, and it is this that explains the coming together of elements like Cosa Nostra and certain financiers who were involved in these movements of capital.
> Q: Are you saying that it was normal that Cosa Nostra took an interest in Berlusconi?
> A: It's normal that anyone who is in possession of a large quantity of capital should look for ways and means of employing this capital, either for the purpose of laundering it, or to invest it gainfully.
> Q: Was Mangano involved in this?

A: Yes, look, I can tell you that he was one of those people who formed the bridgehead of the Mafia organisation in Northern Italy.

The questioner goes on to ask about investigations into Berlusconi's links with the Mafia, and Borsellino makes it clear that he himself is not involved in any such investigations, though he has heard that they are ongoing. The interview took place a matter of days before Borsellino's colleague Giovanni Falcone was blown up, and only a couple of months before Borsellino himself was assassinated. The interview was not shown on Italian television until many years later, and then only on a late-night slot. Given Borsellino's lack of any direct involvement in any of these investigations, it would be wrong to make too much of it, though it does show that serious investigators such as Borsellino did not dismiss the possibility of the kind of links that we have been discussing in this chapter. Borsellino was by no means a man of the left – it is believed that he voted for the MSI party, which was later to evolve into Gianfranco Fini's Alleanza Nazionale, and later still to be merged with Berlusconi's Forza Italia into the People of Liberty (PDL).

New Political Horizons

The victory of Riina had led to a rethink of the Mafia's political strategy. Even before the political system had begun to come apart in the early 1990s, the new leadership of the Mafia had come to feel that the Christian Democrats were not delivering as much protection as they should. In the 1987 elections, Riina ordered the Mafia to transfer its support to the Socialist Party led by Bettino Craxi. Knowing of the close links between Craxi and Berlusconi, he wanted to open some channel of communication with Craxi, and felt that this could be achieved by using Dell'Utri and Berlusconi as intermediaries. Accordingly he sent a senior figure in Mangano's "family", Salvatore Cancemi, to go to Mangano in Milan in 1990 or 1991 and ask him to step aside as an intermediary in relations between the Mafia and the Berlusconi group, and leave it to Riina to handle the relationship directly.[44] Cancemi was later to testify about this meeting, as follows:

> When I went to see Mangano, I said, "Vittorio, listen here, I've spoken to Uncle Totuccio [Riina], and he told me that for these people, Dell'Utri and Berlusconi, since he's got them in his hands, which is a bonus for the whole of Cosa Nostra, do this for me: step aside because this is a matter that Uncle Totuccio is handling, so you should step aside"…Mangano said to me: "But I've had them

in my hands for a whole lifetime, and now I'm to step aside. But why? Is it because I'm not a man of honour and I'm incapable of carrying the matter forward myself?" I said, "Vittorio, please, do this for me, don't insist, don't say anything more about it. If he says that it is in the interests of Cosa Nostra, what can I say? Tell me."[45]

In a similar statement, Cancemi also testified that he had heard Riina say "we can sleep peacefully, I have Berlusconi and Dell'Utri in my hands, and that is a good thing for Cosa Nostra."[46] He also said that he expected legislation that would be favourable to Mafia interests, adding that "we must guarantee [the safety of] these people now, and even more in the future."[47]

The appeal court studied these, as well as a number of other accounts which alleged that Dell'Utri had been involved in some kind of pact, in which Cosa Nostra was to pledge its support to the new party that had been founded by Dell'Utri with Berlusconi as its head, in exchange for the party meeting some of Cosa Nostra's demands which would have made it harder to convict Mafiosi or to confiscate their ill-gotten gains, and would have led to less harsh treatment for those who had been convicted. Most of these statements from *pentiti* showed an impression that Forza Italia would, if elected, be more helpful to Mafia interests than any of the other parties. Some of them allege that Bernardo Provenzano (who took over Mafia leadership after Riina's arrest in January 1993) had spoken of "guarantees" that he had been given by the new political party.

When it had become clear, in the early 1990s, that the political system was disintegrating, Mafia leaders were tempted by the notion of emulating the success of the Northern League, and setting up a regional party in Sicily. For a while, the Mafia encouraged one of its supporters to begin establishing such a party, to be named Sicilia Libera. But this political initiative was almost immediately superceded when news came of Dell'Utri's and Berlusconi's initiative in esablishing Forza Italia. There is no doubt that their new party had, from the start, the enthusiastic support of Cosa Nostra. The issue was whether it had entered into any overt pact in order to get this support.

One *pentito*, Salvatore Cucuzza, claimed that a meeting had taken place between Dell'Utri and Vittorio Mangano, in which Dell'Utri had promised to bring forward "very favourable proposals" concerning legislation on the judicial system. In the original trial, this had been considered as having been confirmed by two notes in the appointments diary kept by Dell'Utri's secretary, which showed that Mangano had been in touch with

CHAPTER 3: THE SCENT OF MAFIA

Dell'Utri in November 1993, though they do not conclusively show that a meeting took place. (In the appeal, though not in the original trial, it was suggested that one of the diary entries may have referred to another person with the not uncommon surname Mangano). There are many puzzles relating to the timing of the meetings alleged by Cucuzza to have taken place, and the appeal court concludes that there is no solid proof that they did take place, or that any pact was reached.

Further evidence hinting at, though by no means proving, the existence of some agreement between Cosa Nostra and the new political grouping came from a *pentito* named Giusto Di Natale, who had made available a room in which senior Mafiosi met. He did not participate in the meetings, but he said that in summer 1994 one of these Mafiosi, Giuseppe Guastella, had arrived there, fresh from a meeting with either Vittorio Mangano or his son-in-law (Mangano's son-in-law was a senior figure in the same mafia family) in a euphoric mood, saying that "things were turning out right, he was happy and he wanted to pass the good news on to Leoluca Bagarella" (an even more senior mafia figure). Guastella went on to say (still according to Di Natale) that "Vittorio Mangano gave assurances he had spoken to Dell'Utri who had been able to give him high hopes... He said there were people looking into it and that Dell'Utri had sent a message saying stay calm, things would turn out right".[48] Suggestive as it was, this evidence could not be given greater weight than the second- or third-hand hearsay that it was.

Another *pentito*, Gaspare Spatuzza, told the appeal court about a meeting that he had had in January 1994 a senior mafia figure named Giuseppe Graviano. Giuseppe Graviano and his brother Filippo headed the Brancaccio mafia family, and they had played a leading role in the terror campaign in mainland Italy that the Mafia had unleashed in the early 1990s. Spatuzza was a hitman, with some 40 murders on his conscience. They were in Rome preparing for a bomb attack on a football stadium, and as he approached the bar in via Veneto were they were to meet, Spatuzza saw that Graviano looked "joyful, like someone who had won the lottery or had a son born." At the bar, Graviano told him that "everything was finalised, and we had got everything we wanted, thanks to the fact that the people dealing with the matter were serious people". Graviano identified one of these people as Berlusconi, at which Spatuzza asked him whether he meant the one from Channel 5, which Graviano confirmed. Graviano identified the other as "our fellow-countryman Dell'Utri". Shortly after this, both Gravianos were arrested, and have remained in detention ever since.

One of the conditions of receiving the protection accorded to *pentiti* who turn state witness is that they must tell magistrates everything they know within 180 days of announcing their intention to turn state witness. Spatuzza had made this announcement in June 2008, but, even when specifically asked about these matters, said nothing about this meeting with Graviano until June 2009. The appeal court judges point out that Spatuzza must have been lying when he signed a declaration in December 2008 saying that he had provided all information that might be relevant in a criminal trial. They hold his credibility to have therefore been undermined, though interestingly they consistently say that he lied in concealing the information, not that he was lying when he told the court about the meeting in via Veneto. As a result of their suggestions, Spatuzza had his protection programme rescinded soon after his evidence. Two other courts – Florence and Caltanissetta – also heard testimony from Spatuzza in different proceedings connected with the mafia terror strategy of the early 1990s, and both these courts, unlike the Palermo court trying the Dell'Utri appeal, judged him to be a reliable witness.

The appeal court's dismissal of Spatuzza's testimony is written in a hyperassertive style. Although many of its criticisms of him are justified, at no point in the document do the judges provide even a hint of a reason, let alone a convincing one, why Spatuzza should have chosen to make allegations that were unfounded – what could possibly have been in it for him? One argument that the judges used against the notion of a pact is odd:

> "So if the country was allegedly delivered into Graviano's hands, and thus those of Cosa Nostra, by Silvio Berlusconi and Marcello Dell'Utri, *"serious"* people, on the basis of an unspecified agreement and supposed promises, one can really not understand why neither the mafia bosses, now all in jail, nor above all the Graviano brothers, who have been detained for 14 years under the onerous regime of 41 bis, whose modification allegedly was one of the basic points of the pact between the mafia and politicians, have never in all those years demanded that the guarantees and undertakings made by those two politicians in that long-ago January 1994 be respected – guarantees and undertakings which for that reason we must conclude were never made."[49]

In summary, the court is saying that because an alleged promise has not been kept, one must conclude that it was never made. There are two things wrong with this argument. Unkept pledges are the stuff of politics – particularly of Silvio Berlusconi's politics. In Chapter 6, we shall see him signing a solemn pledge on national television, committing himself

CHAPTER 3: THE SCENT OF MAFIA

never to stand for office again unless he met four out of five specific goals. He met none, yet stood for office at the next election. The judges' logic would imply that, since the undertaking was not met, all those who thought they saw him making the pledge must have been hallucinating.

The second flaw in the argument is that Berlusconi's government fell after only seven months in office, so that even if he had wished to, he would not have been able to keep the alleged undertaking. One of the reasons for its fall was the unpopularity of some of the changes to the justice system that it had proposed, in particular the so-called "save-the-thieves" law which released corrupt politicians from detention. In September 1994 it proposed other changes to the system of preventative detention which would have met with the approval of the mafia. But once the Northern League had withdrawn its support, it was in no position to deliver on pledges made to anyone.

The Graviano brothers were called upon to testify in the Dell'Utri appeal. Neither of them had turned state's witness since their arrest in January 1994. There was some anticipation about what they might say, since Spatuzza had reported that, in a conversation he had had in jail with Filippo Graviano, the latter had said "If nothing comes from where it should come from, it's better that we too should talk to the magistrates". However, when Filippo testified, he denied ever having said this, and also denied ever having met Dell'Utri. Giuseppe Graviano was also asked to testify. He had previously made it clear that he was unhappy with the conditions in which he was detained – the law regulating the detention of Mafia prisoners, known as "41bis" has long been a bone of contention between the Mafia and the state – and said that his state of health did not permit him to testify, but that he would let the court know when he felt that his health would permit him to speak[50]. A couple of weeks later, Giuseppe Graviano's conditions of detention were relaxed. Whether he would have regarded this as "something coming from where it should come from", who can say? (A curious, but wholly incidental, fact about the Graviano brothers is that both of their wives became pregnant while they were in jail. The export of sperm from jail cells for this purpose is explicitly forbidden by the 41bis rules, but their lawyer says that the sperm had been frozen prior to their arrest, presumably in the expectation that it might come in handy some day).

In March 2011, Giuseppe Graviano came into contact with Spatuzza in the context of a homicide trial in Florence. He publicly said to Spatuzza "I respect your choice", and added "We know very well who are the people named by Spatuzza. I have availed myself of my right to remain silent. I shall speak if there is a trial of me and of those people." He thus seemed to be keeping a sword of Damocles hanging over "the people named by Spatuzza" – Berlusconi and Dell'Utri – and threatening to speak at a later date.[51]

Vittorio Mangano was arrested in 1995 and sentenced to 15 years for drug-dealing. In 2000 he was convicted of a double murder, and died of cancer a few days later. Marcello Dell'Utri claims that, while in prison, he was put under intense pressure to speak openly about his links with Berlusconi, and refused to do so despite being offered a reduction in his sentence. For this, Dell'Utri said in 2008 that Mangano was "in his way a hero", and Berlusconi later associated himself with this judgment.

A Verdict on the Verdict

At the start of this chapter, we described the verdict of the appeal court on Marcello Dell'Utri's alleged connivance with the Mafia as "surprising". Both Mr Dell'Utri himself and his fiercest critics agree about what is surprising in it. It seems to imply that Cosa Nostra, having nurtured a relationship with Marcello Dell'Utri for almost two decades, should have been willing to allow that relationship to vanish at exactly the moment when, as founder of the political party that took power in 1994, his potential value to them had become far greater than ever before. Obviously, different conclusions are drawn. Some hold that the implausibility of the idea shows that Dell'Utri was innocent even before 1992; others that it shows that he was guilty even after 1992.

Although some parts of the verdict seem questionable, its 641 pages make a strong case. It is clear that the mafia offered strong support to Berlusconi's political initiative, and that many senior Mafiosi were under the impression that some kind of undertaking had been made to them. Nevertheless the available evidence does not permit us to pin down with certainty what this alleged pact was, when it was made, by whom and to whom. It may be that the prosecution has further points to make in its appeal to the *Corte di Cassazione*, but not many of us would like to live in a country where evidence of the kind summarised in the appeal verdict for the period after 1992 was considered sufficient for a criminal conviction.

But even fewer of us would like to live in a country where there is such a strong probability that organised crime has enjoyed a cosy relationship

CHAPTER 3: THE SCENT OF MAFIA

with the ruling party. Wise men[vi] have often said that one can't know tomorrow, but historians and judges know that one can also seldom have complete certainty about yesterday. While the probability of a pact may be less than would justify a conviction, it still appears alarmingly high. If one reads the evidence, not for the light that it throws on the appropriate duration of Dell'Utri's jail sentence, but for the light that it throws on Italian politics, then it has to be seen as profoundly shocking. Italy has for many years been in the hands of a man who, when faced with threats, sought protection not from legal sources, but from organised crime, and who paid large sums of money to Cosa Nostra for prolonged periods. His political initiative was, and still is, enthusiastically preferred to any alternatives by organised crime. The ruling party was founded by someone who considers having powerful mafia friends to be a cause for "boasting", and a murderer to be a "hero", and who has been convicted of colluding with the mafia for almost two decades.

Scraps of Letters

During the trial, one of the witnesses whom the prosecution wanted to call was Massimo Ciancimino, whose father Vito had been mayor of Palermo, but had been arrested in 1984 and brought to trial in 1992 for associating with the Mafia and for money-laundering. Gven the slow course of Italian justice, he was not imprisoned until 2001, and died the following year. In his belongings was found a curious scrap of a letter. It was handwritten, and referred to Berlusconi as "Onorevole". The title Onorevole is one granted to members of parliament, and Berlusconi did not become one until 1994. The letter had been taken by police in 2005, but, incredibly, had not previously been brought to public attention.

The scrap of the letter – or rather note – says "...political position, I intend to make my contribution, (which will not be a small one) so as to make sure that this sad event does not need to come about. I am convinced that [in] this event Onorevole Berlusconi will wish to make available one of his television networks".

[vi] Most famously, in Italian, the Medici ruler Lorenzo the Magnificent:
Quant'è bella giovinezza   Youth is a wonderful thing
Che si fugge tuttavia   But it doesn't last very long
Chi vuol'esser lieto, sia!   If you want to be happy, go on!
Di doman non c'è certezza.   Who knows what tomorrow may bring.

The most probable interpretation of the letter is that it is a combination of a threat ("the sad event") in the event that some conditions are not met, a promise of political support if they are met, and a request for space on television. It appears to have been in Vito Ciancimino's possession for onward transmission to Berlusconi, presumably via Dell'Utri. The threat may, as in the past, have been that of harming some members of Berlusconi's family.

Massimo Ciancimino claims that the whole of this letter, and not just the page above, was taken when his father's house was searched. He later produced another letter which was clearly based on the above scrap (which was not in his father's hand). This version reads:

> "...years of prison on account of my political position, I intend to make my contribution (which will not be a small one) so as to make sure that this sad event does not occur. I am convinced that if this event should be verified (whether in a court of law or elsewhere) Onorevole Berlusconi will make available one of his television networks. If much time goes by and I am not suspected of a tort, I will be forced to give up my silence which has lasted for years and I will be forced to call a press conference".

In this form, it is barely more intelligible, but the threat of violence seems to be replaced by the threat of revealing some embarrassing truths. It should be stressed that there are many legitimate doubts about the reliability of Massimo Ciancimino as a witness. Massimo's story is that his father had modified the original draft by Provenzano, and that the threat was to reveal negotiations between Dell'Utri and the Mafia which led to Mafia support being thrown behind Forza Italia. In the event, the judges decided that the link between this evidence and the charges against Dell'Utri was too tenuous to justify calling Ciancimino to testify in the appeal.

Marcello's Strange Behaviour

Ezio Cartotto, who worked with Dell'Utri to prepare the way for Berlusconi's entry into politics, recalled a couple of occasions on which he was struck by Dell'Utri's behaviour in relation to matters concerning the Mafia. One was when it was announced on television that a magistrate named Domenico Signorino had committed suicide. Signorino was a prosecutor in the maxi-trial of Mafiosi in 1987, but had been accused by a Mafia informer of having himself had links with the Mafia. Reported Cartotto:

"Dell Utri's reaction was unexpected, given his cold and detached character: without saying a word, he hurled the TV remote control against the wall, splitting it in two."

Later, in 1994, press suspicion about Dell'Utri's possible links with the Mafia began to come out, and Berlusconi complained that this was damaging Forza Italia's results in public opinion polls. Cartotto said: "I recall that Dell'Utri's reaction surprised me somewhat, in that he said in so many words: `Silvio doesn't understand that he ought to thank me, because if I were to open my mouth…'"

Any politician who lacked Berlusconi's control over mass media would have been compromised beyond redemption by having a best friend and business associate – and founder of his political party – around whom all of these doubts and uncertainties had collected. That Berlusconi's career has continued bears witness to his success in confusing the two types of proof that we distinguished in the introduction. The evidence is inconclusive, but even though the probability of collusion with the mafia when Berlusconi's political career began falls short of what is needed for a criminal conviction, it remains very far from negligible. It is foolhardy to entrust political power to a man surrounded by this miasma of alarming, and till now never disproved, suspicions.

PART II:

WHAT SILVIO BERLUSCONI DID WITH POWER — AND WHAT IT DID TO HIM

"This could be one of the great unspoken themes of history – the shifty, embarrassing reigns that have littered the world, often for decades... all headed up by someone widely viewed as an idiot".
Simon Winder, Germania

CHAPTER 4:
BERLUSCONI'S LEGAL PROBLEMS

This chapter straddles the two parts of this book: Silvio Berlusconi's legal problems themselves for the most part stem from a period before he achieved political power, while the solution to those problems has been the matter that, more than any other, has preoccupied him while he has held power.

Imagine that a criminal were to be elected as Head of Government. How would one expect such a person to govern? For one thing, one would expect that the courts of justice, and all who have to deal with the business of convicting and sentencing criminals, would be regarded with intense hostility. Every effort would be made to discredit them in the eyes of the public. In addition, one would expect the enforcement agencies to be stripped of some of the power that might render them dangerous to those committing the particular types of crime in which our hypothetical criminal has been involved. Finally, one would expect the laws themselves to be revised in ways that would make it less likely that these particular crimes could be successfully brought to a conviction, or, if that were to occur, that they would lead to a jail sentence.

Silvio Berlusconi has at the time of writing never yet been convicted of a criminal offence, yet he has acted, while in office, in exactly these ways. This Chapter sets out the various offences with which he has been charged, and the efforts that he has made to ensure that he remains unpunished. He would say that these efforts are required, not because he has committed any crimes, but because a biased magistracy is intent on bending the laws in order to deprive him of the fruits of his fairly gained electoral victories. Our hypothetical criminal would say much the same.

There are two reasons for being interested in a politician's entanglements with the law. The obvious one is to form a view about whether or not that person is indeed guilty of the crimes of which he is accused. Less obviously, but in this case more importantly, the cases can also throw light in a more general way on the person's qualifications to lead a country. There are many instances in which even Berlusconi's legal defenders have not challenged a fact which, while irrelevant to his guilt in the crime in question, nevertheless highlights the contempt in which he holds the laws of the country that he now governs, his mendacity and the wilful obscurity in which he has chosen to veil the conduct of his business.

Outline of the Cases

Many accusations have been levelled at Silvio Berlusconi in courts of law, and until 2011 – when he was accused of the straightforward crimes of juvenile prostitution and abuse of office in seeking to cover it up – most of them involved matters of great complexity. We have seen the lengths to which Berlusconi went, in setting up his business empire, to make transactions impenetrable. Many of the cases involve attempts to unravel these complex networks of transactions. A full documentation of them would require many volumes. The aim here is to give an overview of the most important of them: the ones that are most typical of the offences of which he has been suspected and accused, and which have had the greatest influence on his actions, as leader of a government, to try to ensure that he remains unpunished.

He has been involved in eighteen cases to date, of which six are still on-going at the time of writing. In three of the remaining twelve he has been found innocent (though in one of these, that might not have been the case had one witness, David Mills, fully divulged all that he knew). In two he was saved by an amnesty declared in 1990. In two more cases the offence that was committed – fraudulent accounting – was a crime at the time it was committed, but by the time the cases came to court, the law had been changed (by the Berlusconi government of 2001) so that it was no longer an offence and could not be punished. Other cases have been timed out, usually when the judges held that because of "extenuating circumstances", and because Berlusconi had no previous convictions, he was eligible for an early application of the statute of limitations (*prescrizione* – see below).

Berlusconi has often said that in his court cases he has "always been absolved". It is certainly true that he has never been punished. But in the cases that were timed out, the evidence often makes it appear highly probable that he had committed the crime. For example, although he

CHAPTER 4: BERLUSCONI'S LEGAL PROBLEMS

was not punished in the criminal court for bribing a judge in the Mondadori case, the fact that he had done so was asserted in the final judgment, and taken into account in a subsequent civil case.

Berlusconi expressed his own attitude to these cases very clearly: "If I am absolved, it will show that there is still justice in Italy; if I am convicted it will show that democracy has been replaced by a dictatorship[vii] against which free men and the parties that represent them have a duty to react in every possible way, from public demonstrations to parliamentary obstruction".[52] He has consistently accused magistrates involved in his cases of being Communists (*toghe rosse*).

Berlusconi and his supporters commonly assert that it is only since his involvement in politics that magistrates have begun to attempt to prosecute him. For example, Angelino Alfano, Minister of Justice in his 2008 government, said in November 2009 that "Nobody has been able to answer one question: how can it be that all the investigations started in 1994?"[53] Not only is it, as will be shown, quite false to suggest that there had been no investigations into Berlusconi's affairs prior to 1994, but it also inverts the true chain of causation. Rather than the investigations being the subsequent *result* of Berlusconi's entry into politics, they appear to have been the precedent *cause* of it. As we have seen, at the time of his entry into politics he told Intro Montanelli that "if I don't go into politics I'll end up in jail and bankrupt". The quest for impunity is fundamental to Berlusconi's political career.

Some Peculiarities of Italian Criminal Law

Under Italian law, there may be three stages of any trial. Someone indicted for a crime is considered innocent until the final stage has been passed. The first stage (*primo grado*) may be followed by an appeal, and there may thereafter be recourse to the highest court, the *Corte di Cassazione* which, however, cannot intervene with regard to the facts of any case, but can only pronounce if there are matters of legal interpretation in dispute. In most countries, someone convicted of a crime is subject to immediate punishment, but in Italy this is not so. Punishment occurs only once the legal process has wound its way to a conclusion.

A second oddity is the way in which the statute of limitations – the principle that crimes committed far in the past may be exempted from punish-

---

[vii] *regime* – the Italian word has a derogatory significance missing from the English word.

ment – is applied in Italy. This is described in more detail below, but as an oversimplification the following gives a rough general idea of how the statute of limitations works: a case can be timed-out (*prescritto*) if the elapsed time since the crime was alleged to have been committed is greater than the maximum sentence for the offence. Thus, if I commit a crime in 2000 whose maximum penalty is 10 years, and the resulting legal proceedings have not been completed before 2010, I get off scot-free. In most other jurisdictions, the clock is stopped once a trial begins, so that, as long as legal proceedings get under way within the time envisaged, they must run their course once they have started. However, under Italian law the clock goes on ticking even after the trial begins. Given that a trial can go to three stages, an accused whose pockets are deep has a good chance of evading punishment by drawing each stage of these proceedings out until the statute of limitations comes into effect. This feature of Italian law has been much criticised, for example by the European Commission, on the grounds that it makes it hard to punish those involved in corruption and white collar crime cases, where the facts of the matter may be highly complex, needing lengthy investigation to establish them, and the defendants may possess resources that enable them to prolong the trials.[54]

Early cases

The account of Berlusconi's early business career in Chapter 1 mentioned the interest shown by the *Guardia di Finanza* in the ownership of Edilnord. Berlusconi said that he was merely a consultant to the firm (though in reality he appears to have been the beneficial owner), and the inspector, Massimo Berruti, called off the investigation, taking a job the following year as tax adviser to Fininvest. A few years later, in 1983, the *Guardia di Finanza* put Berlusconi's phones under surveillance in connection with an investigation into drugs. The investigation turned up no wrongdoing, and was abandoned.

The following year, various people including Berlusconi were investigated by the judge Renato Squillante in connection with radio transmitters that were held to be interfering with Fiumicino airport. Berlusconi's name was quickly dropped from the list of those being investigated, and the rest of the investigation was archived at a later date. A subsequent case showed that Squillante was, at a later date, being paid by Berlusconi's lawyer Cesare Previti, though there is no evidence that he was paid in this earlier case. Later in the same year, Berlusconi's transmitters were prevented by law from transmitting the same programmes simultaneously throughout Italy – as already recounted, Craxi responded by altering the law so as to permit this.

CHAPTER 4: BERLUSCONI'S LEGAL PROBLEMS

The P2 Libel Case

The P2 (Propaganda 2) Masonic Lodge, headed by Licio Gelli, was a secret organisation whose members numbered the heads of all secret services, many generals in the Carabinieri and the armed forces, senior civil servants, some politicians and journalists, and some bankers and financiers (including Roberto Calvi of Banco Ambrosiano, later to be found hanging under Blackfriars Bridge, and Michele Sindona, later to be poisoned in jail) . Its aim was to protect Italy from Communism, and to rewrite the Italian constitution in a way that would permit more decisive, more authoritarian leadership.

It was disowned by the broader Masonic movement in Italy in 1976, but it continued to pursue these aims in a number of illicit ways, including bribery and misuse of the justice system. In 1981 police investigating the collapse of Sindona's banks found a list of P2 members in Gelli's house, and the lodge became known to the public, at which point a Parliamentary Commission of Enquiry into it was set up. Later some documents, including a "plan for the Rebirth of Democracy", were found in a false bottom of Gelli's daughter's suitcase. Licio Gelli was later to be convicted of fraud connected with the Banco Ambrosiano collapse.

Berlusconi had joined the lodge in 1978. To what extent his motives were political, in that he shared the aims and was content with the methods of Licio Gelli, and to what extent they were motivated by the desire to make contacts that would be useful in the financing of his growing business, is a matter for speculation.

In 1987 two journalists, Giovanni Ruggeri and Mario Guarino, published a book entitled "*Berlusconi: Inchiesta sul signor TV*" (Investigation into Mr TV). This was the first attempt to document how his business had grown, and most subsequent accounts, including the very summary version that I have given above, are indebted to the research that they carried out – though the full complexity of his business transactions was not apparent until the investigations by Palermo magistrates in 1998 that were referred to in Chapter 1. Even before its publication, Berlusconi had attempted to bring legal actions against the book, whose publication was delayed from October 1986 to March 1987. One of the authors recounts that he received a visit from an associate of Berlusconi who offered him a blank cheque in return for the rights to publication. In February 1987 Fedele Confalonieri, the head of Fininvest and Berlusconi's longest-standing and most trusted associate, had rung up the publishers to seek to "reach some agreement".

IMPUNITY BERLUSCONI'S GOAL AND ITS CONSEQUENCES

As soon as the book went on sale (it was quickly sold out), Berlusconi initiated a lawsuit for libel against its authors. He lost, and had to pay costs, but also brought another action against them for an article in the magazine *Epoca*. During the legal proceedings, Berlusconi had testified under oath that he had joined P2 in 1981, and had not paid any subscription fee. The journalists then accused him of perjury, since there was ample documentary proof that – as Berlusconi himself had stated elsewhere – he had joined in 1978 and had paid the subscription fee. In the first round of the case, it was held that no crime had been committed by Berlusconi, but the magistrates appealed against the sentence, and the Court of Appeal in Venice found that "the statements made by the accused did not correspond to the truth"; that he had made false declarations on matters that were relevant to the trial; and that his actions completely met the subjective and objective descriptions of the crime in question (*ha compiutamente realizzato gli estremi obiettivi e subiettivi del contestato delitto*) – the crime in question being perjury (*falsa testimonianza*). However, in April 1990 an amnesty had come into force for all crimes committed before October 1989. Before the case, Berlusconi had announced that he hoped that the amnesty would not take away from him the pleasure of seeing the sentence of the previous hearing (to the effect that he had committed no crime) confirmed. However, thanks to this amnesty, he was not put on trial. It is possible that, had he been put on trial for the crime, he might have been acquitted. This is one of the cases in which we need to consider the two levels of evidence that we referred to in the introduction. Without a full trial, we cannot assert with complete confidence that Berlusconi deserved the punishment normally meted out to those who commit perjury. But the circumstances point so strongly towards this possibility that, in most countries, he would be considered unsuitable to hold public office.

There is an interesting comparison to another libel case that occurred in Britain a few years later, when Jonathan Aitken, then Chief Secretary to the Treasury, lied in a libel case that he had brought against the *Guardian* newspaper. In this case, no amnesty came into play to save him from the consequences of his action. He was sent to prison and his political career terminated. Berlusconi's, by contrast, had yet to begin, and, even before it had begun, it appeared probable that he had committed at least one crime, that of perjury.

The case also brings out some other features that were to be characteristic of Berlusconi's future entanglements with the law. First, it was apparent that he had attempted to use the law in this case to muzzle criticism. He may have known that he would lose the libel case, but considered it worth spending money on it simply for the purpose of intimidating and seeking to suppress any future critics. There have been many cases in which he has brought libel cases and lost them – for example, when the Economist published its famous open letter, he sued them, but ultimately lost the case and had to pay costs. Again, when Antonio Di Pietro later accused him of illegally occupying a television channel (see Chapter 6), Berlusconi sued him for libel and lost. Chapter 8 will refer to the flurry of libel threats in which he engaged following the sex scandals of 2009.

While this cynical explanation – that he uses the threat of lawsuits to suppress criticism – has truth in it, another factor may also play a part. The more one contemplates his actions, the more one is forced to the conclusion that he genuinely believes the things he is saying, at least at the time when he is saying them, even if another part of his brain must know them to be untrue. When he is criticised, the egotism that confers on him the remarkable energy with which he is endowed must respond, and can only act on the assumption that the criticism is ill-founded. Facts must be twisted or ignored in order to bring perception into line with this inviolable *a priori* assumption.

That brings us to another characteristic of Berlusconi which this case serves to highlight: his mendacity, but also his ability to project lies in a convincing way – Montanelli's acute observations were cited earlier. When we recount the sex scandals of 2009, we shall see this facility in greater detail. Indeed, it is the mendacity surrounding these scandals that is far more shocking than their substance.

Investigations during Tangentopoli

Virtually all of Italy's major companies were involved in the investigations connected with covert funding of political parties during 1992 and 1993, and Fininvest was certainly no exception. During that period Paolo Berlusconi, Aldo Brancher and Gianni Letta were among the individuals connected with Fininvest who were involved in the scandals. Gianni Letta admitted giving €35,000 to the Social Democrat Party secretary in an envelope. Brancher was arrested for giving €150,000 to the Socialist party in exchange for a contract to transmit AIDS awareness adverts on Fininvest's television channels. Marcello Dell'Utri was convicted of having issued false invoices. In November 1993, Craxi sent a memo to magistrates saying that "economic groups have certainly financed or subsidised political parties, and also individual politicians. From Fiat to Olivetti, from Montedison to Fininvest". It was not until later that the particular modalities in which Fininvest had made most of these payments was to become clear, with the discovery of Fininvest's secret offshore companies.

Late in 1993, a Socialist politician who was also chairman of a football club revealed that the deputy chairman of Berlusconi's football club, AC Milan, had paid him €9.5 mn in addition to €5 mn in secret offshore funds to acquire a player named Lentini. It was this matter that first alerted investigators to the existence of this network of offshore companies.

In February 1994 a Mafioso named Salvatore Cancemi, godson to Vittorio Mangano, alleged that Berlusconi and Dell'Utri had been involved in discussions with the Mafia that had led to the massacres that had taken place earlier that year. As noted in the previous chapter, he also claimed that Totò Riina, then head of the Mafia, had said that according to agreements reached with Dell'Utri, who was Berlusconi's emissary, Riina received €100,000 per year in instalments, and Cancemi also claimed to have been present when instalments of around €20,000 were paid. The matter was extensively investigated over the coming years, and indeed continues to be investigated, but no convincing supporting evidence was found to support Cancemi's allegations that Berlusconi had any involvement in the massacres (though, as we saw in the previous chapter, there is now no doubt that he was paying large sums of money to Cosa Nostra during the late 1970s and throughout the 1980s).

The Mondadori Affair

Chapter 1 recounted Berlusconi's takeover of the Mondadori group, with a judge delivering a detailed sentence in record time, and simultaneously receiving a pay-off from lawyers employed by Berlusconi. This is the case that, until recently, seemed to pose the most potent threat to Berlusconi's political career.

It was not until 1995 that Stefania Ariosto, the partner of a politician in Berlusconi's party, testified that the judge in this case, Vittorio Metta, was a good friend of Cesare Previti, and that she had heard Previti talking about bribes. Not long after the Mondadori appeal over which he had presided, Metta resigned as a judge and went to work with his daughter in Previti's legal office. As so often in Italy, the preparation of the case dragged on for years, and it was only in 2003 that the first round was heard. Before the case came up, the question of whether it could be timed-out by the statute of limitations had to be decided.

CHAPTER 4: BERLUSCONI'S LEGAL PROBLEMS

The Milanese judges who adjudicated on this matter took the view that the gravity of the offences was such that it would be inappropriate to let the matter drop under the statute of limitations. Of the five people under investigation – Metta, Berlusconi and Berlusconi's three lawyers, Previti, Acampora and Pacifico, it was decided that four of them should proceed to trial. However, the judges considered that in Berlusconi's case there were extenuating circumstances which made it appropriate for the charges against him to be timed-out under the statute of limitations (*prescrizione*). Under the law as it existed then (it has since been modified) if there were mitigating circumstances which made the maximum penalty inapplicable, the accusation could be timed-out earlier.

In the Mondadori case, there were four of these "extenuating circumstances". First, it was held that a client employs a lawyer to produce the best possible results whatever the cost, and that if those results can only be obtained by illegal methods such as bribery, that is primarily a matter for the lawyer, and not the client – even if the client is aware that bribery is being employed. Secondly, it was held that the gravity of the offence was diminished by the pre-existing widespread corruptibility of the judiciary – in other words *così fan tutti*, though the judges did not express it this way. Thirdly, it was further diminished by the fact that Berlusconi had handed back a part of Mondadori's portfolio, notably *La Repubblica* and *L'Espresso*, to the De Benedetti group (this followed a revolt by the editors of these papers, who did not wish to be employed by Berlusconi, and a subsequent intervention by then Prime Minister Andreotti). Fourthly, it was considered that "On a subjective level, it is relevant that [Berlusconi] was acting within the framework of an economic and business undertaking on a national scale, whose shadow cannot lead one to an overly negative prejudice against the granting of mitigating circumstances, especially since at present one must take into account the present circumstances of his individual and social life, whose objective profile in itself justifies [the granting of mitigating circumstances]". I may have mistranslated the impenetrable judicial prose (the Italian version is at http://www.giustizia-carita.it/archmag/corr.htm), but the meaning conveyed is that, because he was by then a major national politician and a very wealthy man, he was entitled to a little leniency. Some other legal opinion, extraneous to the case, took the view that some of these – notably the second and the fourth – were not mitigating circumstances at all, but actually aggravated the crime. Be that as it may, this judgment meant that Berlusconi did not take part in the ensuing trial.

The trial of the remaining four wound its way through the various stages of Italian justice, at the end of which, in the highest court (*Corte di Cas-*

sazione), they were convicted and sentenced. In the judgment, it was stated that "the payment of the corrupt judge was undertaken in the interests, and at the instance of, the corrupter", the corrupter in question being the man who is now prime minister of Italy. Once again, Berlusconi did not receive any punishment, unlike the intermediaries who were acting on his behalf, but the judgment made it clear that he was indeed responsible for corrupting a judge, and that therefore the injured party, De Benedetti, was entitled to damages. It was left to a later civil court to assess the exact financial extent of these damages. In the light of the outcome of the trial, the fact that he escaped punishment because of the "extenuating circumstances" that qualified him for the statute of limitations may rightly be held to imply that there was indeed something to be extenuated.

The affair continues to occupy the time of Italian courts some 18 years after the initial events. The damages case reached a conclusion in October 2009, when the courts decided that Fininvest, Berlusconi's group, must pay around €748 million in damages to De Benedetti's group. This assessment took account of the fact that it cannot be said with certainty how an uncorrupted judge would have ruled, so that there was an element of chance in assessing the losses. However, since Fininvest have appealed against this verdict, it will be some time yet before the affair can be said to be over.

It is noteworthy that, in ruling on the damages, the judge reiterated, as the earlier ruling had made clear, that Berlusconi was in part responsible for the corruption of Judge Metta, since there was no doubt that his money was used with his knowledge for this purpose. As in the case of the perjury, culpability has been legally certified, even though there has been no punishment. In an interview in which she protested about the size of the damages, Marina Berlusconi (Berlusconi's oldest child, who now directs Mondadori) did not seek to deny that Metta had been bribed, though she said that the other two judges in the case had shared the view taken by Metta. If that is so, clearly the money and effort spent on bribing Metta was squandered.

The Lentini Case

Although the alleged offence dated back to 1992, and it was first made known to magistrates in 1993, it was not until five years later that Berlusconi was formally indicted for fraudulent accounting (*falso in bilancio*) in connection with the undeclared offshore money used to purchase the footballer Lentini for AC Milan. The case was due to start hearings in July 1999, but the timetable was thrown out by a lawyers' strike which happened to begin on the day of first hearing. As a result, the case did not start until June 2000. By the time of its conclusion, Berlusconi had returned to office in 2001 and the law on fraudulent accounting had been changed in a way that meant that the case was "timed out" (*prescritto*) in 2002.

Cases Connected with the Offshore Empire

The largest group of cases in which Berlusconi has been indicted have been connected in some way or another with the various offshore companies belonging to Fininvest. The Lentini affair was one of the first which provided an indication that Fininvest was in a position to make payments from offshore accounts, and then alerted investigators to the various other uses to which these accounts may have been put. Before describing the individual cases, we need to understand something about this network of companies, the people involved in establishing it, and the functions that it appears to have served.

One of the first – perhaps the first – Fininvest company to be incorporated outside Italy was Reteitalia Ltd, which was set up in March 1980 in London by David McKenzie Mills, who was the company secretary. Mills had trained as a barrister, but then requalified as a solicitor. He is an excellent linguist, fluent in Spanish and Italian, and had been a Labour councillor in Camden, where he got to know and subsequently married Tessa Jowell, who later became a Cabinet Minister in Britain's Labour government. In 1978 he set up the London office of Carnelutti Studio Legale Associati, one of the oldest and best-known Milanese corporate law firms. The joint office, known as CMM or Carnelutti Mackenzie Mills, specialised in setting up offshore companies for a range of clients, particularly Italian companies. He was initially contacted by Massimo Berruti, the man who, while a member of the *Guardia di Finanza*, had conducted an investigation into Berlusconi's Edilnord company some years earlier, and had subsequently, after calling off the investigation, become an adviser on tax matters to Berlusconi's companies. He told Mills that Fininvest wanted to use London as an intermediary in the trading of film rights.

Reteitalia Ltd bought rights from major film companies, and sold them on to other Fininvest television companies at a profit. This profit was not taxable in the UK under the law as it stood at that time, since Reteitalia Ltd was a non-resident company. When UK law was changed in 1988, the activity of trading film rights was no longer carried out through companies registered in the UK, but instead by companies registered in the British Virgin Islands. Various companies were set up by CMM on behalf of Fininvest, and some of them were collectively known as Fininvest Group B, to differentiate them from those companies (Group A) that were consolidated in the overall Fininvest accounts and balance sheet. There were many such companies, and on CMM's summary sheet for each of them were the words "very discreet", as a reminder that the link with Fininvest was not to be made known. Two of the companies incorporated in the British Virgin Islands that traded in film rights were Century One and Universal One. Another company established by CMM was named All Iberian, and was registered in Guernsey. This company acted as the source of funds for the other Group B companies, and itself received money on loan from a company in the Fininvest Group.

Apart from securing more favourable tax treatment on profits made from film rights, the network of offshore companies served two purposes. One was to purchase shares on behalf of Fininvest, without these purchases being declared to Consob, the board regulating the Milan Stock Exchange. (Most stock exchanges have rules declaring that companies cannot purchase more than a specified percentage of the equity in a quoted company without making their purchases public. This was a way of circumventing these rules). The other was to conceal the true ownership of Telepiù, a pay-TV company. Under the Mammì law that then regulated broadcasting, it was illegal for Fininvest, as controller of the three commercial TV companies, to also own or control a separate pay-TV station. The regulatory authority was entitled to make enquiries about the true ownership of any Italian company, but if the owner was a company quoted on a foreign stock exchange, the authority had no power to identify the true owners. It was therefore decided to set up a company quoted on the Luxembourg stock exchange to conceal Fininvest's continuing control of Telepiù, using the companies set up by Mills to do the paperwork and act as a channel for the money.

Thanks to the Lentini case, and to information concerning money received by Bettino Craxi, magistrates began to suspect that this network of offshore companies was being used for improper purposes, and they set out to clarify this complex tangle of companies and find out what they were doing and what they were for. They initially asked Swiss companies to provide material about these companies, but at that point Tanya Maynard, the CMM official who, with David Mills, was involved in administering these companies, asked for all documents being held in Switzerland to be sent back to Britain. The investigation then moved to Britain.

CHAPTER 4: BERLUSCONI'S LEGAL PROBLEMS

In April 1996, police with a search warrant arrived at the offices of Edsaco-CMM (Edsaco, a subsidiary of the Swiss Bank UBS, had taken over CMM, though it was to sell it again once it found out more about the operations that were being undertaken on behalf of Fininvest). They removed boxes of papers that bore on the network of offshore companies that had been set up by Mills.

However, not all of the papers were kept in CMM's offices: Mills had sent several boxes of papers to the Isle of Man prior to the search, and several to Malta. Notes were subsequently found directing that boxes be held "outside our offices". During the search, which lasted four hours, the investigators waited in a room while the documents requested were brought in by employees of Edsaco-CMM, and it appears that several relevant documents were not produced. At this time, Mills was regarded as above suspicion by the Serious Fraud Office who were responsible for the investigation – as it happens, his sister-in-law Dame Barbara Mills had been Director of the Serious Fraud Office from 1990 to 1992. The missing documents related in particular to the purchase of film rights, which were to be the subject of future investigations.

Fininvest's lawyers immediately demanded in the British courts that the documents that had been taken should not be sent to Italy. They said that the investigation was being motivated purely by a political intent to persecute Berlusconi. The argument was dismissed by Lord Justice Simon Brown, who said that it was

> "a misuse of language to describe the magistrates' campaign as being for `political ends', or their approach to Mr Berlusconi as one of political persecution. On the contrary, the magistrates were demonstrating a due independence of the executive, as well as even-handedness in dealing equally with the politicians of all political parties. It is, indeed, somewhat ironical that the applicants here are seeking to be regarded as political offenders in respect of offences committed in part whilst Mr Berlusconi himself was actually in office. I just cannot see corrupt political contributors as `the Garibaldis of today' or seekers for `freedom' or `political prisoners'".

This network of companies was the reason for the allegation that led to the highly embarrassing notification handed to Silvio Berlusconi while he was attending a meeting on organized crime in Naples in November 1994 in his capacity as Prime Minister, that he was to be tried for involvement in bribing officials of the *Guardia di Finanza*. The allegation was that these officials were bribed to give favourable reports while checking up on four of Berlusconi's companies: Mediolanum, Mondadori, Videotime and Telepiù. Money was passed to five officials of the *Guardia di Finanza* by an employee of Fininvest, with a request that the inspections not be carried out "in a heavy-handed way". Apart from these five, six representatives of Fininvest were indicted: Silvio Berlusconi and his brother Paolo, Massimo Berruti, who had previously been a *Guardia di Finanza* inspector at the time of an earlier (1979) investigation into Edilnord, but had subsequently become a Fininvest employee, Salvatore Sciascia, Fininvest's director of fiscal affairs, and two junior employees.

In the first round of the hearing, Silvio Berlusconi was convicted and sentenced to two years and nine months detention. During the hearing, in November 1997, David Mills testified concerning the various offshore companies that he had set up on behalf of Fininvest. However, in his testimony he was rather opaque and discreet about such matters as the true ownership of Telepiù. The appeal confirmed the sentence on Sciascia, who was definitively sentenced to two years and six months of detention. Sciascia claimed that the payments had been authorised by Paolo Berlusconi, but there was no evidence to support this and Paolo was acquitted.

However, doubts had been raised about whether Silvio Berlusconi had himself authorised the bribes, and his conviction was overturned on appeal, on the grounds of insufficient evidence. In particular the hypothesis that Telepiù shares were held by fictitious entities (in order to conceal that the company was really controlled by Fininvest) was held to be "unproven". David Mills' lack of clarity about the true ownership and control of Telepiù may thus have contributed to the acquittal on appeal, and certainly to the fact that no measures were taken to revoke the other licences held by Berlusconi's TV companies, as would have been required under the Mammì law had it been confirmed that he illegally also controlled Telepiù. In his own later words, David Mills had turned some "tricky corners".

While Berlusconi's own guilt in this matter is unproven, what is clear is the contempt in which he held the Mammì law, and his determination to circumvent it. While Mills was being investigated by the British Special Compliance Office about his tax affairs, he explained to them about his involvement in the Telepiù affair, saying that "Berlusconi's actions in this regard violated the spirit of the Italian law".[55]

All Iberian

There were strong suspicions that, in return for all the political help that Craxi had provided to Berlusconi in establishing his dominance of private television, Berlusconi had channelled funds to Craxi for the financing of his political activities. These suspicions led to him being accused of having illegally financed a political party to the tune of about €11 mn. The funds were said to have come from All Iberian. Linked to this accusation was a separate accusation of fraudulent accounting, and the case initiated as a single trial, though subsequently the two channels of the accusation – illicit financing on the one hand and false accounting on the other – were separated.

All Iberian was a company set up by David Mills in 1989. It was based in Guernsey, with the original intention of using it for the sale of film rights. However, it was not in practice used for this purpose. The nominal proprietor of the company was Berlusconi's cousin Giancarlo Foscale. Initially the company was used to purchase shares in other companies in such a way that the ownership of these shares could not be traced back to Fininvest. Later All Iberian became, in effect, the treasury for all of Fininvest's offshore funds.

In 1991 Mills had discussed with various lawyers and financial directors of Fininvest ways of avoiding "the heavy effects of the Mammì law", which, as noted above, made it illegal for Fininvest to hold other companies, notably Telepiù, in addition to its existing commercial companies. "Fininvest's lawyers suggested that, 'in order to avoid the true owners of the company being known' a company should be established in Luxembourg...Mills did not discuss with Fininvest's lawyers the admissibility of this project, saying 'if my clients say it's all right in Italy, then it's all right.'"[56]

During the trial, David Mills was called to testify about the ownership of the companies in Fininvest's Group B, which included All Iberian. The following exchange took place, with the questions being put by the examining magistrate and the answers given by Mills:

> Q: But I don't understand, sorry, who owns this group?
> A: Me. In the final analysis, me.
> Q: But do you have the shares?
> A: No.
> Q: So how do you mean that you are the owner, sorry? That's to say, to go back to what we were saying before, we've seen that this is

a company...
A: That's quite correct.
Q: What's quite correct?
A: That whoever owns the shares owns the company, and I'm not questioning that fact.
Q: So how can you say that you own these companies, if you don't own the shares?
A: In this sense, that the companies either belong to Fininvest or to someone else: the only other person who could own them is me on behalf of my associates....
Q: But excuse me...here we are talking about the ownership of companies, aren't we. So my question is: who currently owns these companies?...Do you have documents to show whether these companies belong to you or not?
A: No. Let me explain. That is, it's not for me to say who is the owner, and who isn't. All I can do is tell the facts, and the fact is that the shares are where they are...
Q: Where are they?
A: They were given to Vanoni, and I don't know where he put them. But I am the person who received the dividends and in that sense obviously the person who receives the dividends is the beneficial owner.
Q: How come that someone who isn't a shareholder gets the dividends?
A: No, sorry, I was...No, sorry, you are doing well in clarifying the matter because I...
Q: I don't understand.
A: I'll explain.
Q: You see? Maybe it's possible...
A: No, let me explain.

The exchange continues in the same vein, as if scripted by Samuel Beckett in order to underline the impossibility of anyone ever comprehending anything. But later on, Mills seems to be more explicit, though still trying to avoid saying that All Iberian belongs to Fininvest.

Q: The thing I can't understand, excuse me if I come back to this point, when you took over the property of this company in the form of its dividends, did you do so as David Mills or on a client's account?
A: No. This matter of the taxation of the dividend was done by me in my capacity as David Mills, that is, as an associate of Mackenzie, no, on my account and that of my associates. So to respond

> to your first question about the ownership, I'd like to clarify the position a bit. The ownership remained a bit unclear, as I was saying earlier, nobody said "I am the owner of this company". Nobody said to me "I'm the owner". However, if you ask me who asked me to form the company, the response, obviously, is the directors of Fininvest. And then, if you ask me on whose account did these societies act, I'd have to answer: they acted for Fininvest. If you ask me, on whose instructions did I form the companies, I must answer: according to the instructions of Fininvest people. If you ask me what initiatives I or my colleagues had, the answer is: we had no power of initiative in these companies, because they existed to respond to the exigencies of clients, and the clients were, as is quite clear from the papers in the case, the client was the Fininvest group. So our role, our meaning me and my employees, was to respond to the needs, the requests for assistance of Fininvest directors in these companies. So, if you put these facts alongside the fact that the shares are at least in the hands of Giorgio Vanoni, and he's put them, I don't know, as collateral or whatever it might be, if this counts as ownership under Italian law, well it is up to you, not to me, to say. All I can tell you are the facts.

These were some of the things that David Mills said. Just as notable, though, are some of the things that he did not say. On the night of November 23rd 1995, when news first came out about the indictment connected with All Iberian, Mills received a telephone call from Silvio Berlusconi. His note recounting the contents of the call was found at a later date by investigators, and runs as follows:

> When I spoke to Berlusconi on Thursday night he insisted that the recent allegations were politically motivated...At the time of the payment, at the end of 1991, Craxi was not Prime Minister. Hence the only accusation that could be made was that an undeclared donation had been made to a political party...Naturally in this country that would not be a crime, as Berlusconi insisted on telling me.

It appears then that Berlusconi's stance at the time of this phone call was that he had indeed passed money to Craxi, but that doing so constituted only a minor offence. Mills, however, did not report this apparent confession when he testified at the trial. In that trial, Berlusconi's defence told a very different, and much more complicated story. He claimed that the money that had been traced to Craxi had in fact been paid to Tariq

IMPUNITY BERLUSCONI'S GOAL AND ITS CONSEQUENCES

Ben Ammar, a Franco-Tunisian film director and trader in film rights, and a supporter of the Palestinian cause. It was claimed that Ben Ammar, who happened to have the same trust lawyer as Craxi, decided to pass the funds directly on to Craxi. Ben Ammar himself went along with this story, though he was unwilling to come to Italy and testify to it under oath. (He says that the Italian courts could have sent a judge to interview him in France, but failed to do so). As Mills wrote in another note to is colleagues:

> It is an extraordinary story, and I don't know whether it's all true or not. It is the case that there was a contract with Ben Ammar. And Fininvest doesn't deny having made the payment via All [Iberian]. It's well known that Craxi was in agreement with various Islamic groups; for example he refused to turn the Achille Lauro terrorists over to the Americans.

After being convicted in the court of first instance on part of the charge of illegal financing of political parties, eventually the highest court determined that, since he had no prior convictions Silvio Berlusconi qualified under the Statute of Limitations for an earlier time-out due to extenuating circumstances, as in the Mondadori affair, and both parts of the illicit financing case were timed out. The final sentence declared that, "on the basis of the mass of documented evidence, it could not be stated that the innocence of those accused was evident, and that they could not be acquitted"[57], though they remained unpunished because of the statute of limitations. Of course, had the first-round conviction in the earlier trial for corrupting the *Guardia di Finanza* survived the appeal stage, he would not have been eligible for these extenuating circumstances. The trial for false accounting dragged on even longer, but in this case, following a change in the law relating to fraudulent accounting brought in during Berlusconi's tenure of power from 2001-2005, he was acquitted on the grounds that what he had done was no longer a crime.

Berlusconi's reaction to public interest in his offshore empire followed a characteristic pattern. For as long as he could, he denied that it existed. Thus, in a television interview in March 2000, he said on a TV programme that he could guarantee that Fininvest had never had recourse to "front" companies (*nomi di copertura*) or to offshore companies, and that all its transactions were undertaken in the clear light of day, and had been subject to taxation. However, once sufficient information (in the form of a report by the accountants KPMG on his offshore empire) had come out to make it clear that this lie was no longer plausible, the story was changed:

"Offshore companies are entirely legitimate things, which my company has since given up, but which at one time it used because it was necessary to find more advantageous ways of paying tax."

As we have seen, the offshore companies were not only used for tax avoidance, but for furtive and surreptitious actions to conceal the ownership of companies, and to circumvent Stock Exchange Regulations. As so often in Berlusconi's business affairs, it is as if one can hear a great deal of squeaking and scratching behind the wainscots, but once you get behind there and shine a torch, the most you can see is some tiny creature scurrying away, perhaps leaving behind a trace of its existence.

The SME Affair

Another battle between Berlusconi's business empire and that of Carlo De Benedetti took place over a food processing firm called SME. This belonged to a state holding company, IRI, then being managed by Romano Prodi. It was to be sold to De Benedetti, but the then Prime Minister Craxi felt that the price was too low. Craxi was also opposed to De Benedetti on other grounds – De Benedetti's newspapers were critical of Craxi, as they continue to be critical of Berlusconi. Craxi therefore asked Berlusconi to put together a consortium to make a competing bid. This was duly done, although it is clear that the objective of Berlusconi's bid was simply to derail the sale to De Benedetti, rather than actually to acquire SME as part of the Berlusconi group. Once again, there were suspicions that judges had been bribed; once again Previti was duly convicted. One part of the case against Berlusconi was timed out, and he was acquitted on another part. However, at a later date it was ruled that the court of Milan had no jurisdiction in this matter, and that therefore the proceedings should never have been started in the first case. All sentences passed by the Milan tribunal were annulled.

Later, as part of his political battles against Romano Prodi, it was to be insinuated that Prodi himself had acted corruptly in agreeing to the original bid. However, no evidence was ever found to substantiate this allegation.

Mediaset Film Rights

Emerging out of the investigation of the All Iberian case, attention focused on the network of offshore companies and their role in keeping funds out of Italy, where they would be subject to taxation. The suspicion is that the film rights were initially being purchased at a low price, but then passed through a chain of transactions among the offshore companies controlled by Fininvest, so that by the time that they were finally sold to Mediaset, the price had been inflated, with the difference accruing to offshore funds under Berlusconi's control. This procedure would have had several advantages for Fininvest. Firstly, it would have reduced tax liabilities, since the gains accrued to companies located in tax havens. Secondly, it provided a pool of hidden funds that could be used for discreet payments to judges and (in the days before Berlusconi had cut out the middleman by becoming a politician himself) to politicians. Thirdly, the capital gains accrued entirely to the Berlusconi family – once Mediaset had become a public company, with the Berlusconi family's stake being diluted by the mass of ordinary shareholders, a higher level of profits would have accrued to these shareholders, and a lower level to the Berlusconi family, had the price of the film rights not been inflated. Finally, during the periods when investment incentives were available to Italian companies, the higher price paid by Mediaset for its film rights would have implied a higher level of investment, and therefore greater incentives from the government. One of the few actions undertaken by the short-lived first Berlusconi government in 1994 was to introduce just such a programme of incentives.

Film rights were traded by companies named Century One and Horizon One. David Mills had been asked about these companies during the All Iberian trial, as follows:

    Q: Do you know who owns these companies?
    A: No. Absolutely not, because you must understand that I didn't follow these companies in detail. It was Tanya Maynard [a colleague of Mills] whose job it was to follow these companies on a day-to-day basis. Certainly I knew, I'd heard about these companies, I'd heard their names, but from the enquiries I made at the time I thought they belonged to Arner, that's to say I was told that at that time they belonged to Arner.
    Q: Do you know what kind of activities these companies were engaged in?
    A: As I've said, I'd heard that they sold rights, but I don't know exactly what kind.

When asked about these companies, Fininvest officials had always claimed that they were completely unconnected with Fininvest or with Mediaset, and one witness had suggested that it was the film companies themselves – the original sellers of the rights – who insisted that these companies act as intermediaries. However, in 2004, when shown a document in which he had set out the "proposed holding structure" of the companies, Mills admitted that they belonged to Marina and Pier Silvio Berlusconi, the two children of Berlusconi's first marriage, but were controlled by Berlusconi himself.

Initially, those investigating these funds had suspected that a substantial part of them had been simply stolen, by an Egyptian-American Film Producer named Frank Agrama. Later, however, it appeared that Mr Agrama was merely holding these funds on behalf of Mr Berlusconi. The magistrates investigating this case consider that the period over which taxes may have been avoided and minority shareholders defrauded may have extended until 2001. Consequently the case will not be timed-out in the near future, and investigations are still ongoing. One thread of this investigation led into the Mills affair, described below.

The Mills Affair

On February 2nd 2004 David Mills asked for a meeting with his personal accountant, Bob Drennan, of Rawlinson & Hunter. Drennan had dealt with his tax affairs for many years, and his offices had been adjacent to those of Mills. Mills began his explanation, but when Drennan began to take notes Mills said there was no need, as he had set out the relevant facts in a letter. He then signed and handed over the following letter:

> Dear Bob,
> The brief relevant facts are these.
> In 1996 I ended up with a dividend from Mr B's companies of around £1.5m after all the tax and fees had been paid.
> This was all done on a personal basis: I took the risk, and kept my partners right out of it.
> Wisely or otherwise, I informed my partners what I had done and, since it was a substantial windfall, offered to pay them (I think) around £50,000 or £100,000 each as what I though [sic] was a pretty generous gesture.
> Which shows you how wrong you can be, as they insisted the transaction should be treated as a partnership profit. To avoid litigation (we had just merged with Withers) I agreed to put the money on deposit in my bank until they were satisfied that there would be no third party claim.

By 2000 it was clear there would be no claim (I knew that all along) and the money was taken off deposit and paid out; I kept just under £500,000 out of what was then getting on for £2m.

So all that risk and cost for not very much. The greatest cost was leaving Withers. I was not asked to leave it, but felt so uncomfortable there, not least because my Mackenzie Mills partners had taken most of the benefit for none of the risk, that I really couldn't stay.

I spent 1998, 1999 and 2000 as a sole practitioner, and it was evident that the trials were going on, there would be lawyers to pay and there was always the risk of being charged with something – which is actually about to happen now as a result of the latest investigation, which you know about.

I kept in close touch with the B people, and they knew my circumstances.

They knew, in particular, how my partners had taken most of the dividend; they also knew quite how much the way in which I had been able to give my evidence (I told no lies, but I turned some very tricky corners, to put it mildly) had kept Mr B out of a great deal of trouble that I would have landed him in if I had said all I knew.

At around the end of 1999, I was told I would receive money, which I could treat as a long term loan or a gift. $600,000 was put in a hedge fund and I was told it would be there if I needed it. (It was put in the fund because the person connected to the B organisations was someone I had discussed this fund with on many occasions, and it was a round about way of making the money available.)

For obvious reasons of their own (I was at that stage still a prosecution witness, but my evidence had been given) it needed to be done discreetly. And this was a roundabout way.

At the end of 2000 I wanted to invest in another fund, and my bank made a loan of the amount, secured on my house etc., of around €650,000. I paid it off by liquidating the $600,000. I attach a copy of the dollar account.

I regarded the payment as a gift. What else could it be? I wasn't employed, I wasn't acting for them, I wasn't doing anything for them, I had already given my evidence, but there was certainly the risk of future legal costs (as there have been) and a great deal of anxiety (as there certainly have been).

This has been going on for more than eight years now. My con-

CHAPTER 4: BERLUSCONI'S LEGAL PROBLEMS

tract was aware of how my income earning capacity had been damaged, and in 1998 and 1999 I was able to send bills from my practice to certain companies, which were paid and increased my income. But this was different.

Because I was pretty sure my CGT [capital gains tax] position was negative overall, I stupidly made no returns on my transactions. If they are closely looked at (i.e., where did the money come from to buy the Centurion shares?), I am obviously concerned about what to do and how this should best be handled.

I attach the key documents.

Yours sincerely

David Mills

Having read the letter, Drennan was in a dilemma, and called a meeting to discuss with his partners what he should do. The conclusion that they reached was that, since there was such a strong suspicion of a link between the money received and the evidence given, the matter should be handed over to the authorities for an opinion. The letter was sent by the British authorities to the Milan magistrates, who interviewed Mills on July 18th 2004. He confirmed what was in the letter, saying that Carlo Bernasconi had told him that Berlusconi had decided to make this gift to him in consideration of the way in which Mills had been able to protect him. Bernasconi was an old friend of both Mills and Berlusconi who worked for the latter from Switzerland in connection with the acquisition of film rights, and who had died in 2001.

Subsequently Mills retracted this statement. He said that in reality the money had come to him from Diego Attanasio, a shipping magnate, but that he had made up the story about it having come from Berlusconi in order to show that the money was a gift, and therefore eligible for a more concessional tax rate. Attanasio denied giving the money, and this second story was not accepted as truthful by the judges.

Both Mills and Berlusconi were charged with corruption, the former for having received, and the latter for having given, money in exchange for a testimony that was less than the whole truth. However, before the case came to a conclusion, Berlusconi had won the 2008 election, and a bill (known as the *Lodo Alfano*, after the Justice Minister Angelino Alfano) was passed giving the President, the Prime Minister, and the Speakers of the upper and lower houses of parliament immunity during their tenure of office. Berlusconi was therefore duly struck off as a defendant, and the case proceeded against Mills alone. He was convicted and sentenced to

4 years and six months detention in the first round in February 2009. The appeal was heard, with great dispatch, in the autumn and at the end of October the sentence was confirmed, with the only change to the original decision being that it was specified that the corruption was subsequent to, and not prior to, the misleading evidence. The final stage at the *Corte di Cassazione* ended in February 2010, with confirmation that he had been corrupted, and a fine of €250,000, but no further punishment since the case was deemed to have been timed-out under the "ex-Cirielli" law described below.

It is not possible to study Berlusconi's offshore empire without being forced to the conclusion that this is a very shifty way to do business. His attempts to deny that his offshore companies existed were matched by an equally implausible statement in 2006 that he "didn't even know" David Mills – "they say he came to Arcore – I may have shaken hands, but I never had a work relationship with him". This contrasts with Mills' statement that he met Berlusconi on three occasions – once at Arcore, once in Milan itself, and once at the Garrick Club in London. And Mills' note of his telephone conversation with Berlusconi in April 1995 is hardly compatible with the notion that they were strangers to each other. While Mills' guilt in having been corrupted by Berlusconi has now been irrevocably established in Italian law, Berlusconi's guilt will require further hearings, given that Berlusconi's part in the trial was suspended by the various legal manoeuvres described below. These manoeuvres were found to be unconstitutional, and the hearing resumed early in 2011.

Outstanding cases

Apart from the Mills case, the most notable case currently outstanding against Silvio Berlusconi at the time of writing is the trial for juvenile prostitution and abuse of office described in Chapter 7. In addition, the Mediaset film rights case remains to be heard, as does a similar, but more recent case (Mediatrade film rights). A civil case also remains to be heard, concerning the reparations due to Carlo De Benedetti's company, as a result of Berlusconi seizing control of Mondadori after a judge had been bribed.

Berlusconi's Search for Impunity

Soon after both the 2001 and the 2008 elections, one of the first actions of the Berlusconi government was to introduce laws making the prime minister immune from prosecution. On both occasions, the constitutional court overturned the law, declaring it to be in violation of the principle (which is displayed in each Italian court) that the law is the same for everybody. After the disappointment in the 2001-2006 parliament, Berlusconi's lawyers had hoped in 2008 that they had found a way to get around the objections that the constitutional court had made, and when the constitutional court again overturned the immunity law, Berlusconi alleged that both the lawyers and the president had been biased against him (he indicated that the president had told him that he would use his influence with the judges to make sure that the law passed, and it does seem to be the case that lawyers in the President's office had given help with the drafting of the bill).

Prior to the judgment of the constitutional court in 2009, Berlusconi's lawyers had indicated that it would not be possible for him to govern effectively if he faced the distraction of prosecution, and that he would have to resign. This, however, he gave no sign of doing, when, by a majority of nine out of fifteen, the Constitutional court again judged that the bill was unconstitutional. Two of the judges who had voted with the minority had, controversially, taken part in a dinner party together with both Berlusconi and the Minister of Justice Angelino Alfano, the author of the bill, a couple of months before the judgment. Their presence there seemed to violate the usual principle that judges should avoid social contacts with those who are about to be affected by their decisions.

In an unfortunate slip of the tongue, Berlusconi, complaining about the amount of his time and attention that were occupied by the – allegedly – politically-inspired attempts to prosecute him said that he had to spend €200 million a year on "judges – excuse me, lawyers".

Reform of Corporate Law

Apart from these direct attempts to legislate for his immunity, all of Berlusconi's terms of office have been dominated by a flurry of legislative activity aimed to ensure that he is not convicted in any of his trials. A pressing need when he was elected in 2001 was to reform the law on false accounting so as to decriminalise some of the activities in which he had been implicated. At the time, the law specified that anyone who committed accounting fraud could be fined €1,000 to €10,000, and imprisoned for between one and five years. Some changes were introduced as soon as Berlusconi entered office, and by April 2002, the following changes were made by a legislative decree:

First, in cases in which no potential harm to shareholders or creditors could be shown, the penalty was reduced to not more than one year and six months.

Second, if the fraud was capable of harming shareholders or creditors, the penalty was six months to three years for non-listed companies, and one to four years for listed companies.

Third, shareholders or creditors must lodge a formal complaint if they wish the harsher penalties applied in the second case to be applied.

Fourth, where no harm is shown to shareholders or creditors the crime is reclassified as a misdemeanour (*contravvenzione*) rather than a felony (*delitto*). This reclassification reduces the statute of limitations from ten years to three years.

Finally, margins of toleration are introduced, excluding punishment if the profit and loss account is falsified by less than 5% or the balance sheet by less than 1%.

Thanks to these new regulations all of Berlusconi's indictments for false accounting fell away or were timed out. There was some uncertainty about whether these more permissive rules were acceptable under European law, and the European Advocate General suggested that Italy's judges should ignore the new law, since it was too lax and gave too much discretion to be compatible with European regulations. However, in 2005 this opinion was not accepted by the European Court.

Reform of Law on Foreign Documents

Another early step in the search for impunity made by the incoming Berlusconi government in 2001 was to require that financial evidence obtained from foreign sources (*rogatorie*) should be admissible only if the documents supplied were originals, or, if not, were stamped on every page of every document with official stamps. While it lasted, this regulation greatly impeded the investigations into Berlusconi's off-shore empire. However the Constitutional Court found it to be inadmissible.

The "ex-Cirielli" Law

A more lasting change in the law that was to speed many of Berlusconi's trials into the safe harbour of impunity was the reform of the statute of limitations that was undertaken in 2005. Until then, the law had specified that the statute of limitations would come into play according to the following schema:

> After 20 years if the minimum penalty was 24 years;
> After 15 years if the minimum penalty was 10 years;
> After 10 years if the minimum penalty was 5 years;
> After 5 years if the minimum penalty was less than 5 years or a fine;
> After 3 years in other cases,
> After 2 years if the penalty was community service.

The new law introduced a relationship between the time for cases to lapse and the maximum penalty for each crime. It would be wrong to say that this law always caused cases to time-out earlier than they had under the previous law. For some of the cases with heavier penalties, the new rules could actually delay the statute of limitations. But in general it led to a sharp reduction in the time available to the courts in cases where the penalty was between 5 and 10 years, and notably in such cases as corruption, including corruption in legal processes, perjury, aiding and abetting – crimes of the kind which many members of the political class in general, and Berlusconi in particular, had at one time or another been suspected of having committed.[58] The new law also reduced the amount of discretion available to judges in determining whether aggravating or extenuating circumstances might impact on the time available to the courts to bring a trial to its conclusion. Another provision that was inserted into the bill as it passed through parliament was a clause excluding detention for those over the age of 70, except for "habitual delinquents". An immediate effect of this was that, a few days after Cesare Previti had been admitted to prison for corrupting a judge, he was able to come out again. For this reason the law was sometimes referred to as the "save-Previti" law, though it is more often referred to as the "ex-Cirielli" law. Cirielli was the name of the deputy who originally introduced the legislation with the aim of making the statute of limitations less freely available to serious criminals, but withdrew his support for it after it became clear how it was being altered in order to promote the goal of impunity for Berlusconi and his friends.

The Cirami Law

Another concern that exercised the Berlusconi government of 2001 to 2006 was the desire to have Berlusconi's cases tried, if they must be tried at all, in courts that were thought more likely to be sympathetic to the defendant. The Milan magistrates had spearheaded the *Mani Pulite* programme, and had a long history of investigating Berlusconi's affairs, in particular his use of offshore funds for the various purposes that have been described. A bill was introduced in November 2002 to allow cases to be transferred from one regional jurisdiction to another, if either the defence or the prosecution could show that there was a "legitimate suspicion" that the judge in the case was not impartial. The final decision on whether a case should or should not be transferred rested with the Supreme Court (*Corte di Cassazione*), but it was possible for repeated applications to be made in the event that new reasons for suspicion could be shown.

The law specifically stated that it could be applied to trials that had already begun, and it was immediately used to seek the transfer from Milan to Brescia of two of the trials in which Cesare Previti was suspected (and subsequently convicted) of corrupting a judge. The law provided that if a trial was stopped because the Supreme Court decided to transfer it, then the clock should be stopped, as far as the statute of limitations was concerned, until such time as it had reached the same stage in the new court as it had in the old one before being suspended. Nevertheless, it would appear possible that unsuccessful applications could delay matters, and speed up impunity under the statute of limitations, while they were being decided on. In practice, the Supreme Court proved to be hard to convince in cases where the defence sought to prove legitimate suspicions about the impartiality of the judges.

Indeed, the peculiar circumstances of Italy make it uniquely difficult for judges to be impartial, when the institutions of justice are under almost daily attack from the executive. In an interview with Boris Johnson for The Spectator in September 2003, Berlusconi had said that judges were "doubly crazy, firstly because they are politically crazy, and secondly because they are crazy anyway. In order to do that job you need to be mentally disturbed, you need to have some psychic derangement. If they do that job it's because they are anthropologically different from the rest of the human race." It would be surprising if members of a profession described in this way by the leader of a political party were to go out of their way to vote for that party. The judge who presided over the civil damages suit connected with the Mondadori affair was apparently seen in a restaurant after Prodi's election victory in 2006 behaving in a festive mood and opening champagne bottles. This fact was held by the Berlusconi press to be proof that he could not be impartial in any case involving the leader of the party who had expressed these views about his profession. It is routine for Berlusconi to refer to any judge who prosecutes him or any magistrate who investigates him, as being "politically motivated". But if any members of these professions are indeed politically motivated, it is most likely to be Berlusconi's own pronouncements that have made them so.

The issue of "legitimate suspicion" cuts both ways. If a citizen has the right to feel certain that a judge in his case is unbiased, then he must also have the right to feel certain that the government, when it makes new laws, is also unbiased, and is not making these laws purely in order to benefit its members. Since Berlusconi entered politics, that certainty has no longer been available.

The Pecorella Law

A further change enacted in early 2006 was a law that made it impermissible for the prosecution to appeal against a "not guilty" verdict. Such appeals are not permissible in many countries, but given that in the Italian system the prosecution must win three trials before a conviction becomes definitive, this reform further tipped the balance against the prosecution, and was warmly welcomed by criminals of every type. It was held to be of doubtful constitutionality by the then President, Carlo Azeglio Ciampi, and was sent back to parliament for reconsideration before eventually being passed. It was indeed heavily modified by the constitutional court, and has been abolished in most of its essentials. All that remains of it is a provision that if a court holds that there is no case to answer (*non luogo a procedere*), then this decision cannot be appealed.

Brief Trials

Following the Constitutional Court's rejection of the *Lodo Alfano*, various new wheezes were studied by Berlusconi's lawyers. The immunity law may, if Berlusconi lasts that long, be proposed once again, in the form of a change to the constitution. But that will take time: a constitutional change requires either the support of two-thirds of the members of parliament, or a referendum. Meanwhile consideration is being given to passing a law which will put an end to all trials that have been going on for longer than a specified time. Italian law is famous for the long delays and backlogs of cases, and some reform is overdue.

The simplest method, of course, would be to abandon the lengthy three-stage process, and make the first round (*primo grado*) definitive, except in cases where the defence can produce specific reasons why the trial should proceed to an appeal. If there is one principal reason for the lengthy delays in bringing cases to a final conclusion, it is this curious practice, unique to Italy, of an automatic right to three separate trials before punishment is inflicted. But this method, of course, is anathema to Berlusconi and his lawyers, as being likely to produce the opposite effect to the impunity that they are striving for. They are approaching the case from the other end, and plan simply to abandon cases that have exceeded some arbitrary time limit. This will make it easier for criminals to avoid being punished in cases of great complexity, such as fraud and corruption charges, and will also reward those who can afford lawyers sufficiently guileful to find ways of causing delay in the courts.

A common tactic in the past has been to propose some change in the law which, in addition to ensuring Berlusconi's impunity, will also put an end to many other cases. In order to avoid the malign consequences of sweeping de facto amnesties, some opposition politicians have been willing to vote for legislation which is more precisely directed at Berlusconi's impunity. This was the tactic used in order to get wide support for the Alfano immunity law in 2008. It was also used following the failure of that law. The threat of a law that would cancel thousands of cases is being held over parliament, as a way of inducing the opposition either to vote for a constitutional change, or for some other *ad personam* law to keep Berlusconi out of the law courts.

Legitimate Impediment

One such law, passed in February 2010, reforms legislation concerning "legitimate impediment" for an accused person to absent himself from hearings. On a number of occasions, the courts have declared themselves satisfied with reasons advanced by Berlusconi for being unable to attend a court hearing, connected with official duties that he is obliged to perform at the time proposed for the hearing. However, under the legislation existing until 2010, each case needed to be presented separately. Berlusconi sought, and parliament delivered, a much more permissive system by which those "whose activities are connected with the function of government" may defer hearings for up to 6 months on up to three separate occasions (18 months in total), provided that the charges concerned are unconnected with their official functions. It is not yet clear which ministers and officials would come within the scope of the new law, but it would certainly include the Prime Minister. The significance of 18 months is that by then, it is hoped, some permanent constitutional change will have put the Prime Minister beyond the reach of the law.

In December 2010, this measure was judged to be unconstitutional – it was to be left to the judges in individual cases to decide what kind of impediment was to be legitimate, but the notion of an automatic entitlement by Ministers not to turn up in court was dismissed. It is for this reason that a backlog of blocked cases emerged out of the deep freeze in early 2011.

Stop the Telephone Interceptions

A further investigation was started in March 2010 by magistrates in Trani, near Bari, who had been undertaking an investigation into excessive interest rates charged on American Express cards. This led them to intercept some conversations at AGCOM, the authority responsible for regulating the television industry. In one of these Berlusconi was heard asking the head of AGCOM to work out a strategy for getting off the air a television programme called *Annozero*. The case will be discussed in Chapter 6, but, as so often with Berlusconi scandals, an attempt was made by his supporters to divert attention from what had been discovered and instead to create a scandal about how it had been discovered. Inspectors were immediately sent to check on the magistrates in Trani to find out whether the matter came within their jurisdiction, and whether they had misused their powers to intercept phones.

This brought back into focus the idea of drastically limiting the powers of magistrates to tap telephone conversations. A draft law to this effect had already been put forward, but had been put on the back burner because of more pressing business, and because of opposition by President Napolitano. There have been numerous occasions, some of which are referred to elsewhere in this book, on which telephone interceptions have uncovered Berlusconi's involvement in matters of questionable legality, and it looks likely that the government will act fast to prevent this happening again. The draft law makes an exception for investigations into organised crime, but of course many of the trails that lead to organised crime start off as investigations into more routine crimes, and these trails will never be uncovered if the law is enacted. There are many other crimes that have only been uncovered as a result of telephone interceptions, and if the law is passed all of these will in future go undiscovered and hence unpunished. The tight conditions that must be passed before interceptions can be carried out will be the answer to many a criminal's prayer, while the new restrictions that are to be imposed on reporting of cases will further choke the flow of information on which a democracy depends. In response to Berlusconi's indictment for juvenile prostitution and abuse of office in early 2011, the bill to limit the use of interceptions came back to the top of the agenda.

Questions of Competence

A further response to this indictment – whose background will be discussed in Chapter 7 – was the argument that Parliament's privileges were being infringed by putting the Prime Minister on trial in this way, and that the only organisation competent to indict him was the Parliamentary Tribunal, because (Berlusconi's parliamentary supporters argued) the Prime Minister was acting in an official capacity when he undertook the actions for which he stands indicted. This Tribunal comprises magistrates, not parliamentarians, but it can only be activated by a vote of Parliament, which, given Berlusconi's majority in the house, would not be forthcoming. While Parliament is free to raise these issues about which court is competent to make the indictment, it is not clear that it has the right to determine the outcome. Most legal opinion holds that it is for judges, not parliamentarians, to determine whether a particular action was carried out in an official capacity.[59]

Proposals for a far-reaching reform of the justice system were tabled in early 2011. They involved many ideas that had been aired before, such as separation of careers between judges and prosecutors, and restrictions on phone tapping, and some that had not, such as making judges personally responsible for damages in cases of miscarriage of justice, and automatic early application of the statute of limitations to those over 65 who have never been convicted (tailored to meet Berlusconi's needs in the Mills and Mediaset cases). Some of these proposals will require reforms to the constitution, and will be hard to enact. However these proposals may come out, one thing is clear: reform of the legal system, however urgently it may be needed, can never be entrusted to a government about whom there is even the suspicion that changes are being made specifically in order to ensure the impunity of its members. To put legal reform into the hands of those who share any of the same interests as criminals is as absurd as to entrust economic reform to monopolists – and it is to this that we now turn.

CHAPTER 5:
THE ECONOMY UNDER BERLUSCONI

In 2009, Tony Barber, of the Financial Times, said on the Financial Times website: "In the court of public opinion, some may consider it surprising that Berlusconi has not been convicted of being one of the worst stewards of the Italian economy since 1945. His first, short-lived government in 1994 achieved nothing. His five-year spell in power from 2001 to 2006 was notable mainly for its failure to introduce the liberalising reforms that Italy desperately needs to make itself competitive in the eurozone. Now, he is presiding over a decline that the International Monetary Fund thinks may make Italy the only eurozone country to experience three consecutive years of recession, from 2008 to 2010[viii]. Worst of all, Italy's public debt is set to soar to 116 per cent of gross domestic product by 2010, according to the European Commission. In other words, Italy will be back where it was in the late 1990s. Noemi or no Noemi, this is Berlusconi's real sin." We shall consider this judgment in the light of a few specific issues, after first reviewing the economic performance of his governments to date.

The Pledge to the Electors

Berlusconi's first period of government, for seven months in 1994, was too short to have any measurable economic impact. There is inevitably a long time lag between government action and economic results: even taxing and spending decisions take time to implement, and the time required before one can judge structural reforms is still longer. Still, the five years during which Berlusconi held power from 2001 were long enough to provide a basis on which his economic legacy can be judged, and far enough in the past to guarantee the availability of the economic statistics on which to judge that period, and to a limited extent also the period since he regained power in early 2008.

[viii] Economic prospects subsequently improved, and the economy grew by around 1% in 2010, though public debt has exceeded Barber's estimate, and stands at 118% of GDP.

During the 2001 election, Berlusconi made much of his "contract with Italians", which covered the following five points:

- Reducing the share of taxes in national income, and specifically exempting all incomes less than €11,000 from income tax, with a 23% tax on those between €11,000 and €100,000 and a 33% rate on those over €100,000.
- A plan for neighbourhood policing, leading to a major reduction in crime.
- Raising minimum pensions to about €500/month.
- Cutting unemployment in half and adding one and a half million new jobs.
- Starting at least 40% of the investments covered in a ten-year plan for major public works.

The contract ends with the words: "In the event that at least four of these five goals have not been attained, Silvio Berlusconi formally undertakes not to stand as a candidate in subsequent general elections". He publicly signed the contract in a television programme shortly before the election.

The Berlusconi Effect: *Più Stato, Meno Privato*

Let us start with his tax-cutting pledge, and in general with his pledge to reduce the size of the state – one of his slogans when he entered the political arena was "*più privato, meno Stato*" (more private, less state). The pledge was specific in terms of one particular tax – income tax – but general in terms of reducing the overall burden of taxes ("fiscal pressure" is the term used in the contract, meaning the share of taxation in the overall economy). During his subsequent period of government, there was some simplification of income tax rates, though the goal of exempting all incomes below €11,000 was not reached. In addition the 33% tax rate came in at €29,000 rather than €100,000, and it was not the highest rate of tax: a 39% tax rate came in at €33,500, and on incomes over €100,000 an additional 4% was levied.[60] (These changes relate to the 2005 budget, by which time Berlusconi had had plenty of time to fulfil his pledges). However, pledges that are specific to income tax could in principle be met simply by shifting the burden of taxation onto other taxes, such as value added tax or other indirect taxes. What is of greater significance is to assess whether Berlusconi has the right to present himself as a politician who is able to achieve the stated goal of reducing the overall tax burden ("fiscal pressure"), and of cutting the size of the state.

CHAPTER 5: THE ECONOMY UNDER BERLUSCONI

The purpose of taxes, of course, is to pay for public spending. However, not all of public spending needs to be paid for out of current taxation. Some can be paid by borrowing – by selling government bonds and bills. This in effect postpones the pain of paying for public spending and leaves it for future generations, who will have to pay higher taxes in order to find the money to pay the interest, and repay the capital, as the debt matures: as Herbert Hoover said, "Blessed are the young, for they shall inherit the National Debt". It may seem immoral to penalise the next generation by racking up government borrowing, but in the context of a growing economy, it makes good sense to do so to a limited extent. If the economy is growing, the next generation will be better off and better able to afford the taxes required for servicing the debt.

In other words, it is not so much the absolute level of public debt that needs to be stabilised, but the ratio between public debt and the overall size of the economy. In Italy this ratio has long been well over 100%, much higher than any other major countries (except Japan, Belgium and more recently Greece) and well above the level of 60% which was originally proposed as a criterion for membership of Europe's single currency.

To be able to reduce the proportion of national income that the government takes in taxation, it is necessary to reduce the proportion of national income that the government spends. The only circumstances in which governments can safely and sustainably cut taxes without cutting spending is if they have the good fortune to inherit a situation in which their predecessors have been excessively prudent in keeping public borrowing below the sustainable level. This is not a situation in which any Italian government has found itself for many years.

Therefore, if we want to be able to assess whether Berlusconi is sincere in wishing to cut the share of national income that is taxed, we need to focus first and foremost on the proportion of national output that is spent by the government.

In the chart below, we show that proportion. It is the red line in the chart, and that is the one to which we need to pay attention. The chart also shows, in green, the proportion of taxes to national income, but it is the red line which tells us whether tax cuts are sustainable, or merely opportunistic. (There is also a dotted line, whose significance will be explained later – ignore it, and the right hand axis, for the time being). The parts

IMPUNITY BERLUSCONI'S GOAL AND ITS CONSEQUENCES

of the chart that are shaded in blue denote the periods during which Silvio Berlusconi has held power. Data for the chart, as for others in this Chapter, are derived from Oxford Economics' database.

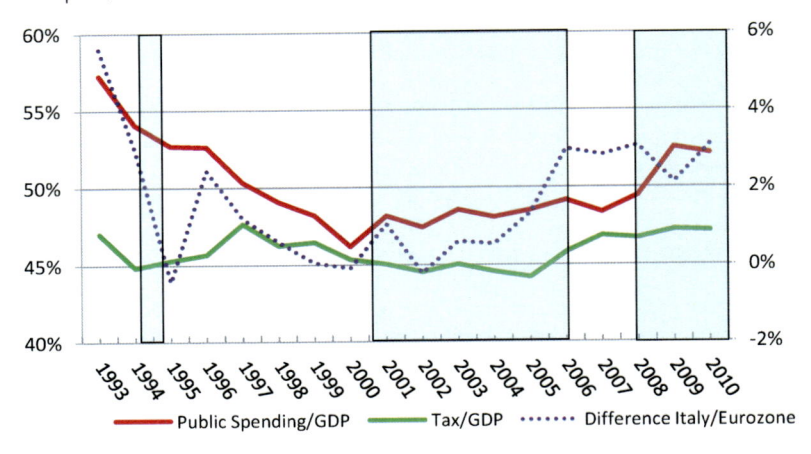

Italian Government Revenue and Spending (% of GDP)

The first striking thing about the chart is the steady decline in the ratio of public spending to GDP that *preceded* Berlusconi's return to power in 2001. More than 6% of national output was returned from the government to the private sector between 1995 and 2000, by which year the share of the economy spent by the government had fallen to "only" 46%. The fiscal rigour of this period – with taxes rising even as public spending fell during the mid-1990s – had the specific aim of qualifying Italy for membership of the single European currency, and that goal was achieved. The closing gap between the red and green lines shows that by 2000 there was hope of a more sustainable future.

As soon as Berlusconi arrived in office, *the decline in public spending* (relative to the rest of the economy) *came to an immediate halt*. Government spending began to drift upwards once again, while government revenue initially did not. The share of the economy spent by the government continued to drift upwards throughout his first term of office, and by the end of the period there was no alternative but to increase fiscal pressure (the share of taxes in GDP). After a period of stability during the 2006-2008 government, Berlusconi returned to office in 2008 and the share of public spending rose again. By the end of 2010 it was right back where it had been in 1994, when Berlusconi first made his promise to cut back the size of the state.

CHAPTER 5: THE ECONOMY UNDER BERLUSCONI

It is inevitable that, when global economic conditions deteriorate, as they did from 2007 to 2010, public spending will rise as a share of the economy. Equally, when economic conditions are relatively favourable, it should fall back. It is interesting to "control" for the changes in the global climate, and this can be done by comparing the outcome in Italy with the outcome in comparable countries. Now it is time to look at the dotted line in the chart. When this reads 0% against the right-hand axis (as in 2000), it means that the share of public spending in Italy's GDP was exactly the same as in all the other countries in the Eurozone. When it reads 3%, this means that the proportion of the economy that is being spent by the Italian government is 3% more than the proportion spent by all other Eurozone governments. So while the continuous lines are telling us what happened in Italy over time, the dotted line tells us how this compares with other countries.

But the general conclusion is still the same – whatever the point of comparison, the Berlusconi years have seen the private sector's share of total spending fall, while that of the state has risen. When Berlusconi came into office in 2000, he inherited a situation in which Italian finances had been brought into a reasonably sustainable state, and public spending had been steadily falling as a share of the economy, so that Italy was now exactly in line with its partner countries in the Eurozone. By the time he left office in 2006, other countries in the Eurozone had used the favourable economic conditions to reduce public spending as a share of GDP. Italy had not, so that an extra 3% of GDP was being spent in the Italian public sector, compared to the partner countries.

Nowhere is the emptiness of Berlusconi's claims to be the bringer of a liberal economic revolution clearer than in this chart. Absolutely no effort was made to deliver on the promise of a sustainable tax cut. Like other promises (such as "I have decided to sell all my companies" in 1994), its only function, once it had fulfilled its electoral purpose, was to be forgotten as quickly as possible.

Cutting Crime, Cutting Unemployment

Although it is not strictly a measure of economic performance, it is worth casting a glance at crime rates, since these had figured in the second of the five pledges. Crime rates had in fact been gradually declining in the years up to 2001, and it may have been this that gave Berlusconi the confidence to make the pledge (though more probably, he made this pledge, like the previous one, in the confident and correct conviction that it would be immediately forgotten once the election was over). The total number of crimes reported stood at 2.2 mn in 2001, down from 2.4 mn in 1996. However, five years later they had risen to 2.7mn. Whether or not the pledge to get more policemen on the beat – always popular, never effective – was achieved, it certainly did not lead to the promised major reduction in the crime rate.[61]

The commitment to cut unemployment in half, and to create 1.5mn new jobs, was not met, but the record on employment during the first Berlusconi government was quite positive. In the last full year before he took power, unemployment had stood at 10.1%, with 2.4 mn seeking work. During most of the 1990s, job creation had been very slow, but this changed towards the end of the decade: from just 70,000 new jobs per year in 1996 and 1997, this rose to 200,000 in 1998, 247,000 in 1999, 384,000 in 2000 and 392,000 in 2001. To meet his target of 1.5 mn new jobs over the five years of the government, it would be sufficient to create 300,000 per year. However, in the event the pace of new job creation slackened to 170,000 in the final two years of the government, so that the total number of jobs created over the period as a whole came to 1.35 mn rather than 1.5 mn. Quite a near miss. However, with the labour participation rate rising – as it always does when employment prospects improve – this fell far short of halving the unemployment rate. By 2005 it had fallen to 7.7% of the labour force, rather than the 5% implied by the pledge. It bottomed out at just over 6% under the ensuing Prodi government, and then began to rise again in response to the deteriorating global economy. By the final quarter of 2010 it was back at 8.6%.

Reform of the labour market was one of the relatively few economic measures that were introduced under the Berlusconi government that started in 2001. A law was introduced in 2003, following some (but not all) of the suggestions that had been made by Marco Biagi, an expert on labour law, who had been called upon to advise on labour market reform, and who had been assassinated by the "New Red Brigades" in 2002. The aim of the reforms was to reduce the level of protection legally accorded to employees, which was deterring the creation of new jobs, and to make it easier to take on employees temporarily or for limited periods. One of the most-criticised aspect of the reforms is that they failed to make corresponding reforms in the social security system, with the result that "Italy's social security net is generous for some workers, but virtually nonexistent for (most) others ... a rising share of workers faces high employment risk but little income insurance"[62], as stated in a recent IMF study.

CHAPTER 5: THE ECONOMY UNDER BERLUSCONI

The labour market reforms undertaken during the Berlusconi government followed an earlier reform, undertaken in 1997 by the then Labour Minister Tiziano Treu, which had introduced temporary contracts and incentives for part-time work, as well as permitting the establishment of private employment services. The chart below shows a very clear break in trend following these reforms, with unemployment falling steadily after 1997. By contrast the reforms of 2003 appear to have caused at best a temporary and slight improvement in unemployment.

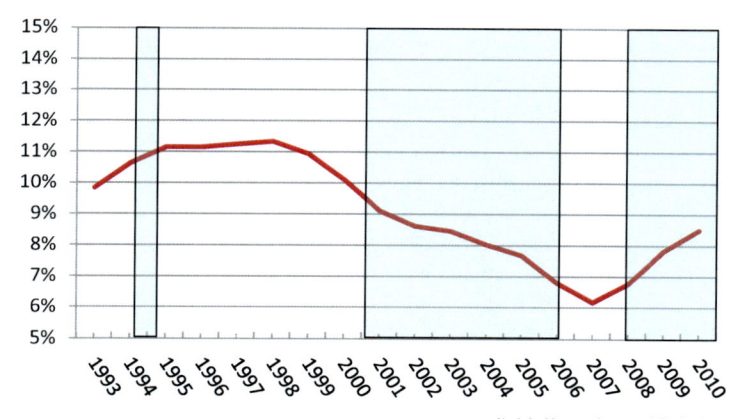

Italy's Unemployment Rate (percent)

The main conclusion of the IMF study of Italy's labour market regulations is worth quoting: "In this context, liberalizing product markets is of first-order importance as it can help improve labor market outcomes, induces little to no fiscal cost, and may increase the political feasibility of subsequent labour market reforms."

The Macro-economic Disaster

Liberalising product markets is one of the activities that one would expect from a centre-right government, with a view to improving the overall level of economic performance. Although it was not one of the five specific pledges, such an improvement in Italy's overall economic performance was certainly one of the more general claims that Berlusconi made. It is therefore important to review this performance during the Berlusconi years. The growth rate of the economy as a whole – gross domestic product (GDP) – provides a useful summary measure of the success of economic management. There are some well-known criticisms of using

IMPUNITY BERLUSCONI'S GOAL AND ITS CONSEQUENCES

GDP as a measure of welfare: it omits issues relating to the sustainability of growth (a high growth rate, if purchased by imposing costs on future generations through, for example, environmental damage, is worth less than a lower growth rate without such costs) and it omits issues relating to distribution and subjective welfare (if all the growth accrues to a small class of super-rich, the subjective benefit to the members of that class may be outweighed by the frustration and resentment of those who are left out). This is not the place to discuss these issues: suffice it to say that there is no sign that they rank very high on the agenda of the political party headed by Berlusconi. With that proviso, we shall use GDP growth to assess how Italy has fared under Berlusconi's economic management.

It would be too crude simply to look at GDP growth rates in isolation. Italy, like any other trading nation, is heavily influenced by the world economic environment in which it finds itself. For example, in the Spring of 2008 when Berlusconi took office once more, the global economy faced a severe shock because of banking problems whose epicentre occurred in the "Anglo-Saxon" economies, and particularly in the USA, but which influenced world trade as a whole. It would obviously be wrong to blame the slowdown in Italy's economic performance since he took power in 2008 on Berlusconi's government. Equally, a similar shock occurred when the combination of the end of the "dot-com" boom and the attacks on the World Trade Centre took place around the time that Berlusconi was forming his first administration. We must find some way of controlling for these external factors before we can pass judgment on his economic record.

The best way of doing this is to consider, not Italy's GDP growth rate in isolation, but *its rate relative to other countries, and particularly to the rest of the Eurozone*. The Eurozone provides the obvious point of comparison. Any shocks, such as the ones we mentioned in the last paragraph, or the commodity-price shocks of 2007, will have exerted the same impact, negative or positive, on the other members of the Eurozone to more or less the same extent. (There are, of course, some differences – for example France, by virtue of its large investment in nuclear power, is less exposed to oil-price shocks than Italy or other members of the Eurozone; Germany with its large exports of capital goods is more vulnerable to a global slowdown). Equally, since they share the same interest rate environment and the same exchange rates, monetary conditions are broadly similar.

Looking at individual years produces a "noisy" chart from which it is hard to see the wood for the trees, and is also not particularly relevant to the

CHAPTER 5: THE ECONOMY UNDER BERLUSCONI

issue which we are trying to address – is there evidence that the Berlusconi governments have been able to unleash the potential of the Italian economy more successfully than their predecessors? For that reason the chart shows, not single-year, but five-year growth rates (so the reading of 10% in 2000 means that average income in 2000 was 10% more than in 1995). As before, the Berlusconi years are shown shaded in blue.

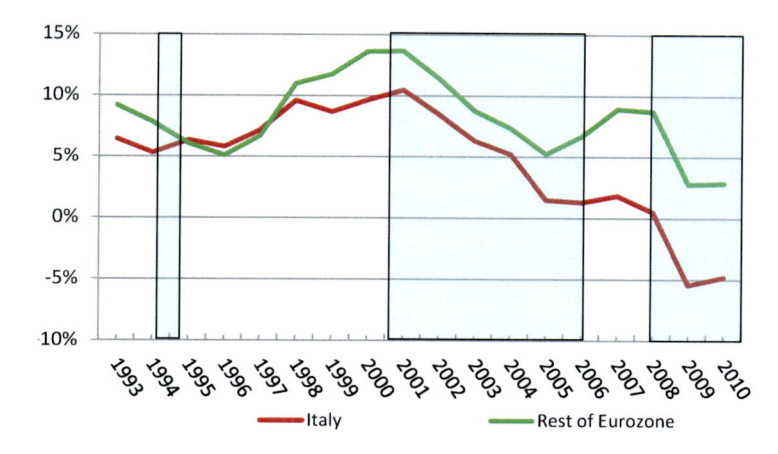

Italy's Growth rate Compared to the rest of the Eurozone

The relationship between the rate of growth of an economy, and the activity of its government, cannot be defined with precision. Some policy actions by a government – for example, a decision to cut taxes or boost public spending – will create additional demand which may feed through almost immediately into a higher growth rate. Others – for example, trying to improve the quality of the workforce by increasing expenditure on education – will take many years to have an effect. In any given year, the overall outcome for the economy depends on many decisions taken years ago by previous governments, as well as more recent decisions taken by the one currently in power. And, of course, factors which no governments can influence, such as the global environment and the choices made by individuals, may dwarf any impact that governments can have.

Despite these uncertainties, the chart does seem to tell a clear story. By the time Berlusconi took power in 2001, Italy had begun to lag somewhat behind the rest of the Eurozone. By the time he left power, the gap had widened substantially, and it has not closed since then. In 2010 average income in Italy was some 5% below the 2005 level, while in the rest of the Eurozone it was some 3% above that level. Economic growth in

IMPUNITY   BERLUSCONI'S GOAL AND ITS CONSEQUENCES

Italy ground to a halt at the start of this century, and declined during the recession. Unlike their counterparts in the rest of Europe, Italians are now worse off than they were in 2000. When they persist for long periods, differences in rates of economic growth can gradually bring about cultural chasms, such as the one which separated East from West Germany in 1989. This is beginning to be palpable in Italy.

The same point, about the deterioration in Italy's economic performance since 2001, is made, perhaps more simply, in the Chart below.

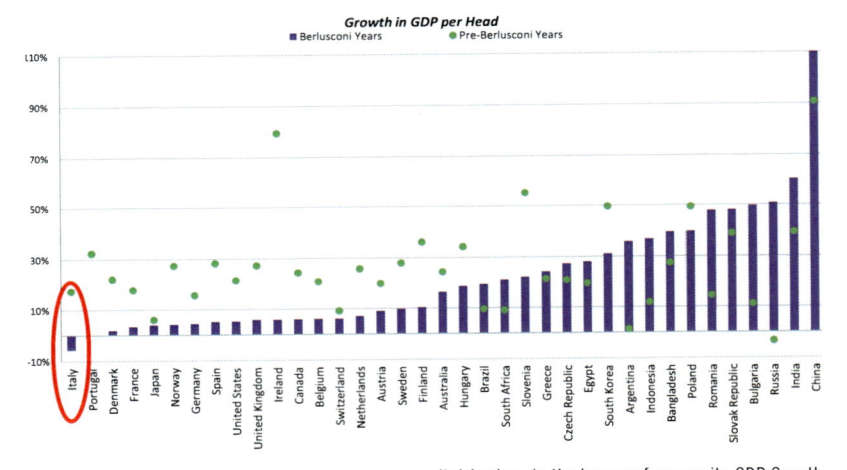

Growth in GDP per Head
■ Berlusconi Years   ● Pre-Berlusconi Years

Italy's place in the league of per capita GDP Growth

The Chart compares Italy at the foot of the world league table of per capita GDP growth in the eight years from 2001 to 2009 (during most of which period Berlusconi was in power, and hence labelled "Berlusconi years"), with its performance during the eight years prior to Berlusconi's first major spell in government (labelled "pre-Berlusconi years"), when it had been much closer to the OECD average.

The world contains 120 countries with populations of more than 4 million. Out of these, only two – Mugabe's Zimbabwe and Berlusconi's Italy – had a smaller economy in 2009 than in 2001. If one focuses on per capita income rather than on the overall size of the economy, then one can find two other countries which have fared worse than Italy over this period: Haiti and the Côte d'Ivoire (their GDP grew more rapidly than Italy's, but their population growth was much higher). But apart from these three, no other country in the world has fared worse than Italy since Silvio Berlusconi took office in 2001.

To reiterate: this underperformance during the period in which Berlusconi has been in power cannot be explained away by reference to global economic conditions, which by definition were the same for all countries. It might be objected that the price of tackling the severe problems afflicting the Italian economy is a period of pain, with the pay-off occurring only after some delay – just as the early years of the Thatcher government in Britain produced severe economic pain, but were followed by a period in which economic performance was better than for Western Europe as a whole. But that, too, won't wash. Rather than taking the pain early and getting the gain later, the reverse happened under the 2001-2006 Berlusconi government, with the gap separating it from the rest of Europe widening towards the end. Difficult decisions were avoided – the burden of public debt, which had been reduced (relative to the economy as a whole) under the previous government, was once again allowed to grow after Berlusconi had taken office. The gain was taken early and the pain happened later, as a result of the failure to address difficult problems.

To be sure, these problems are tough and intractable. An over-reliance on industries which are vulnerable to competition from China and other emerging economies, a weight of pensions obligations that is exacerbated by an ageing population, a public debt that is too big to allow for any fiscal stimulus when times are bad – the list could be extended.

Membership of the Euro may also have been a problem, in that it was no longer possible to have recourse to the devaluations which periodically offset Italy's loss of competitiveness before the mid-1990s. But that problem was also faced by many other countries in the Eurozone, who still managed to outperform Italy. Indeed, Germany itself, in the early years of this century, seemed to be suffering from a very intractable competitiveness problem in the aftermath of reunification. But it was addressed by means of the difficult decisions which were taken by the German government, but avoided in Italy.

Silvio Berlusconi has always tried to project himself as someone whose background of business success make him uniquely well qualified to tackle Italy's economic problems. The data show, though, that these problems have become worse during his period in office, and the gap in economic performance that separates Italy from the rest of Europe has widened.

Since Tony Barber made the judgment with which we opened this chapter, it has become a little harder to share his view that economic mismanagement is "Berlusconi's real sin". But that is not because there is any reason to view Berlusconi's economic management in a more favourable light.

It is simply because the extent of the damage that he is inflicting in realms other than the economy is turning out to be much worse than seemed likely at the time that Tony Barber wrote. Nevertheless, it may well be that when his career in government is seen in a longer historical perspective, what will stand out as the most significant result of his administration will be the impoverishment – both absolute and relative – that Italians suffered.

Alitalia

One economic issue that threw a clear light on his characteristic approach to economic issues was the privatisation of Alitalia, the country's "flag-carrying" airline. It had long been making crippling losses, and the centre-left government that preceded Berlusconi's return to power in 2008 had been negotiating to sell it to Air France, which had already allied with the Dutch KLM. An attempt to sell the company, in which the Italian government held a 49.9% stake, had failed in 2007. In mid-March, about a month before the election, after tough negotiations, it was announced that a deal to sell the company to Air France for €138 mn had been agreed in principle. Air France was to take over Alitalia lock, stock and barrel, and assume responsibility for all of its debts, which amounted to upwards of €1.2 bn. It was also to inject €1 bn of fresh capital to rejuvenate the airline. Air France specified that Alitalia would retain its national identity within the Air France-KLM group following the takeover.

However, on March 21st 2008, at the height of the election campaign, Silvio Berlusconi said that, if he won, he would respond with "a curt no" to an Air France bid that he described as "arrogant and unacceptable". "We cannot give up our flagship carrier" he declared in an election speech. The future of Alitalia became one of the main issues in the election campaign, with Berlusconi saying that he was confident that an alternative Italian bid would be tabled "within a few days". Later, on March 25th, he had lengthened this forecast to say that the bid would be forthcoming "within three to four weeks". The takeover of the national airline by a foreign one was presented as a severe blow to national pride – Berlusconi accused Air France of "colonialism" and raised the prospect that the Italian tourism industry would be at risk from visitors being routed to France. At one stage he said that his own children were willing to join a rescue bid, though he quickly backed down on this statement.

The Northern League were equally hostile to the Air France bid, but for a different reason. They had long wished to turn Malpensa, the white-

CHAPTER 5: THE ECONOMY UNDER BERLUSCONI

elephant international airport near (but not quite near enough) to Milan, into a major hub, and they knew that this was not part of Air France's vision for Alitalia.

Air France was thus faced with a clear prospect of intense opposition from the government that was widely expected to emerge after the election. At this stage, Air France was also negotiating with the unions about the number of job cuts that would be necessary if their bid were successful. Air France Chairman Jean-Cyril Spinetta had said that the plan would involve only 2,100 job cuts. In the talks between the unions and Air France, both sides had every incentive to hang tough – Air France knew that it would have enough trouble on its hands from the declared opposition of the next government, and would have been foolish to make concessions to save a deal which looked doomed for other reasons.

On April 3rd, the talks between Air France and the Unions broke down and Air France withdrew its offer (its share price rose sharply immediately afterwards). Whether the deal would have gone through if Berlusconi had not declared his intention to veto it is a counterfactual question which cannot be answered with any certainty. Berlusconi now claims that it was the unions, not he, who shipwrecked the Air France deal. As we shall see, a similar breakdown in talks between the unions and a potential buyer was to occur later in the year, but with a different political climate and, as a result, a different outcome.

As the summer wore on, it became clear that, contrary to Berlusconi's declarations, no alternative bid was ready to be tabled, and that, in order to summon one into being, the government would have to offer terms that were significantly more favourable to the buyer than in the case of the Air France offer. An emergency bridging loan that had been granted to tide Alitalia over looked likely to be judged illegal by the European Commission. The crushing weight of Alitalia's debts continued to rise, and the company was declared bankrupt at the end of July.

By that time, the government had tabled a proposal to split Alitalia into two companies. A "good company", consisting of the hardware and the landing rights was to be sold, while all of Alitalia's debts were to be put into a "bad company", which was to be presented to the Italian taxpayer to clear up the mess. On these terms – fundamentally different from the terms offered by Air France, which would have taken over the debts as well – it was possible to find a group of Italian businessmen who were willing to take away the planes and the routes for a bargain price. The consortium included Air One, a privately owned domestic carrier that was itself close to bankruptcy, and badly needed to be able to neutralise any potential competition from Alitalia; also Roberto Colannino, a successful entrepreneur who had turned round the scooter and van manufacturer Piaggio, and who was to manage the new Alitalia, the Benetton family, who also had a stake in Rome's Fiumicino airport, Pirelli and several other leading industrialists. All of those who took part in this consortium were well aware of doing Berlusconi a huge favour by turning his fantasy of an Italian consortium into a reality; each of them would have had some other issue on which they would hope that the government could see its way to returning the favour. But none of them were rich, or foolish, enough to be able to do what Air France would have done, and assume responsibility for paying Alitalia's creditors. The amount of cash which the consortium committed was well under half the €2.4 bn of the Air France offer.

They also needed to know that no anti-trust authority was going to interfere. Alitalia's monopoly of the Milan-Rome route was one of the few profitable parts of the operation, though the arrival of a high-speed train service, combined with the continued delays, overbookings and cancellations on the Alitalia service has meant that the future value of this route cannot be taken for granted. In addition, on many of the other national routes, the merger of Air One with Alitalia had removed any chance of competition. The government duly indicated that anti-trust issues would not adversely affect the consortium, thus leaving consumers to pay an additional cost which they would not have incurred under the Air France deal. It also indicated that the bankruptcy laws would be changed to allow the deal to go through – normally the protection of creditors requires that no asset should be sold at less than its market value. But Alitalia's assets had a greater value if sold individually – in other words, dismantling the company – than as part of the whole. For example, many of Alitalia's landing slots had a market value which the consortium could not have afforded to pay for, but which were necessary for the continuation of the company – and these slots were not included in (or to put it another way, given a zero value in) the valuation made by the consortium.

Negotiations with the unions were again very tough, particularly because the number of redundancies that was required to make the deal attractive – around 7,000, including those at Air One – was much higher than the 2,100 on which Air France had been insisting when its talks with the unions broke down. Just as Air France's talks with the unions had broken down, so did the consortium's, and in mid-September the consortium left the table, announcing that they were abandoning their bid. However, this time the political climate was totally different, and with plenty of cajoling

CHAPTER 5: THE ECONOMY UNDER BERLUSCONI

and arm-twisting the government was able to persuade the unions that no better deal would be available, so that an agreement was reached.

It was also clear that the consortium could not manage without an alliance with a major international airline. The Northern League hoped that it would choose Lufthansa, since they expected that Lufthansa would assign a greater role to Malpensa. However, in the end the consortium decided to offer a 25% stake to Air France. In order to prevent the consortium from simply selling their shares directly to Air France, and retiring from the scene having pocketed the difference between what they paid the government and what they knew Air France was willing to pay, the government had required that they undertake not to sell their shares for five years. However, knowing that sooner or later Air France is likely to wish to take over completely, the members of the consortium are unlikely to want to antagonise the minority shareholder. (If it should wish to acquire a majority interest before the five years are up, Air France will find it easy to get around the "lock-up" clause simply by making a rights issue). In other words, Air France has effective control of the company, even without a majority of the equity. By the end of the year, then, Air France had secured pretty much what it wanted, and at a fraction of the cost that it had been prepared to pay. The difference was to be paid by the Italian taxpayer.

One part of the plan under which the consortium had undertaken to revive Alitalia involved increasing the number of international and intercontinental routes. In mid-2009, the new Alitalia announced that it had, in accordance with this plan, added 13 such new destinations – but that every one of these involved flying from Italy to France or Holland and changing planes there. Even a passenger wishing to fly Alitalia to Berlin will have to change planes in Paris – though it is hard to see why any should wish to do so, given the large number of far cheaper and more reliable airlines already flying directly to Berlin from Rome, Milan, Naples, Venice, Pisa and Cagliari.

The fear that Berlusconi conjured up during the election campaign – that people wishing to visit Italy on the national flag-carrier would be routed via Paris, threatening Italian tourism – has thus become a reality. The failure of Berlusconi's policy is complete in all respects but one: it certainly helped him to win the 2008 election. As a consummate salesman he cannot, of course, admit to this. Indeed, he includes the "saving" of Alitalia as one of the proudest achievements of his government. To make this remotely plausible, he must, and does, now insist that he was in no way responsible for the collapse of the original negotiations with Air

France the week after he had announced that he would veto them. As we have noted, this assertion rests on a counterfactual – nobody can say for sure what would have happened if he had kept his mouth shut.

Two points are, however, beyond dispute: firstly he was lying when he said that he knew that an Italian consortium was ready to make an offer within days (later modified to weeks). Secondly, as Gianni Dragoni wrote in *Il Sole 24 Ore* (Italy's equivalent to the Financial Times), on September 28th 2008, the deal that was struck under his government was inferior to the Air France offer in every single respect, including the dubious appeals to patriotism. Two years later, Alitalia continues to make losses.

This episode highlights two general points about Berlusconi's approach to economic issues. Firstly, he is no uncritical admirer of the operations of a free market. There is a sharp contrast here between his views and those that one would expect to find in a politician of the right in the US, Britain or even Germany. What the market was suggesting was that the individual assets owned by Alitalia had a greater value than the company as a whole. In particular, its "slots" (take-off and landing rights) were much in demand, particularly at Fiumicino and Milan's Linate airport. A year earlier Alitalia had sold six slots at London's Heathrow airport for €92 mn. Yet, as we have seen, a zero value was attributed to these slots in the offer by the Italian consortium. Had the slots and other assets been auctioned off as normally required by bankruptcy laws, the administrator would have received more money, and the cost to the taxpayers and to Alitalia's debtors would have been lower. But this would have been politically unacceptable, since the appeal to national pride which had helped Berlusconi to win the election would have been shown up for the farce that it was. Politics comes first, the market comes second.

The other, related, lesson from this episode is that it shows Berlusconi's vision of the normal way to business success: get the state to help you. Just as he was helped in his business career by the sweeping aside of all the safeguards that were intended to ensure competition in the commercial TV industry, so he planned to help the consortium by sweeping aside the anti-trust restrictions which would normally have applied in a case like this, as well as by seeing that they were given the assets at less than market value.

Tax Evasion and Tax Havens

Financing Italy's public expenditure has always been a problem. During the latter half of the last century, it seemed that some kind of equilibrium had been reached along the following lines: households underdeclared the value of their incomes and capital gains in order to minimise direct taxes. They derived a warm glow from the fact that they were successfully outwitting the government. At the same time, households were relatively cautious in their expenditures, and saved a high proportion of their disposable income, investing it, directly or indirectly, in government debt. By allowing relatively high rates of inflation, the government was able to reduce the value of this debt, in effect appropriating a large part of household savings, and deriving a warm glow from the knowledge that it was successfully outwitting households. However, with the advent of the Euro, the rate of inflation became a variable that was determined at the European level, rather than at the national level, and it became necessary to find a more conventional way of balancing the budget. A legacy of the old system was a massive burden of outstanding government debt which might, under that system, have eventually been inflated away. When plans to set up the common currency were originally drawn up, it was considered unlikely that Italy would qualify, and it was proposed that member countries should undertake that the level of outstanding government debt should never exceed 60% of GDP. In Italy, outstanding government debt has exceeded 100% of GDP for many decades.

Under the Amato and Prodi governments in the mid 1990s, strenuous efforts were made to put Italian finances into shape – the first chart in this chapter showed how the gap between government revenue and government spending was narrowed at that time. Various methods were used to increase public revenues, many of which were seen as being essentially one-off measures needed to clear the hurdles to Euro membership, which would not be repeated once this goal was achieved. These measures often consisted of a pardon (*condono*) for past offences in areas like planning permission or tax evasion, in exchange for a one-off payment. Similar measures are occasionally practiced by many governments, and are not unique to Italy (though, of course, pardons constituted a major source of export earnings for Italy in the middle ages). But, given its serious problems with public finance, Italy has had recourse to them more often than most other governments in the period since 1990.

One of the problems with this policy is that the expectation of future pardons provides an incentive to illegal activity. The law is flouted in the present, in the confidence that exemption from punishment can be purchased in the future. For this reason, during the 2008 election campaign, Giulio Tremonti, now Finance Minister as he had been in the previous Berlusconi government, promised[63] that he would end the policy of raising funds in this way. "Today the conditions for them no longer exist. In the past I certainly didn't use them voluntarily, but because I was forced to by hard necessity. Pardons are a thing of the past".

This message would have dismayed at least some of those considering voting for Berlusconi. One of the things that many of them admire about him is the adeptness with which he himself has devised schemes for tax-evasion. We have seen how profits from film rights bought for Mediaset accumulated in offshore locations: Berlusconi was accused of evading taxes of around €60 mn by this scam in the period up to 1999. Many voters, far from deploring the idea that the government could be directed by a man who himself has so much to lose from being tough on tax evasion, vote for him precisely because they expect him to display to them the leniency he expects for himself, when it comes to punishment for such peccadilloes.

And they are right to expect this. An article by Silva Maria Giannini and Maria Cecilia Guerra in February 2009[64] showed that, despite the rhetoric about being tough on tax evasion, many controls which aimed at identifying tax evaders were actually being dismantled. For example, when filling in VAT returns, it is no longer required that the counterparties to the sales and purchases be identified – although the *Corte dei Conti* – roughly equivalent to the UK Audit Office – said that, given the widespread computerisation of accounts, providing this information did not impose a great administrative burden on businesses. Similarly, restrictions on the amount that could legally be paid in cash (in other words, untraceably) were removed. The article provides other examples. Measures announced to combat tax evasion on a large scale turn out to consist merely of writing into the legislation a series of measures which were already being taken in practice – nothing will change. A decline in the ratio of VAT collected to economic activity suggests that already the results of loosening controls are beginning to have an adverse effect on public finances. As Tito Boeri, Professor of Economics at Milan's Bocconi University, has pointed out, "the tradition of the Berlusconi cabinets has always been one of declining tax revenues even at unchanged tax rates."[65]

Berlusconi had expressed his opinion on the matter during a talk to tax inspectors in 2004: "There is a law of natural justice which says that, if the State asks you for more than a third of what you have earned, that is an abuse of power, and then you can do your best to find ways around this, or even ways of evading taxes, which you feel to be in accordance with your own personal sense of morality, and which don't make you feel personally to blame".[66] The clear message is that tax evasion is acceptable if the payer's "personal sense of morality" tells him that the amount demanded is in his view excessive.

In July 2009, Tremonti backed down on his commitment not to instigate new pardons, and introduced a measure offering immunity from prosecution for those declaring foreign holdings that were previously undeclared. On offer was freedom from prosecution from fraudulent accounting, fraudulent bankruptcy, and all offences relating to tax evasion. The fee for this comprehensive pardon was a payment to the treasury of some 5% of the money being repatriated into Italy.

Tremonti had pleaded "hard necessity" as the reason for instituting pardons in the past. And it is true that public finances remain in a dire state. By the end of 2009, the *scudo fiscale* – the indemnity for repatriated capital – was being hailed as an outstanding success, and the deadline had been extended to the end of April 2010 (though with a slightly higher penalty for those bringing in capital after the original deadline). The amount of tax revenue raised through the measure is likely to amount to about 0.3% of GDP – not a negligible amount, but, for a government that regularly spends over 50% of GDP, too trivial a sum to justify the moral hazard involved in yet another pardon.

It seems a curious gift to make, both to small wrongdoers who may have stashed away some "black" money in a bank account in Switzerland or Liechtenstein, but even more to organised crime. In seeking to defend the measure, Tremonti said that it was very similar to one recently taken by the Obama government in the US.

Yet on inspection, it was radically different, and much more valuable to organised crime. The Italian pardon allowed one to bring money in *anonymously*. Indeed, it is not clear how it could be established that the money was in fact brought in from outside. Somebody in possession of illicit money could simply hand it in at a bank and say that they had bought it in from overseas, thus benefiting from the immunity offered by this pardon. In the US, there is no anonymity – in their scheme someone benefiting from the immunity must declare it on his tax form. In Italy, by contrast, in return for handing over a small percentage of the illegal money, the offender is given a kind of "get-out-of-jail-free" card, which he can produce if at any future period he is charged with some offence relating to that money, to prove that he has purchased immunity against those charges. He has complete immunity against any future tax liabilities relating to that money; while in the US scheme any taxes that have been avoided must be paid.

Money-laundering is an expensive business: normally if one holds illegal funds in some obscure tax haven as a result of some illegal activity, and wishes to convert these funds into usable funds in one's own country, one would expect to pay some 40% of the value to whoever performs the service of laundering this money. As Marco Travaglio pointed out[67], with this tax pardon the Italian state in effect set itself up as a cut-price money-launderer, performing the same service at a heavily discounted price.

To understand this extraordinary abdication of any sanctions against criminals and tax evaders, we need to see it in two separate contexts. The *first* of these relates to the man in the street, who may have committed minor offences such as concealing some of his revenue from the state. The state has always been seen as a hostile entity, perhaps more so in Italy than in most other countries. Berlusconi is the first leader of the state who knows how to create a bond between himself and the minor offender: you have committed a small crime and are worried about being punished, but you can know that I have committed much larger ones and you can rest assured that, with me in office, neither of us is going to suffer humiliation and loss. Though never explicitly stated, that is the bond that binds and endears Berlusconi to many of his countrymen, and helps to account for his unique popularity.

The *second* relates to organised crime. Any leader of an Italian government must make the right noises about fighting the various organised crime groupings. He must pay homage to Falcone and Borsellino and the other mafia-fighters who have been assassinated. Organised crime knows and understands that these are the rules of the game. They judge a politician on what he does, not what he says. During 2009, there had been growing signs that organised crime in general, and Sicily's Cosa Nostra in particular, were feeling that Berlusconi had not done enough to deliver on the implicit (possibly even explicit, as Chapter 3 discussed) pledges in return for which he received an overwhelming preponderance of Sicilian votes. Two very different characters, the blogger Beppe Grillo and the leader of the Northern League Umberto Bossi, even hypothesised that the "escort" D'Addario (see Chapter 7) was put up by the Mafia to create difficulties for Berlusconi – but this seems to me a conspiracy theory too far. However, there were other signs of discontent: the declaration by the imprisoned ex-boss Riina that the murders of anti-mafia judges in 1993 had been commissioned by third parties, rather than indepen-

CHAPTER 5: THE ECONOMY UNDER BERLUSCONI

dently decided on by the mafia; the emergence of the letter from the Mafia to Berlusconi (discussed in Chapter 3); the threat of a separatist political party of the South.

Although the promise of reform to the rules affecting phone-tapping has gone a long way to giving organised crime what it had wanted and expected from the Berlusconi government, it is a demanding taskmaster, and clearly expected more tangible economic help. During the 2001-2006 Berlusconi government, the Minister for Infrastructure, Pietro Lunardi, had said that "we must get used to living with the Mafia", and some similar sentiment may have been expected from the second one. This is not to suggest that any open negotiations took place between the Italian government and representatives of organised crime syndicates that led to this pardon; merely that it was part of a strategy for ensuring that the government could continue to count on the overwhelming support that it enjoyed at the last election in the areas where organised crime is powerful. In the photograph above, Antonio Di Pietro, wearing a Mafia-style cap, protests about the pardon with a placard saying "The Mafia is grateful".

The *Corte dei Conti* estimates the deadweight loss of corruption to the Italian economy as around €60 billion a year, and in early 2011 reported a 30% increase in the number of cases of corruption reported over the last year. The encouragement given to the corrupt by the fiscal pardon will have cost the Italian economy, and indirectly the Italian exchequer, far more than the €4.5 billion that the exchequer is estimated to have received from that pardon.

The need to drastically reform public finances is a pressing one, as can be seen by considering the level of confidence that global investors currently show towards Italian government undertakings. For a long period following the introduction of the Euro, the "spreads", or interest-rate differentials, between, say, German public debt on the one hand and

Italian or Greek public debt on the other remained very low. Investors took the view that, since all of these debts were denominated in Euros and would therefore suffer identical risks of having their value eroded by inflation, and since it seemed unthinkable that any of the governments should default, any government debt was worth as much as any other. If the Italian government sold a bond offering 4% interest, it would trade at about the same price as a similar bond sold by the German government, though typically the Italian government would have to offer about 0.3% more interest to compensate for the greater perceived risk.

This gradually began to change as the financial system sickened in late 2007. From just 0.3%, the extra interest that was needed to persuade investors to prefer an Italian government bond to a German one steadily increased to a peak of 1.5% in early 2009. Throughout 2010, financial markets were spooked by the debts of the "PIIGS" – Portugal, Ireland, Italy, Greece and Spain. The spread between the rates at which Germany can borrow and they can borrow has fluctuated as European leaders attempted to reach agreement on the circumstances in which the governments of Eurozone countries might extend funds to other governments in difficulty. Italy is not at present in the front line, but in Spring 2011 a ten-year Italian bond still had to pay that 1.5% premium over a German bond.

An Italian default remains a very low-probability event, but the financial crisis that began in 2007 has taught the financial markets a painful lesson about how to distinguish the really unthinkable from the merely not-yet-thought. And the greater the market's concerns, the more pressing the need for the Italian government to increase taxes or cut spending, because the interest payments on its massive burden of outstanding debt are higher than they would otherwise have been. Populism has its price. The first Berlusconi government didn't last long enough to have to pay the price, and the second occurred at a time when favourable world economic conditions made it possible to postpone paying the price. But those times are over, and the third Berlusconi government that started in 2008 will face decisions that it will be very difficult for Berlusconi to pretend not to have ducked (though we can be confident that he will try to duck them).

Berlusconi and the Market

We have seen that, when he first entered the political arena, Berlusconi presented himself as being the man who would carry out in Italy the kind of market-friendly reforms that had been introduced by Reagan in the USA and

CHAPTER 5: THE ECONOMY UNDER BERLUSCONI

by Thatcher in Britain. His political pronouncements have always been in favour of market forces (at least until these forces began to get a bad name for themselves in 2008), and many of his critics have also described him as being part of the "neo-liberal" revolution of the 1990s. Yet the criticism made by John Barber at the start of this chapter was the exact opposite: that he had failed to bring in the "liberalising reforms" that Italy needs.

Barber's criticism is just. We saw that the growth under the 2001-2005 government, not just of public spending, but of the *share* of public spending in the economy as a whole, was very different from what you would expect if the government had indeed been committed to "neo-liberal" principles. Again, in the case of Alitalia, the choice that the market indicated was rejected in order to exploit the popular appeal of economic nationalism.

The Alitalia case showed that the commitment to the market is weak in the very place that you would expect with a monopolist in power: the anti-trust system. Competition regulations were sidelined in order to allow Alitalia and Air One to merge and remove the element of consumer choice in the large number of internal flights where they were competing. When we consider the television system, we will see that court decisions aimed at creating more competition have repeatedly been ignored, both by Berlusconi's businesses and by his government.

Nor do Berlusconi's political allies have a stronger commitment to the market than he does. Those that came out of the old Alleanza Nazionale inherited the Mussolini tradition of state involvement in economic matters. They have disowned other parts of Mussolini's political heritage, but not that part. The Northern League, for its part, shares the anti-business instincts of any populist party.

An example of this anti-market populism is the way in which opponents are frequently derided as being members of an elite. A popular tactic used by defenders of Berlusconi against well-known critics – Beppe Grillo or Marco Travaglio for example – is to make known how much they earn, as if high earnings were automatically a proof of evil-doing, rather than a proof that these people are doing things that others value.

Where reforms have been carried out to dismantle restrictive practices and give freer rein to competition, these reforms have almost always taken place under governments of the centre-left, particularly when Romano Prodi was in charge, and almost never under a Berlusconi government. It is characteristic of such reforms that their benefits are spread thinly over a large number of people, while their costs, though much smaller than the benefits in absolute volume, are borne by a small and concentrated group of people, who have every incentive to create a powerful pressure group to resist such changes. Prodi's tentative steps towards liberalising the pharmacy retail industry, and the rules for taxi-drivers, created violent resentment from those benefiting from long-established restrictive practices. Some of Berlusconi's keenest supporters, paradoxically, are the taxi-drivers and pharmacists whose restrictive practices were threatened by Prodi's liberalising reforms, and safeguarded by Berlusconi. Carrying out a liberalising reform of the economy – something that Berlusconi frequently promises – requires a large measure of political courage. And, while he has shown courage in some of his other dealings, Berlusconi simply does not possess the type of courage that is required for this task. Nor would it be in his interest: any actions that damage his popularity also damage his chances of preserving his impunity.

Macro-economic policy lends itself to few photo-opportunities. An earthquake can provide scope for pictures of a leader with an arm round a sobbing sufferer who has lost house and family in the tragedy. A refuse crisis can provide a photo-opportunity cutting the tape on a new incinerator, or even helping load garbage onto a truck. But the dull and important matters of public finance provide no mirror in which the ego can be reflected, and for this reason do not attract much attention from Silvio Berlusconi, except to the extent that he is conscious of having to deliver on the unwritten and unspoken pledges that make tax-evaders, large and small, vote for him, or to the extent that these economic policies have a direct impact on his own businesses. Nothing could be less likely than that a Berlusconi government should get to grips with Italy's underlying economic problems. Instead, the steady return of corruption, after the anti-corruption revolution of 1993 was first diverted and then reversed, acts as a steadily-increasing deadweight on the Italian economy, and in large part accounts for the dismal economic performance that was illustrated at the start of this Chapter.

CHAPTER 6:
TELEVISION AND GOVERNMENT

La 7 – the competitor that might have been

By the time he had entered the political arena, Berlusconi had three television channels which dominated the commercial television market. He did not have a complete monopoly: there remained TeleMonteCarlo, broadcasting in Italian from the principality, until it changed its headquarters to Rome in 1999. The company passed through various hands: it was owned by the entrepreneur Raul Gardini in 1993, but after Gardini committed suicide during the Mani Pulite trials, ownership passed to Vittorio Cecchi Gori, who was also a senator in the People's Party. Its market share was diminutive, at about 2-3% of viewers.

In 2001 it was acquired by Telecom Italia, which was then being run by Roberto Colannino (who was later to play a role in the Alitalia sale discussed in Chapter 5). Telecom, as the sixth largest telecommunications company in the world, had the resources to turn it into a true competitor to Mediaset. The station's name was changed to La 7, and Colannino began to recruit talented TV performers who had audience appeal. Colannino's political affiliations were with the centre-left – his son was to be the Democratic Party's spokesman on industrial affairs at the time of the Alitalia sale. It seemed that a "third pole" was about to emerge – a television company that would gain some of the advertising revenue currently split between RAI and Mediaset, and would have a political slant that would contrast with Mediaset's, preserving an element of balance and a greater plurality of information sources, while leaving RAI to remain politically neutral as befits a state-owned company.

It was not to be. In August 2001, Pirelli, the tyre and cable company, launched a takeover bid for Telecom Italia. This takeover was a vastly ambitious, highly leveraged, and in the event, ill-starred financial manoeuvre. Telecom's market capitalisation, which was at a peak at the time that Colannino had made the original takeover, was to fall steadily both before and after the takeover was complete, and by 2003 about half of the market value of the company had disappeared. However, naturally Pirelli had high hopes at the time that the takeover would succeed. Whether it was to be profitable for Pirelli depended on matters that had little to do with the new venture into television, which was yet to be launched and was therefore a very minor part of Telecom Italia's attraction for Pirelli. By this time Berlusconi was back in government, and had the final voice on a range of matters that were crucial to the outcome of the deal, including in particular the maximum rates chargeable for both cellphone and land-line calls.

A deal was struck, and it was a deal which illustrates as well as any why those in government should be debarred from retaining their business interests. Telecom Italia agreed to take over Berlusconi's old building company, Edilnord, for a figure (€300 mn) three times its estimated market value. In addition, it agreed to take over a Berlusconi group publication called *Useful Pages*, which competed with Telecom's own Yellow Pages. This appeared to raise some anti-trust issues, so Telecom also agreed to pay a €55mn penalty to Berlusconi's group if the deal was blocked by the anti-trust authority. This did indeed happen, and Telecom paid the penalty, leaving the publication in Berlusconi's hands. Telecom also agreed to sponsor Berlusconi's football team, AC Milan, to the tune of €24 mn. As Alexander Stille notes, "since Telecoms' new head, Tronchetti Provera, is an avid soccer fan and vice-president of the other Milan soccer team, archrival Inter, this deal seemed nothing less than a humiliating kind of feudal vassalage, a declaration of total loyalty to the king".[68]

More significantly, Telecom agreed to dismantle the plans to invest resources in building up La 7 into a serious challenge to Berlusconi's own channels. The famous names who had been hired by Colannino were paid off and sent back. Giuliano Ferrara, who is politically very close to Berlusconi, took over a news programme[ix]. The channel's market share has remained where it was before, namely at around 2 - 3%.

For his side of the bargain, in addition to refraining from intervening in the domestic telecoms market in a way that might have prejudiced Telecom, Berlusconi used his good offices as prime minister to intervene

---

ix In February 2011 Ferrara appeared at a bizarre meeting entitled "In Underpants but Alive", at the Worm Theatre (sic) in Milan, at which he seemed to claim that the philosopher Immanuel Kant would not have opposed juvenile prostitution and abuse of office. A few weeks later he was awarded a €1.5 mn/year contract to host a talk show on RAI.

CHAPTER 6: TELEVISION AND GOVERNMENT

with the Turkish authorities to grant roaming rights to the mobile phone company that Telecom had recently purchased in Turkey.

Squatter's Rights - Rete 4

In 1994, the Constitutional Court had ruled that private television companies may not possess more than two television channels that broadcast over the airwaves (as opposed to digitally). Since acquiring Rete 4 from the Mondadori group in 1984, Berlusconi had owned three. This anomaly therefore needed to be corrected. However, the government was slow to take action. It was not until 1998 that a new regulation was passed, which called for television companies wishing to transmit over the airwaves to submit bids for approval. Bids were duly held, and the frequencies occupied by Rete 4 were assigned to a new channel, Europa 7, which was proposed by an entrepreneur named Francesco di Stefano. Rete 4, if it wished to continue transmitting, was supposed to become digital and to vacate the space it was occupying on the airwaves, but it was allowed to continue transmitting for a transitional period, until satellite antennae were available in "adequate" (*congruo*) numbers to permit it to move to digital.

The other existing Mediaset channels had won their bids, and were to continue broadcasting. In the case of Europa 7, it was told to wait until the minister responsible had completed the process of assigning frequencies before it could start transmitting.

Despite protests from Europa 7, this "temporary" situation dragged on indefinitely. The matter was again brought before the Constitutional Court, which in 2002 decreed that an absolute deadline of 31 December 2003 must be fixed, after which Rete 4 must be transferred to digital transmission only, if it wished to continue in existence. After Berlusconi had been re-elected in 2001, his minister for Telecommunications, Maurizio Gasparri, drafted a new law which, in defiance of the ruling by the Constitutional Court, gave Rete 4 permission to continue to transmit over the airwaves until such time as the whole of the television system was switched over to digital. The President has the power to ask parliament to look again at a law which he considers may be unconstitutional, though, if they pass the law again, the President has no further delaying powers, unless the Constitutional court confirms it as unconstitutional. The President, Carlo Azeglio Ciampi, used these powers to delay the law, but it was finally passed in April 2004. A temporary decree, known as the "Save Rete 4" decree, had been signed by Berlusconi to cover his TV station over the period between the expiry of the deadline set by the Constitutional Court and the entry into force of his new law.

Mammì had dreamt up the fiction of pretending that there were 12 stations, in order to veil the reality of the Berlusconi group's dominant position. It now fell to Gasparri to dream up another novel wheeze to try to save his boss's TV channel from the antitrust authorities. He came up with the following: rather than looking at shares of the TV market, relevant market was defined as being the overall media market, including, in addition to TV, newspapers, magazines, even posters and the internet. But this didn't convince the European Court, which in January 2008 declared that the Italian authorities, in continuing to deny Europa 7 the promised frequencies, did not have objective selection criteria and were continuing to deny access to new entrants to the market. In response, and in order to avoid a threatened fine of €350,000 per day backdated to January 2006, the Italian government said it was willing to transfer some frequencies, not from Rete 4 which had been occupying them, but from the state broadcaster RAI 1. However, the coverage of these frequencies fell well short of what was available to Rete 4, and also of what Europa 7 considered would be financially viable.

Various publications have referred to the illegal (*abusivo*) occupation of frequencies by Rete 4, describing it as a "squatter", and it has always been Mediaset's policy that anybody using these terms should be sued for libel. Mediaset has always lost the ensuing cases. Antonio Di Pietro was the latest to have been sued in this way, but the judge ruled that this was indeed an appropriate description of what has been occurring. One hopes that the policy of suing has now been dropped. But the squatting has not ceased: it will continue until the final analogue switch-off in 2012.

Mediaset – A mediocre stock

The 1990s were the heyday of Berlusconi's financial empire. During the first few years of that decade, his companies were almost submerged with debt. By its end, it was one of the most profitable media businesses in the world, and Berlusconi ranked no. 14 in Forbes rich list. Since then, the financial performance of his companies has been distinctly lacklustre, and by 2010 he had slipped down to no. 74. The chart below shows how the value of Mediaset, his most important company, has evolved since 2003 in comparison with that of the Dow Jones Eurostoxx 50 (an index of the most important stocks in the Eurozone, of which Mediaset is one component). You can see that if you had spread your investment funds across all

CHAPTER 6: TELEVISION AND GOVERNMENT

of these 50 stocks, you would have ended up eight years later with 20% more money (though, had you been lucky enough to sell up in mid-2007, you would have been 80% richer). However, if you had invested all your wealth in Mediaset, you would have ended up 40% poorer.

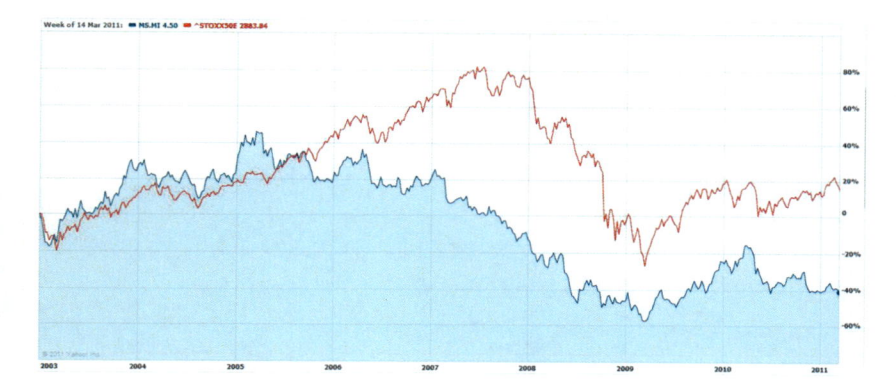

Mediaset's Share Price Compared with Eurostoxx 50

Mondadori's performance, shown overleaf, was worse still – you would have lost 60% of your your cash if you had invested there in 2003. It is surprising how little press attention has been given to the underperformance of Berlusconi's companies. Most Italians still think of him as a financial wizard. His achievements until the turn of the century do justify this opinion, (although financial wizardry is always against the public interest when undertaken by a monopolist) but many seem unaware that the performance has taken a drastic turn for the worse. Of course, it should be recalled that stealing from Mediaset shareholders by artificially inflating the price of film rights is one of the charges against him that have yet to be tried.

What has changed? The answer is: the internet. It is not that television viewing habits have altered all that drastically in response to the arrival of the internet. In the US, for example, the number of hours spent watching TV has stayed relatively static, at about 13 hours per week, even as the time spent on the internet has soared to an almost identical number. But the advertising revenue on which commercial TV must rely is spread much more thinly.

The internet offers more targeted ways of spending advertising outlays. As a result it has attracted a steadily rising proportion of those outlays. In the UK, the internet has overtaken TV as the most important advertising medium, accounting for 23.5% of all advertising spending, against TV's

IMPUNITY   BERLUSCONI'S GOAL AND ITS CONSEQUENCES

21.9% in 2008. This cross-over has not happened in Italy, or indeed in most other countries, but the trend is clearly there. Globally, TV is estimated to have accounted for about 40% of advertising spending in 2008, and the internet for about 9%, with internet spending rising by about a quarter over the year, despite the gloomy economic conditions that prevailed. During the first half of 2009, Nielsen reports that TV advertising in Italy fell by 14%, while internet advertising rose by 8%. Advertising in newspapers and journals has been hit even harder than TV advertising, which explains the underperformance of Mondadori.

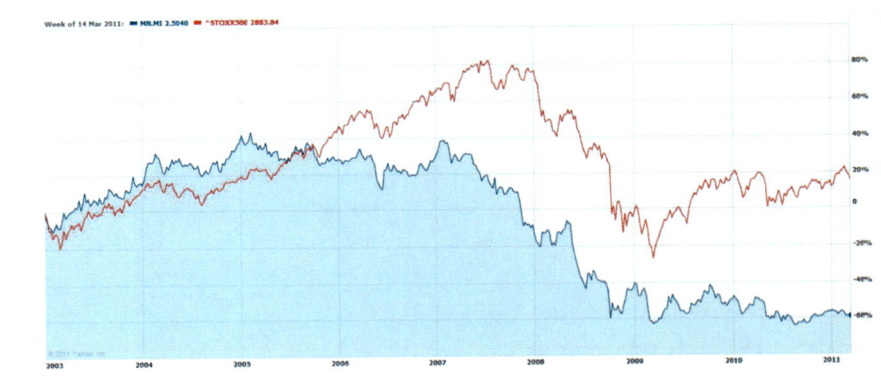

Mondadori's Share Price Compared with Eurostoxx 50

Moreover, even if the number of hours spent in front of the TV remains broadly constant, the way in which those hours are spent is changing in a way that is unfavourable for TV advertisers. Time shifting, by downloading programmes from the internet or by inbuilt hard drives, is becoming simpler, and the DVD is becoming more popular. Single-screen devices – TVs with an inbuilt internet connection – are in their infancy, but they are expected to become increasingly popular.

Italy, it is true, lags behind in these trends. Internet World Statistics estimates Italian internet penetration at 50.1%, ranking 20th within Europe, behind Poland, Hungary and Slovakia, but ahead of Greece, Portugal, Croatia and the Czech Republic. Southern Europe as a whole has much lower internet penetration than Northern Europe. But the fact that Italy is behind can only mean that the trend has further to go. That signals more tough times ahead for companies like Mediaset whose income derives in large part from television advertising.

Who provides Mediaset's cash?

Spending on television advertising is highly concentrated – a small number of advertisers account for a large proportion of the spend. Three cellphone companies – WIND, Vodafone and Telecom Italia Mobile – provide between them some $290 mn out of the €2.2 bn of Mediaset's total advertising revenues, or 13%. Seven companies supplying food and household products – Unilever, Ferrero, Barilla, Unilever, Procter and Gamble, L'Oreal, and Reckitt Benckiser – provide a further €360mn, or 16%. These ten companies alone provide about 30% of Mediaset's income. Five car companies – Fiat, Volkswagen, Ford, Peugeot-Citroen and Renault – between them account for about a further 8%. Almost any one of these companies could, if it were to change its advertising policy, precipitate large problems at Mediaset. The cellphone companies, in particular, use Mediaset much more heavily than most other companies. The overall average split of TV advertising revenues is currently a bit less than two-thirds to Mediaset and rather less than one-third to RAI. However, the cellphone companies, along with Unilever, spend more like three quarters of their TV advertising budget with Mediaset.

Another company with a large advertising spend (about 1½% of Mediaset's total income) is Sky, which spends over 91% of its TV advertising money with Mediaset, and only 9% with RAI. Sky has developed over the last few years into a formidable rival. Mediaset's usual reaction to competition is to legislate it out of existence, as we have seen with La7 and with Europa 7, but this has been harder going in the case of Sky.

The Government's Publicity Budget

The public sector itself, which includes such large Treasury-controlled companies as ENI (the oil company), ENEL (the electricity company) and the Post Office, spends a large amount of money on advertising. It is instructive to read a report, published by Nielsen in mid-2009, about how this budget had changed, since it is here that the conflict of interest is most apparent. The Nielsen report estimates that Mediaset's publicity revenues would have fallen in 2008, had it not been for the diversion of an increasing part of public sector spending away from competing companies and in favour of the one owned by the prime minister.

In the case of ENI, its total TV publicity spending declined from €52 to €48, but the share directed towards Berlusconi's channels rose from 25% to 37%, bringing an additional €5mn for Mediaset. Enel also increased its spending with Mediaset by €3mn. The Post Office, which had directed two-thirds of its spending to RAI and one-third to Mediaset in 2006, had by 2008 reversed these proportions, generating an extra $1.9mn of revenues for the prime minister's company.

It may be, of course, that these decisions were motivated, not by any base desire to curry favour with the source of political power, but by a conviction that the cost-benefit ratio of spending had changed decisively in favour of Mediaset in the year following its owner's accession to power. Certainly this conviction appears to have been held even more strongly by central government itself than by the state-controlled corporations. Between 2007 and 2008, Publitalia's (i.e. the Berlusconi group's) share of central government spending doubled from 29% to 58%. There were a number of government campaigns on such matters as road safety, sexual tourism (just to be clear, the Minister of Equal Opportunities is opposed to it), the anniversary of Garibaldi and so forth. RAI is obliged by its charter to transmit such advertisements free, but Mediaset can and does charge for them, and received an additional €2mn from this source, at the expense of newspapers and magazines, whose share of government publicity spending dropped sharply.[69]

It is instructive to compare what happened to Mediaset's Italian revenues, which were cushioned by the sudden decision of the state to switch vast swathes of advertising revenue in its favour, and what happened to the advertising revenues of Berlusconi's Spanish channel Telecinco. These fell by 37% in the same period – a reminder of what can happen to a business when there is no friendly government around to prevent the market from functioning freely.

The relationship with Sky TV

In 1990, Berlusconi established the first Italian pay TV station named Telepiù. In 1995, a concessional rate of value added tax, of 4% rather than the normal 19%, was agreed to by the Government. Initially there had been a suspicion that he had offered bribes in order to get this concession, but the investigation into this matter, which was undertaken by the Rome magistrates, found no evidence of this and the matter was archived. The VAT rate was raised to a higher, but still concessional, rate of 10% in 1997. Even with this concession, the business did not prove particularly profitable, and in 1997 90% of it was sold on to the French company Canal+, a subsidiary of Vivendi, with 10% being retained by Mediaset. In May 2002 Vivendi itself collapsed, and the Italian pay-TV

CHAPTER 6: TELEVISION AND GOVERNMENT

operations were acquired by News International, the Murdoch media empire. They were merged with a cable TV operation called Stream TV, and Sky Italia was born.

Sky TV is a minority taste in Italy, with 4.9 mn subscribers, compared to 1.3 mn at the time it began operations. This represents a market share of about 9%. It is available to subscribers via ADSL and cable modems, as well as via satellite. Despite its relatively small market share it had, by 2008, overtaken Mediaset in terms of Italian television revenues, though not in terms of total income. Of the three principal TV operators, the state broadcasting company RAI had revenues of €2.7 bn in 2008, comprising €1.6 bn from the licence and €1.1 bn in advertising revenue. Sky's revenues were €2.6 bn, mainly from subscriptions but with a small contribution from advertising. Mediaset earned €2.2 bn from advertising and €0.2 bn from its still nascent pay-TV operations – Mediaset established a pay-TV station called Mediaset Premium in 2005 to compete with Sky, though its operations are mainly on a pay-per-view basis rather than annual subscriptions.

The success of Sky TV appears to have come as a surprise to Mediaset, and since 2008 Berlusconi's government has given increasing attention to state intervention in order to protect Mediaset's revenues and market share from the competitive threat posed by Sky. One step was the revocation of the 10% concessional rate of VAT: it was doubled in November 2008. The timing was strange: this was a time when the global economy was in extreme difficulties, and most governments were doing their best to put spending power back into the hands of consumers by reducing taxes.

Berlusconi claimed that this tax increase could not be held to result from a conflict of interest, since it damaged his pay-TV enterprises as well as those of Sky. However, the comparison is invalid, since pay TV represents almost all of Sky's income, but only a very small part of Mediaset's income. Increasing the burden of tax on pay-TV is bound, other things being equal, to slow down the rate of growth of pay-TV customers, and therefore to increase the audience for the free-to-air-TV on which the bulk of Berlusconi's advertising revenues are based. In addition, the tax increase affected only the subscription part of Mediaset's pay-TV business, and not the pay-per-view business funded by smart cards.

A further blow aimed at Sky TV was to follow six months later. Until mid-2009, all RAI programmes were available to Sky viewers, using their existing decoder (just as, for example, subscribers to Sky's UK operations can get BBC channels as well as Sky channels). Sky paid to RAI some €57 million in fees for the RAI programmes that were available to its viewers. In July 2009, RAI changed its strategy. It decided to participate, with Mediaset, in a new satellite, to be called Tivusat. (Mediaset and RAI own 48% of Tivusat, with Telecom, owner of the La 7 channel, owning 3.5%). Content viewed on Tivusat will be free, but viewers will need a decoder and smart card that are separate from those used for Sky. The cost of the decoder is to be less than €100, but of course for those using Sky, or contemplating using it, the main disadvantage will not be the financial one of buying an extra decoder, but the nuisance value of having to have two separate decoders when previously they had one. For the present the free-to-air channels of RAI and Mediaset will continue to be available via the Sky decoder, but the fear that this may not continue to be the case is a clear deterrent for Sky subscribers. They will also be used to getting the premium RAI programmes as part of their existing package, and may be deterred from continuing to subscribe to Sky, not only by the increase in the value added tax, but also by this reduction in their content.

One Sky subscriber wrote on a technical forum as follows, soon after the announcement: "I'm a bit unhappy about the thought of adding another decoder under the TV...I see myself continually zapping between decoders and changing the input to the TV...what do you advise? Should I renounce my contract with Sky? Throw away my TV and devote myself to transcendental meditation? Or is there another solution?" That was very much the type of reaction that the Mediaset government would have been hoping for.

At the same time, or soon after, announcing its participation in Tivusat, RAI also announced the termination of its deal to make its premium programmes available to Sky subscribers. This decision thus creates a €57 mn reduction in the revenues available to RAI. Defending this decision, RAI's director Mauro Masi said that the further growth of Sky would cost RAI a multiple of this amount in lost advertising revenue, since the growth of Sky would reduce RAI's viewing figures.

This is an odd argument. The real competitor for RAI, in terms of advertising revenue, is not Sky but Mediaset. Sky has some 5% of the market for TV advertising in Italy, with Mediaset having 58% of the total and RAI most of the rest. Being a subscription service, Sky is not reliant on advertising revenue in the same way as Mediaset, which has competed ruthlessly with RAI in this area. On one occasion Berlusconi, as prime minister, said that he couldn't understand why anybody advertised with RAI. Certainly the market's reactions to the Tivusat deal were unequivo-

CHAPTER 6: TELEVISION AND GOVERNMENT

cal. "In the medium term, this is a move that may benefit Mediaset" said a Milan-based media analyst following the announcement.

The fact that the state-owned corporation was taking decisions whose only rationale seemed to be to improve the competitive position of the prime minister's businesses was shocking to many Italians. The President of the Republic called for further reflection on the decision, but seems to have had his misgivings allayed. A few weeks later, Sky announced that it had produced a plug-in "dongle" which could be attached to its decoders, as a result of which Sky subscribers would, quite legally, continue to have access to non-premium channels broadcast on Tivusat. RAI, which had selflessly given up €57mn of its revenue in the attempt to make life harder for the prime minister's main competitor, now appeared to have made this sacrifice for nothing.

A further obstacle was placed in the way of Sky at the end of 2009. It was announced that the proportion of time that pay-TV channels could devote to advertisements was to be cut in three steps from 18% to 12%, at the same time as this proportion was raised for other TV channels from 18% to 20%. At the same time, it was announced that channels that broadcast the same material an hour later, as well as Mediaset's pay-TV channels, did not count in terms of the laws regulating the number of TV channels that can be owned by a single operator, thus liberating Mediaset from a potential regulatory worry. Finally, it was announced that X-rated material (which earns Sky $62 mn a year) could not be broadcast between 7 am and 11 pm.

The campaign against Sky had begun to produce fruits by the end of 2009. In the final quarter of that year, Sky Italia announced that it had suffered its first ever net loss of subscribers, down by 63,000 to 4.7 mn, and that it had lost $30 mn.[70] Insofar as Sky purveys an ideology, it is, of course, an ideology very similar to that espoused by Berlusconi. Fox News, the sister network of Sky in the USA, is capable of producing material every bit as tendentious as Mediaset. The issue here, though, is one of competition. If television has to be dominated by right-wing media moguls, it is better if there are two of them competing with each other, rather than one possessing a monopoly - and much worse if the one possessing a monopoly is at the same time in charge of the government.

Spectrum Auctions: The Taxpayers' Gift to the Prime Minister

As television broadcasting has become digital rather than analogue, it has become possible to auction off large parts of the radio spectrum that were previously used for analogue transmission. The sale of frequencies to mobile phone companies has brought in billions of Euros of revenues in all of the countries where frequencies have been auctioned off. In Italy, mobile phone operators need these frequencies even more acutely than elsewhere, as the existing frequencies are fully utilised.

However, Italy's special situation – with a Prime Minister who is also the beneficial owner of the main private television company – has led to a rather different procedure being followed. Some parts of the spectrum are indeed being auctioned off to mobile phone operators, but other parts are being given away to the existing television companies. Mediaset and RAI are each being given five "multiplexes", while others are to be allocated, still free of charge, to other television companies on the basis of a "beauty contest".

There has been much manoeuvring to try to exclude Sky from qualifying for this beauty contest, whose timing remains uncertain. The European Commission ruled in July 2010 that it was illegal to exclude Sky, but the current Minister in charge is seeking other methods of ensuring that competition for the Prime Minister's business is eliminated.

Telephone and internet operators have left no doubt that, if Italy is to be rescued from its current deficit in internet access, and the mobile phone network is to be freed from its current congestion, these frequencies are urgently needed to be released from television operations – yet more channels showing old films or selling jewellery – and allocated to telecommunications. If this were done, more money could be raised from auctioning the frequency, and the burden on taxpayers correspondingly reduced. This, however, would pose a threat to the profitability of the Prime Minister's business, which is better served by ensuring that it is given, at zero cost, the frequencies that it might want.

In effect, the operation can be seen as equivalent to the levying of a tax, whose amount is equal to the revenue that would have been raised by selling additional frequencies to telecommunications operators. Some of the proceeds of the tax go back to the taxpayers in the form of a subsidy to RAI, which is being given free frequencies. But the majority constitutes a gift to private television operators, and of course the largest beneficiary of that gift from taxpayers is the prime minister who has overseen the operation.

Control of RAI

The state broadcasting company RAI, unlike the BBC, is permitted to sell advertising space on its radio and TV channels, which it does through a subsidiary called SIPRA. But, as we have seen, it earns only about half of what Mediaset does from advertising, with over 60% of its revenues coming from a licence fee or tax payable by anyone possessing a TV.

RAI is governed by a council of nine members, seven of whom are elected by the parliamentary committee responsible for oversight of RAI, and two of whom are nominated by the Ministry of Finance, which owns 99.5% of the shares in RAI. Prior to Tangentopoli, there was an agreed carve-up of political influence over the three television channels of RAI, according to which the Christian Democrats controlled RAI Uno, the Socialists RAI Due, and the Communists RAI Tre.

One of the first symptoms of direct interference in the affairs of RAI came in 2002, when Berlusconi, then on a state visit to Bulgaria, criticised three broadcasters who had been critical of him. Berlusconi said "The use which [Enzo] Biagi and – what's that other one called – Santoro – and that other one – Luttazzi have made of public television, paid for by everybody's money, is criminal. And I believe that it is a specific obligation on the new board that it should not permit this to happen". This pronouncement was known as the "Bulgarian Edict", and not long after it the three who had been named were duly removed from television. Biagi was told that his show was too costly, and when he offered to accept the wage of the lowest-paid RAI journalist, provided this wage was paid to an old people's home instead of to him, he was told instead that his programme couldn't go out because of advertising considerations. Biagi died in 2007, and soon afterwards Berlusconi said that "I struggled to keep Biagi in television, but in the end Biagi's desire to retire with a handsome golden handshake prevailed". Luttazzi has never returned to television. Santoro returned in 2006, and his programme *Annozero*, put out by RAI 2, continues to attract large viewing figures, and equally massive vituperation from Berlusconi and his allies.

While criticising one of Santoro's programmes in 2009, Berlusconi said that he had commissioned a survey showing that 50% of viewers would refuse to pay their TV licence to the RAI. At the same time, *Il Giornale*, the family newspaper, launched a campaign urging its readers not to pay the licence fee, which it described as the "Santoro tax". The head of government was thus using his influence to urge citizens to break the law.

IMPUNITY   BERLUSCONI'S GOAL AND ITS CONSEQUENCES

During the Berlusconi government that started in 2008, top-level personnel at RAI have been frequently changed, with the result that its ability to present a truly balanced view of the world of politics in particular has been undermined. A characteristic move was the posting of the journalist Augusto Minzolini, apparently at Berlusconi's direct behest, to take charge of TG1, RAI's principal news source. The results of this move will be documented in Chapter 8.

The second attempt on Santoro

As part of an investigation into credit card fraud, magistrates in Trani had been intercepting some phone calls made by AGCOM, the agency regulating the broadcasting industry. In one of these conversations, intercepted in 2009, and revealed in March 2010, Berlusconi could be heard complaining that Santoro's programme *Annozero* had not yet been removed from the airwaves. The programme is the most widely-watched current affairs discussion on any schedule, and consists of investigative reports by journalists interspersed with studio discussions, in which representatives of Berlusconi supporters are as numerous as his opponents. The programme had covered the Mills affair (see Chapter 4), the D'Addario and bunga-bunga affairs (see Chapter 7), and Spatuzza's testimony in the Dell'Utri appeal (see Chapter 3). Berlusconi's objection was that some of these matters were the subject of judicial proceedings, and should therefore be discussed only in the courts and not on television. Of course, as Chapter 4 documents, he has also been at great pains to make sure that they are not discussed in the courts either.

RAI's role is to defend, and not to attack, its own programmes, so although the managers of RAI were fairly sympathetic to Berlusconi, they couldn't simply remove the programme in line with his requests. ("Not even in Zimbabwe" said RAI's general manager). They would, however, have to respond to any protests made by AGCOM, the supposedly independent authority responsible for seeing that all broadcasters kept within the rules. Berlusconi therefore called Giancarlo Innocenzi, an ex-employee of his who was now on the board of AGCOM and fulminated, saying that "he wasn't earning his salary" if he couldn't keep a programme like Annozero off the air, and asking Innocenzi to formulate a strategy for its removal. The magistrates then said they were investigating Berlusconi for abuse of office (*concussione*) and Innocenzi for aiding and abetting (*favoreggiamento*). The investigation was denounced by Berlusconi as an attack on liberty, and another attempt by magistrates to derail the elected government. However, Berlusconi's goal was in part obtained, when it was decided that RAI would suspend all current affairs talk shows in the run-up to the 2010 regional elections.

Summary

Berlusconi's critics often, and understandably, focus on parts of his record about which it is difficult to arrive at the truth – questions such as:

- Does the wilful complexity of his business arrangements conceal wrongdoing?

- What is his degree of guilt in connection with the various accusations of law-breaking for which he has been indicted?

- What should one make of his association with Marcello Dell'Utri, and of the latter's involvement with organised crime?

These are all complex and often obscure matters that deserve to be investigated, and it is to be hoped that further progress can be made in reaching objective and impartial judgements on them. In contrast, the matters discussed in this Chapter are all clear and open. There is no doubt about the actions that Berlusconi's government has taken to protect Berlusconi's businesses, and to place obstacles in the way of those that seek to compete with them or to undermine his popularity. It is here, even more than in the racier matters discussed in the next Chapter, that the shame and squalor of Berlusconi's government is exposed to the full light of day.

CHAPTER 7:
SEX SCANDALS

Berlusconi's Degeneration

One of the themes of the second half of this book is: what did power do to Silvio Berlusconi? An important part of the answer is to be found in his relationship with women. When he entered politics, he was ten years into what seemed to be a stable second marriage. After ten years in power, his second wife had left him, describing him as "ill", and his emotional life seems to have become dominated by a series of superficial encounters with women young enough to be his grandchildren. Feeling in the sense of emotion has been replaced by feeling in the sense of touching up. The image of Berlusconi that we will encounter at the end of this chapter – an old man sitting in a chair, feeling the private parts of women half a century younger as they strip, wriggle and writhe, pole-dancing and belly-dancing, sometimes in pretend police or nurse uniforms – is symptomatic of the general debasement of his personality brought about by too much power.[x]

His recent encounter with the child Karima el-Mahroug, known as "Ruby", has triggered off the most violent showdown yet between Berlusconi and the justice system. The outcome of this showdown will not be known when this book is printed, and many of its details have yet to emerge. As well as describing the main features of that case, this chapter will try to put it into the context of the gradual changes in his personality that lay behind this breakdown of a stable home life, and will focus on what these matters have to tell us about his ability to govern, and about his willingness, and his need, to dismantle the rule of law in order to remain in office.

---

[x] A similar decline is portrayed in the aged Mao in the opera "Nixon in China", where, in the final act, Mao is shown being sexually satisfied by venal young women.

Do Sex Scandals Matter?

It is often argued that the way in which politicians conduct their sex lives is entirely a private matter, without relevance to their political performance. However, when we select a politician, we are always making some judgment about his or her personality, as a basis for trying to assess how they might behave in circumstances that cannot be foreseen in advance. The way in which they conduct themselves in their private life carries some valuable information about their personality. Moreover there are plenty of virtues, such as truthfulness and reliability, which are highly significant in judging a politician, and which may be directly revealed in their private lives.

A typical, and sensible, view is that taken by one journalist who declared in 1994 that "A politician is a public man at every moment of his day, and ought to behave like one…he ought to know that every aspect of his life is public. If he does not accept this rule he should give up being a politician".[71] The journalist was Augusto Minzolini, now the presenter of the flagship TV news programme, who, as we shall see in the next Chapter, was to take a very different view of the episodes recounted in this one.

The argument that one's private life is irrelevant is, of course, not open to any politician who has already claimed that his or her life beyond politics demonstrates evidence that qualifies them for high office. Silvio Berlusconi is in this category. He printed off a brief biography of his life, entitled *An Italian Story*, and distributed it to every Italian household as part of the 2001 election campaign. He frequently claims that his business career demonstrates his qualifications for running the economy. There have been plenty of photo-opportunities demonstrating him at the heart of a happy family, for as long as he had a wife who was willing to appear on such occasions.

Just as Berlusconi's court cases repay study, not only for the light they throw on whether or not he has committed any crimes, but also for the indirect light they cast on his integrity and credibility, so his private life also provides useful information, and gives plenty of examples of his idiosyncratic relationship to the truth. For this reason, it is worth recounting the episodes that have recently distracted and amused the world. They exemplify Darwin's theory of sexual selection in a way that brings to mind the barcarolle at the start of Act II of Donizetti's *Elixir of Love:*

Io son ricco, tu sei bella,	I am rich and you are lovely.
Io ducati, vezzi hai tu.	I've got cash and you've got charm.

CHAPTER 7: SEX SCANDALS

The Spy's ex-wife

During Berlusconi's first sustained period in office, from 2001 to 2006, there was nothing similar to the series of sex scandals that erupted around, and disrupted, his tenure of office from 2008. There was, however, one matter that gave a foretaste of what was to come. In 2003, he became friendly with an aristocratic young announcer on RAI television named Virginia Sanjust. Virginia was separated, though amicably, from her husband, Federico Armati, who was an agent for SISDE, the Italian secret service. From 2003 to 2007 she benefited from Berlusconi's generosity, receiving many presents, including a gift of €50,000 and the use of an apartment in the centre of Rome.

After first meeting her at RAI in 2003, Berlusconi sent her a bunch of flowers, and her husband encouraged her to pursue the relationship. She met Berlusconi at Palazzo Chigi (the official residence of Italian Prime Ministers), and asked him to promote her husband. Berlusconi said that this would be very difficult, but nevertheless he did it, and also offered her a job in his press office. She accepted, but soon afterwards gave this up in favour of another job at RAI.

For the next couple of years, Virginia and Berlusconi enjoyed a genuinely affectionate relationship, seemingly more profound and less fleeting than some of the others discussed in this chapter, and worthy of the respect that John Betjeman evoked in his sensitive little poem:

> "Let us not speak for the love we bear one another –
> Let us hold hands and look."
> She, such a very ordinary little woman;
> He, such a thumping crook;
> Yet both, for a moment, little lower than the angels
> In the tea-shop's inglenook.[72]

Relations between Virginia and her husband Federico gradually deteriorated as the two quarrelled about custody of their son. At one point she told him that she hoped that he would be reduced to poverty, so that she would have a better chance of being awarded custody. Some time after this – and in her husband's view because of this – SISDE decided in 2006 to demote Federico, and transfer him to a quite different and much less well-paid (€1,700 a month instead of €4,500) post in the Ministry of Justice. Before the transfer came into effect, he decided to try to use his wife's relationship with Berlusconi to get this transfer annulled, and told a magazine that he had some red-hot news about the prime minister.

Berlusconi had advance warning of this threat, and told Virginia about it: this was a sensitive time, since elections were about to be held.

Virginia met her husband in a bar and, with a concealed recording device, recorded him threatening to ruin Berlusconi. At this point, miraculously, Armati's transfer was annulled – the blackmail appeared to have been effective. Later, Armati's complaints about being taped without his consent, and his suspicions that Virginia had engineered his demotion, became the matter of a legal case, from which nothing conclusive emerged. SISDE argued that his demotion was for extraneous reasons, and the court judged that too much time had elapsed between his wife's threat and his demotion for the one to be likely to have caused the other. The investigation did not enquire why he had been reinstated at that particular time, beyond establishing that it was at the bidding of the head of SISDE. It did not ask any questions about why the head of SISDE had come to this decision, and whether anyone else had put him under pressure. Despite the inconclusiveness of the court case, there is, though – and this is one of the most worrying points about the matters that we shall discuss in this section – a strong hint that the threat of blackmail may have influenced Berlusconi's actions as prime minister. As a footnote to this episode, Virginia Sanjust gave an interview in early 2011 in which she said that her relationship with Berlusconi had ruined her life.

Jobs for the Girls

In 2004 magistrates in Naples began to investigate a suspected case of tax evasion involving a producer who was thought – wrongly as it turned out – to have been issuing inflated invoices to the state broadcaster RAI. As part of this investigation, some telephone conversations with the Manager of RAI fiction, Agostino Saccà, were intercepted for six months from June 2007. Saccà was a long-standing ally of Berlusconi – it was he who, following the "Bulgarian Edicts" discussed in the last Chapter, saw to it that Biagi, Santoro and Luttazzi vanished from the screens. Saccà was also the instigator of the scheme, also discussed in the previous Chapter, for a joint RAI-Mediaset satellite to compete with Sky.

Berlusconi's conversations with Saccà covered many topics – for example, he wanted Saccà to make it clear to Umberto Bossi that RAI was doing everything it could, at Berlusconi's instigation, to back the historical epic film *Barbarossa* of which RAI was co-producer. (The film deals with a matter dear to the mythology of the Northern League: the battle of Legnano in 1176, in which Milanese forces defeated the Holy Roman

CHAPTER 7: SEX SCANDALS

Emperor Frederick Barbarossa after a dispute about taxes. It was released in cinemas in 2009, and was a flop).

Saccà was hoping eventually to leave RAI and to set up his own company to produce fiction programmes. Berlusconi, as owner of Mediaset, was of crucial importance to the success of any such plan. What the telephone conversations suggest is that, in exchange for offering his support to this scheme, Berlusconi was pressuring Saccà to hire various young women whose career he wished to advance for a variety of reasons. In one case the reason was "to keep the boss's pecker up (*sollevare il morale del Capo)*".

In another case, the reason was more political. This was a time when Prodi's government, with its tiny majority in the Senate, seemed particularly vulnerable. In December 2007 he asked Saccà to hire two actresses, Elena Russo and Evelina Manna, saying to him: "Evelina Manna has nothing to do with me, I'll tell you what's with her, I'm trying to get a majority in the Senate, you see? This Evelina could be...I've been asked about her by someone I'm negotiating with. Because I'm involved in this operation. If you could call her, and also Elena Russo."

Subsequently Berlusconi claimed that these actresses had been unfairly penalised because they were not of the left, and that the only people who got jobs at the RAI were "people who prostitute themselves and people on the left".[73] If we take Berlusconi's words to Saccà at face value, he was trying to use an employee of the state broadcasting company to participate with him in a plot to bring down the government. However, the magistrates decided not to take these words at face value, and went with an interpretation suggested by Saccà, who said to them: "If I remember rightly, when Hon. Berlusconi spoke to me about Evelina Manna, he vaguely mentioned that some senator on the left was interested in her, but I have to say that it was my impression – only an impression mind you – that maybe Hon. Berlusconi, out of personal discretion, and fearing that I should think him personally interested in the actress, had told me an innocent lie". Although this version of the story confirmed Berlusconi as a liar, it was less damaging than the supposition that he might have been speaking the truth to his friend.

On another occasion, the reason for recommending a particular actress was even more alarming. Berlusconi rang Saccà to say: "That crazy woman Antonella Troise – she's got it into her head that I hate her, and that I've blocked her artistic career. She's gone around saying crazy things. Do me a favour, ring her up and say that I've been on to you for several weeks telling you to get her a job. Sorry, make it clear that I'm playing an active role. Because I keep telling her that I am, but she says and thinks that I am the obstacle, which is mad because I've never ever been an obstacle to anyone in my entire life. Well, but it's crazy, so do me this favour, because she's getting dangerous".

Here again we have a situation analogous to that with Virginia Sanjust's husband. Berlusconi must use his power in order to try to stop someone from saying dangerous things…again that hint that, whatever one may think of his rackety lifestyle, one of its problems is that it renders him susceptible to blackmail.

The Bimbo Candidates

Following this episode, attention was thankfully diverted away from his private life for the first year or so of his new administration. But this was not to last long. The sex scandals of 2009-2011, which brought the most severe embarrassment yet to a man not easily embarrassed, began with two disputes between Berlusconi and two of his longest-standing bedfellows – his political bedfellow and his actual bedfellow, Mrs Berlusconi.

The first dispute was with Alleanza Nazionale, the neo-fascist party which had merged with Forza Italia at the end of March 2009. *Farefuturo*, a think-tank headed by Gianfranco Fini, had become concerned after a report in *Il Giornale*, the Berlusconi family newspaper, about candidates for the forthcoming European elections. The report said that "the *soubrette* Barbara Matera, 27… an announcer on RAI and actress in the series *Carabinieri* on Canale 5 will be a candidate for the PDL in the European elections." This was followed on 22nd April by the following report in *Libero*, another daily paper close to Berlusconi, then edited by Vittorio Feltri (who within a matter of months was to move to *Il Giornale*):

> Beautiful and young: adjectives which come up like a mantra whenever there is talk of the PDL candidates for the European elections. ..It's the third day of the training session for the aspiring PDL members…The list is all female, as is well known: the showgirl Elisa Alloro, the head of the "We miss you Silvio" committee, Emanuela Romano, Angela Sozio from *Big Brother*, the Mediaset journalist Rachele Restivo…

Ms Restivo was famous from a TV programme called *Passion: Eroticism for women*. The list continued, with names like the twins Eleonora and

CHAPTER 7: SEX SCANDALS

Imma de Vivo, who had been on *Isola dei Famosi*, the Italian equivalent of *"I'm a Celebrity Get me Out of Here"*, Cristina Ravot, a singer who had performed at Villa Certosa, Silvia Trevaini who in 2005 had been in the finals of a beauty competition, and it ended with "a mysterious young lady about whom we know only her name, Giada [Jade] and her origin: Lithuania".

The choice of these candidates was discussed in the same paper under the title: "The Knight's Deeds: the Showgirl candidates *in pectore*". The word I have translated as showgirl was *velina*, which literally means tissue paper, something flimsy without substance. The word was to be much in use as the year progressed. Berlusconi's tendency to promote the political advancement of young showgirls had already produced a Minister of Equal Opportunities, Mara Carfagna, whose background had been as a topless presenter of TV programmes, and, according to one much-witnessed clip on You-Tube, knickerless ballroom dancer. (The picture of her on the right below, from the Livorno satirical journal *Il Vernacoliere*, shows a woman breaking the law and a minister enforcing it).

A sinistra: una trota che batte illegalmente. A destra: un ministro che si batte per la legalità.

A couple of years earlier, Berlusconi had publicly said to Ms Carfagna that, if he wasn't already married, he would marry her – a remark which understandably produced a rift with his wife, though on that occasion the rift was, at least publicly, patched up. (The Argentine newspaper, El Claron reported that it was common knowledge in Rome that Ms Carfagna had performed sexual services for Berlusconi[74], and this led one satirist, Sabina Guzzanti, to sing a song at a public meeting about lusty men wanting an Equal Opportunity to have her perform this service for them also).

A three-day training course was arranged to give the showgirl candidates the political information that they would need for their candidacy. The course seems to have been run on lines familiar to any school teacher or pupil: speaking of his role in the course, the Minister of Public Administration, Renato Brunetta, said that he had had to tick one of the students off for chewing gum in class; that they had raised their hands when they wanted to seek his permission to go to the bathroom; and that he had passed around hand-outs and asked questions about them the next day. "No other party has organised a course with teachers of this calibre", he said, though without mentioning the obvious reason – that no other party had dared to put forward candidates of this calibre.[75]

Alarmed by this tendency, Sofia Ventura, a political scientist from Bologna, wrote an article for the *Farefuturo* think-tank. The article, entitled "against *velinismo*", after speaking generally about the under-representation of women in European politics, went on to mention a

> "specifically Italian phenomenon which makes the situation even worse. I refer to the practice of co-opting young, sometimes very young, women who are undoubtedly comely but with a background which could hardly justify their presence in an elective assembly like Parliament, nor in even more responsible roles. There's no doubt about the need to make room for a new generation in Italian politics, but is this, we ask, the way to do it?...We are seeing a way of making politics with women's bodies. The fact that image is crucial is well known, and applies to men as well as to women, but here we are dealing with a different phenomenon... Here we are witnessing the leadership of a party using the pretty faces and bodies of people who don't have much to do with politics, with the aim of projecting a (phony) image of freshness and rejuvenation ... women are not playthings to be used to entrap, nor are they fragile beings in need of protection and promotion by generous and paternal males. They are just people. We should like those with important political responsibilities to remember this from time to time".

The whole episode is only comprehensible in the light of the electoral law described in Chapter 9, and the entirely top-down nature of the political

CHAPTER 7: SEX SCANDALS

party headed by Berlusconi, which gives very little say in the choice of representative to those who are supposedly being represented.

Fini made it clear that he had not approved the article, but nor did he reject Ventura's views. In response to this criticism from Berlusconi's political bedfellow came unexpected support from his actual, or at least recent, bedfellow, his second wife, Veronica Lario. But she, by then, had another cause for complaint, and before we resume the story of the *veline*, we must touch on this issue, which was to become a focus in the early summer of 2009.

A few days after the *Farefuturo* article, Silvio Berlusconi suddenly appeared at the 18th birthday party of a young woman called Noemi Letizia. The birthday party was being held in Casoria, a less-than-chic suburb of Naples located in the heartland of the Camorra. Berlusconi's presence there was widely photographed, not only with the family, but with the cooks and anyone else within range of the cameras.

It was to this surprising appearance by her husband, as well as to the issue of the *veline* candidates, that Veronica Lario reacted. She said that she wanted to make it clear that she and her children were victims, and not accomplices in this situation. "We have to put up with it, and it hurts". On the subject of the candidates, she said that "what comes out of this, and is even more serious, is the aggressiveness and the lack of restraint in wielding power, which damages the credibility of all women … Someone has written that this is all in the cause of amusing the emperor. I agree: what is apparent from the newspapers is a shameless load of rubbish, all in the name of power". On the subject of her husband's appearance at the 18th birthday party, she said; "What do I think about it? It surprised me a lot, especially because he never came to the 18th birthday party of any of his children, despite being invited". She made it clear that she was seeking a divorce, and emailed a press statement to this effect. The press agency, Ansa, was so astonished that it sat on the statement, and contacted Berlusconi privately about it before publicising it. One part of the statement described Berlusconi as a "pig" (*maiale*). This struck Ansa as being so strong that they rang her up and asked if they could remove it. She said she had her reasons for using but, but that as long as the substance of her statement was clear they should do as they thought best. The word was omitted.

Berlusconi was at the time in Warsaw for a meeting of the European Popular Party (the confederation of centre-right parties in the European Parliament), but seems to have spent much of the day in phone calls to party organisers in Rome. By the end of the day, all of the *veline* candidates had been dropped except for three. Almost as remarkable as the fact that they had been put forward in the first place was the fact that they were dropped, not in response to any outcry from the rank and file, but because the leader's wife objected. Berlusconi responded to his wife's statement by saying "even the *signora* believed what was in the papers, which upsets me. Sometimes it happens that women can get a little irritable."

Many of the potential candidates who had been dropped had harsh words about Veronica Lario, correctly identifying her statement, rather than any political pressures arising from Ms Ventura's article, as the reason for their disappointment. Cesare Romano, whose daughter Emanuela had been hoping for a seat, went so far as to sprinkle alcohol on his shirt and hands and attempt to set fire to himself in front of Palazzo Grazioli, Berlusconi's residence in Rome[76], but was saved by the carabinieri. Another, Angela Sozio, who had been on *Big Brother*, said "I didn't expect to be treated like this, and by a woman!"[77] Yet another, Chiara Sgarbossa, who had been Miss Venice six years earlier and had gone on to present a programme of national lottery draws, gave an interview which appeared to show that her real political sympathies lay more with the Northern League, for its tough stance on immigration, than with the PDL for which she had hoped to stand, saying: "it's a disaster, I've no words for it… Thanks, Veronica, if you hadn't intervened we would all be in the list…I'd like Silvio Berlusconi to give me an explanation of all this…Barbara Matera never said anything on the training course, while I asked questions".[78]

A few days later, on May 3rd, more in response to the 18th birthday party to which we will turn in a minute than to the *veline* affair, Veronica gave two headline-catching interviews. To *La Repubblica* she said:

> "I am closing the curtain on my married life. But I want to do it like any ordinary, honest person, without noise. I'd like to avoid arguments. Now I feel more tranquil. I am convinced that at this point it wouldn't be dignified for me to stay. My marriage has run its course; I can't stay with a man who goes around with under-age girls. Enough, I can't go on arm-in-arm with this spectacle of virgins offering themselves to the dragon in search of success, fame and economic growth. Thanks to some strange alchemy, the country allows everything and justifies everything that its emperor does. I ask myself what country we are living in, how it could be possible to accept the kind of political methods that led to the centre-right electoral lists, and how it could suffice for two of my statements

to bring about an immediate about-turn. I've done my best, I've done everything I thought possible. I've tried to help my husband, and I've begged those who are close to him to do the same, as one would for a sick person. It's all been useless. I thought they had understood, but I was wrong. Now I say 'enough'".[79]

To *La Stampa*, on the same day, she said:

"I've been forced to take this step, I don't want to say any more. I certainly don't want to get into an argument about the *veline*, even though I'm convinced that whoever puts himself forward for public service should have the right background, based on the work they have been doing beforehand. But to read in newspapers that he frequents an under-age girl (because he knew her before she was 18), to read that she calls him *Papi* [Daddy] and talks about their meetings in Rome and Milan, with parents who seem to have no objections, well, that really is unacceptable. How can you stay with a man like that? Despite all this my husband remains popular and hasn't been damaged by the affair. Noemi? If only she was his daughter".

This last remark refers to some (false) speculation that the young woman in question was the result of an earlier liaison between Berlusconi and her mother. On his return from Warsaw, Berlusconi cancelled other appointments to try to talk to his wife, but she had asked his secretary to tell him not to approach her, since she had nothing more to say or hear: all the words had been used up.

Before leaving, for the time being, the matter of the bimbo candidates, we must note that, in an interview on May 5th, Silvio Berlusconi claimed that he had not been directly involved in drawing up the candidate lists. Later he was to refer to this claim again, both to repeat it, and also to contradict it. In the same interview, he said that he had tried to select female candidates who were young and not unattractive (he didn't mention any other desirable qualifications), thus appearing to suggest that it was, in fact, his hand behind the selection of these candidates – as indeed had been suggested by newspapers that were firmly within his camp (*Giornale* and *Libero*). Later in the interview he mentioned that the women representing his party in parliament had a better attendance record, and were more reliable at voting, than the men, clearly implying that lobby-fodder was all he expected from a member of parliament.

IMPUNITY   BERLUSCONI'S GOAL AND ITS CONSEQUENCES

The Under-Age Girl

At this point, we need to revert to the matter which, along with the *veline* affair, triggered these divorce proceedings: Silvio Berlusconi's appearance at Noemi Letizia's 18th birthday party on April 26th 2009, just before he left for Warsaw.

Before telling at some length this story – a complicated web of accounts which partially overlap but more frequently contradict each other – we should be clear that what makes it worth telling is the light that it throws, not mainly on Silvio Berlusconi's relationship with this young woman, but more significantly on his relationship with the truth; on the weapons he has at his disposal when people tell truths that are not to his taste; and on the way in which these weapons are deployed. This affair was a showcase in which Berlusconi's uniquely cynical and relativistic attitude to the truth would be displayed, not for the first time, but in a more concentrated fashion than ever before.

The most plausible of the stories about this matter does, indeed, indicate that he behaved in a reprehensible way, using his power to impress and dazzle a vulnerable young girl – though there is no suggestion that the relationship went beyond that[xi]. But what really casts a light on his suitability to govern a country is what the story tells us about his willingness, and indeed his impressive ability, to tell lies when the truth is of a kind that is uncomfortable to his own personal interests, and conflicts with the fantasies that he wishes to believe about himself, and that he wishes others to believe about him.

While Berlusconi was still in Warsaw, on April 29th, he explained his presence at the birthday party by saying that Noemi's father, Elio Letizia, had been Bettino Craxi's chauffeur. This story was quickly denied by Craxi's son Bobo – although later Bobo indicated that he would have kept his mouth shut if he had known the extent of the damage that he was inflicting on Berlusconi by speaking out. The following day Berlusconi's press office denied that he had ever said that Elio Letizia had been Craxi's chauffeur, to the bewilderment of those press correspondents in Warsaw who had heard both conflicting statements.

[xi] In 2011, Karima el-Mahroug ("Ruby") said that it was common knowledge among the young women who frequented Berlusconi that his relationship with Noemi had been sexual. This was denied by Noemi, who said she would sue Ruby.

CHAPTER 7: SEX SCANDALS

A second story came forth a few days later, in an interview on television with Bruno Vespa (most of which can still be seen on You-tube). The interview is notable for the absence of any real questioning by Vespa, who is content merely to prompt Berlusconi when he pauses. In this version, Berlusconi said that he had known Elio since the days of the Socialist party (which ceased to exist in 1994, following Craxi's disgrace, flight from justice and exile), and had asked to have a discussion with him about the choice of candidates to represent his area in the European elections. (There is an obvious conflict with his denial, in the context of the *veline* affair, that he had been involved in selecting the candidates for the European elections).

He mentioned to Elio that he would be in Naples on the following day to inaugurate a new incinerator, and at that point Elio told him about the planned birthday party. He said that the phone call from Elio seeking to have this discussion had come while he was at a motor show at which people had started chanting "Thank Heavens for Silvio" and "You're really great". At one point a woman had started saying "you're magic" and everybody joined in, shouting "magic, magic". All this, he modestly said, had made him really embarrassed, so that when his helicopter pilot had warned him that a storm was coming up and would threaten the planned trip to Naples, he was happy to be able to duck out of these trying scenes of adulation and leave early. When he got to Capodichino airport at Naples, according to his account, he asked the local police if it was true that the restaurant was just three minutes' drive away, and when they confirmed this, he decided to go.

Once there, he says, he decided to have himself photographed with everyone in sight, and this shows, in his view, that there cannot have been anything dubious about his relationship with the young girl – if there had been, he would have kept the matter secret rather than having all these photographs taken. He says that all the clamour was got up by left-wing newspapers, and even suggests that some of these had alleged that the photos were all photomontages. The interviewer – who throughout gives the impression of a solicitous butler, frequently rubbing his hands as he leans forward in his concern that the great man is at ease – ventures at this point to ask why it was not only the left-wing papers that were making these claims, but also his wife, whereupon Silvio says that he is not going to discuss anything to do with his marriage.

This version of events also met with incredulity. Nobody in his party seemed to have heard of Elio Letizia, least of all the two politicians whose candidacy he had apparently been seeking to advise the Prime Minister about. There was no trace of him ever having been active in the Socialist Party, and a number of people who had been high-ranking figures in that party specifically excluded the possibility that he had ever been involved. Yet Berlusconi continued to state that "I am a friend of the father: that's all. I swear it. The matter seemed to me so plain and simple that I would never have thought it possible to build such a castle of lies on it."

Berlusconi's second story also seemed hard to reconcile with what Noemi herself had said in an interview a week earlier. She said that Berlusconi had given her a gold necklace, and that "I adore him. I keep him company. He rings me up, tells me he's got a moment free and I join him. I stay and listen to him – that is what he wants from me. Then we sing together...I often sing with Daddy Silvio at the piano or at the karaoke." Later she is asked when she will get into politics – will it be at the next regional elections? "No, I'd rather be a candidate in the House of Deputies, in Parliament. Daddy Silvio will see to it".

As time went on, the press began to learn more about the Letizia family. They had suffered a tragic loss of their son Yuri in a car accident in 2001. Although the father was employed in a fairly modest role as a Naples council employee dealing with finance from the EU and with "innovative finance", they owned three houses as well as a perfume shop, all of which were in their daughter's name. The father had been arrested in 1993 ("at the time of the Socialists") under suspicion of having taken bribes, along with a number of other council employees. All were found not guilty on appeal, but it turned out that Letizia had somehow got dropped from the list of those charged. His file was completely lost from sight, whether by accident or design. All of the remainder were acquitted in a sentence which stated that "it seems evident that for all the crimes mentioned, the illegal conduct can with certainty be ascribed only to Letizia". So he was considered to be the only one responsible, but at the same time remained mysteriously unpunished, though he was suspended from holding any public office until 2007.

Mystery remained, not only about this affair, but also about the exact way in which the family had got to know Berlusconi, who initially insisted that he had only ever met Noemi in the presence of her parents. Berlusconi's lawyer, Niccolò Ghedini, took part in an episode of the *Annozero* television programme in which he vociferously maintained this, although it wasn't clear what role the parents had played in the karaoke sessions which Noemi had mentioned. As we shall see, it also turned out that this certainly wasn't true, though it is uncertain whether Ghedini had been lied to by his client Berlusconi, or whether Ghedini himself knew that he was lying. In the same programme, Ghedini was asked how Berlusconi happened to have a gold necklace to give to Noemi as a birthday present, when by Berlusconi's own account he had changed his plans to go straight from the motor show to Naples. (Ghedini responded that Berlusconi must have dropped in at one of his houses to pick it up on the way, though no such stop was mentioned in Berlusconi's account).

In mid-May, *Chi*, a gossip magazine belonging to Berlusconi's Mondadori group, published pictures of Noemi with a young man called Domenico Cozzolino, who said he had been her fiancé for ten months, and was shown kissing her passionately, in the presence of her parents who were also depicted fondly entwined with each other. In an interview about the alleged link between Berlusconi's divorce and his relationship with Noemi he said "she used to cry every evening, but I am close to her and try to make her understand that what's been written is nonsense, that we know the truth. We've known each other for two years, but we've only really been together for a month. Do we plan a future together? She tells me she hopes so, and sometimes she talks about the joy of marriage. Even though she's only 18, she's got the mind of an adult". In the interview, Noemi says that she "gave Domenico her first kiss, and I hope that I'll do it the first time with him. Virginity is an important value. I very much believe in God and I'm a practising Catholic". This picture of Noemi in a stable relationship, supervised and sanctioned by her parents, cooled off some of the speculation about the nature of her relationship to Berlusconi. At the same time, it caused some bewilderment among her immediate circle. None of her Facebook friends or the rest of her circle knew that she was involved with Cozzolino, whose background was that he had appeared on a TV show called *Men and Women* on Berlusconi's Channel 5 (an equivalent to the show called *Blind Date* that used to be shown on British television, with Cilla Black presiding).

These doubts came to a head when Noemi confessed to a facebook friend that she had never loved Cozzolino, but she had to wait until the European elections on June 6th before she could dump him, after which there would be an interview ending the relationship. But she didn't want to be with him much even before then. This message ended up in the *Corriere*, whereupon Noemi said she would put the police onto the hacker who had stolen her identity and invented this false message. However, she did indeed end the relationship immediately after the European elections. Then, on June 30th, Cozzolino gave an interview in which he admitted that "it was all a lie, our engagement was a complete fake. The truth is that it was all set up. It was Noemi who asked me to pretend to have this phoney relationship, though I think someone else suggested it to her. I was contacted three or four days after her 18th birthday party". He also admitted that he had not been at the birthday party, contradicting what he had said in the interview to *Chi*. [80]

At this point, let us review the various conflicting stories about how the relationship between the prime minister and the young girl had come about. We have noted Berlusconi's initial, quickly withdrawn, story about Elio, the father, being Craxi's chauffeur. In Berlusconi's second account, in the TV interview, he indicates that there is a political content to the friendship (he wants to discuss candidacies) but doesn't mention how it came about. Initially the mother had confirmed Berlusconi's account, saying that the friendship "dated back to the days of the Socialist party", which was dissolved in 1994 after Craxi's disgrace. On May 5th the father declined to say anything about how he had got to know Berlusconi, but on May 25th he gave an interview to the Naples daily newspaper "*Il Mattino*". The previous day, Berlusconi had said "you'll see that the father will make everything clear in an interview, he will tell about the origin of our relationship. I've known that girl's family for more than ten years". So he clearly had some foreknowledge that Letizia was going to make a statement, and most likely also of its contents.

At the start of the interview, Elio Letizia said that he wanted to make two things clear. Firstly, that politics had nothing at all to do with it (apparently contradicting Berlusconi's claim that a political discussion about candidates was the reason for the meeting). Secondly, that Noemi was *illibata* — a rather old-fashioned Southern word meaning that she was still a virgin – and that he was proud of this. (Later, the website *Voglioscendere* was to show a cartoon in which a child asks a mother "*Che cosa vuol dire illibata?*" – what does *illibata* mean – to which the mother replies "*vuol dire che non è stata ancora candidata*" – it means she hasn't yet been put up for election).

Letizia then said that the first time he met Berlusconi was in 1990, when he went up to him in a street in Milan and shook his hand, but that he didn't really get to know him until May 2001, when Berlusconi was at a meeting in Naples. Knowing that Berlusconi liked old books and picture postcards, he asked if he could give him some, and was told to contact his secretary. Later he went to Rome to deliver them. That July brought the tragic accident that killed his son, and he says that two days later he got a handwritten later from Berlusconi himself, a letter that was heartfelt and touching. Elio says he felt that it was on that day that his relationship with Berlusconi was born; he felt that he was sincere, close to him, sharing his sorrow. In December of that year he went Christmas shopping

CHAPTER 7: SEX SCANDALS

in Rome and decided that would be a good chance to introduce his wife and daughter to Berlusconi. On that occasion, according to Elio Letizia, Berlusconi said to Noemi "consider me your granddad" (*nonnino*), but Elio said granddad sounded too old, and suggested she call him Daddy (*papi*).

At this point, the interviewer asked about various meetings and phone calls that had been referred to by Noemi's ex-fiancé, whose account we will review shortly, and Letizia's lawyer intervenes to say that all of this is the subject of a criminal case which he is undertaking on Letizia's behalf.

The interviewer then asks about Noemi's presence, without her parents, at a dinner in Palazzo Madama, in Milan, which had been noticed by various other people present at the dinner. Letizia explains that there is no mystery: Noemi had often wanted to visit a model parade, and he had asked Berlusconi whether he could help her. They were invited to Rome and took a taxi to Palazzo Grazioli, Berlusconi's private residence. Noemi went on to Villa Madama, an official house outside Rome used for functions, thinking to find a model parade, but instead there was a dinner. Letizia says he stayed at Palazzo Grazioli with Alfredo, the butler, to watch an Italy-Greece football match on the TV there. Then Noemi got back at 11:30 and they returned to spend the night in Naples.

Finally, the interviewer asks about Noemi's presence, along with her mother, at a party in Milan, where they were photographed next to Fedele Confalonieri, the CEO of Mediaset. Letizia says that was the day when she had been called for a screen-test by Emilio Fede, the TV presenter close to Berlusconi, to whom a publicity book of photos of Noemi had been sent in the hope of getting her a TV job. She went with her mother, and afterwards both of them were invited to the party. They stayed the night at a hotel and returned the next day. For the record, says Letizia, she didn't get the job.[81]

That is the father's account of the friendship, in which there is nothing to suggest why somebody who had given some postcards of Naples should be consulted about candidacies in the European elections. His statement that the family's friendship with Berlusconi dates from 2001 conflicts with his wife's earlier statement, that it dates to the "time of the Socialist party". A completely different account was given by a Gino Flaminio, a young man who had been Noemi's boyfriend until the start of 2009.

According to him, the relationship between Noemi and Silvio dated from around October 2008. Noemi had told Gino that she had made a book of photos, and sent it to an agency in Rome. Gino said that Noemi had told him that Emilio Fede had taken the book, along with others, and had left it on Berlusconi's desk. (This part of the account thus fits to some extent with Elio's subsequent story). After sending the book, Noemi heard nothing for four or five months. Then, suddenly, Berlusconi calls Noemi on the phone, directly, without the intervention of a secretary. This happens about 5 or 6 pm one afternoon while Noemi was studying. Berlusconi says that he has seen the pictures and is struck by her angelic face, by her purity, and tells her that she should stay as pure as she is. This first call happened in Gino's absence, and what Gino recounts is what Noemi had told him.

Later, though, when she gets another phone call, she holds out the phone to Gino who hears Berlusconi talking about her purity. In the first phone call, Berlusconi didn't tell her who he was, but asked her a lot of questions – how old she was, what she liked doing, what her parents did, whether she studied. A long, quiet call. Later when Noemi said, "excuse me, but with all these questions, who are you?" He said "if I tell you, you won't believe it", and then "can't you hear who I am?" Gino says that he couldn't believe it the first time she told him, but later when he also heard his voice, how could he not believe it? Noemi said that the calls always originated from Berlusconi. She always called him *Papi*. Sometimes when they were together Noemi picked up the phone, said *Papi*, and Gino immediately realised it was the prime minister. Gino confirms that the relationship was like one between a father and a daughter, and is particularly clear that he doesn't wish to be misunderstood on this point.

At one point, a call came in with both Berlusconi and Emilio Fede on the line – Gino knew this because he was in the car with Noemi at the time. Earlier, Emilio Fede had said that he too was acquainted with Noemi's mother, but Gino dismisses this as absurd. He doesn't know why Berlusconi put Fede on the phone, but assumes it has to do with a screen-test.

Soon, Gino begins to feel uncomfortable about the situation. He says he felt like the butcher on the corner being engaged to Britney Spears. He told Noemi about this, and worries because she is still so young and childlike, never separated from her little blue teddy-bear with a cross round its neck. A quiet, straightforward girl with principles. Gino began to separate from Noemi in December, and says that the thing that he really couldn't take was the long holiday that she went on in Sardinia, at Berlusconi's Villa Certosa. Noemi had told him in December that *Papi* had invited her there, and that she could bring her friend Roberta. She went there around December 26-27 and came back around January 4-5.

When she got back she told him how well Berlusconi had treated her and her friends, how they had joked and laughed. There were about thirty or forty girls there, accommodated in bungalows in the park. In the bungalow that she had shared with Roberta there were also the "twins", though Gino doesn't know who the twins were. (Possibly, though this is only speculation, they could have been Eleonora and Imma de Vivo from *I'm a Celebrity Get me out of Here*, who had featured in the list of *veline* candidates, and were later to feature in the bunga-bunga parties). She said that Berlusconi had been with them only for New Year's Eve, though Gino is not inclined to believe this. They left, according to Noemi, on the prime minister's private jet along with the other girls. Gino's relationship with Noemi broke up after her return.

This account conflicted head-on with all other accounts, particularly that of the prime minister. It was the first account that mentioned Noemi's visit, without her parents but with her friend Roberta, to Berlusconi's villa in Sardinia – which makes it clear that Berlusconi and his lawyer were lying when they said that Berlusconi had only ever met Noemi in the presence of her parents. Berlusconi admitted as much after Gino's story surfaced, saying "It is true that Noemi was my guest at New Year, together with many other guests, and I can't see what's scandalous about it. It's only used to make insinuations. About what? Sex? For heaven's sake, you must be joking".

By bringing to the forefront the allegations – alleged allegations, since there is no trace of them to be found in any newspaper – concerning sex, Berlusconi seeks to move to the background the truly important fact, which is that he had been lying to the public. (This was a man who, in 2006, had accused then prime minister Prodi of lying, and had said that a prime minister who lies should resign).[82] Despite the evidently paternal nature of the relationship, any normal person would share Gino's unease about an immensely powerful septuagenarian seeking to dazzle a seventeen-year old girl whom he has rung up out of the blue.[83]

We have seen that Noemi's father's lawyer spoke of bringing legal action against Gino, and this was just one part of the immediate campaign that was mounted to seek to discredit him. He had, as he had admitted in the interview, had a brush with the law – he had been using a stolen motor which had been put into his car. There was no indication, though, that he had ever committed any crime as serious as the one which magistrates had blamed on Elio Letizia.

The Berlusconi family newspaper *Il Giornale* paid him for an interview, and photographed him while he was taking banknotes, thus insinuating that he had been paid by *La Repubblica* to concoct a false story. On May 31st he wrote a letter to *Il Corriere* in which he apologised to Noemi and the prime minister. It ends like this:

> My point of view has been used by those who, being unable to attack the Man of the People (that's what I call the prime minister), use gossip and tittle-tattle, the story of my love for Noemi. Now they are insinuating that he had sexual relations with her, which I exclude *a priori* as impossible. Can't a man of the people have his private life? What's wrong about being friends with a normal family? The great thing is that he is different from the usual politicians – he is the friend of the bosses, the workers, the employees, the beggars, the poor, in fact of EVERYONE. I am sorry, I could never have imagined what would be made out of my story. I publicly apologise to Noemi and to everyone for all the ruckus that has been caused by our love story and I wish her ALL THE BEST. This is the simple truth. For the rest, please leave me in peace.

And it begins like this:

> Everything started with an interview with two journalists, and I would like to make it clear that it was they, not I, who initiated the contact. They asked me about Noemi and about our love story, saying that they only wanted to ask a few facts about us. The journalists from *La Repubblica* asked me to make a video in which they would put questions to me. I spoke only the truth. Out of this video came an uproar, people saying I was a libeller, a liar, and I had only done it for the money. I would like to ask, who or what have I libelled? I want to make it clear that I neither took nor sought a cent from *La Repubblica* (though I've had offers from other journals for my inconvenience).

In other words, he is a fan of Berlusconi and is unhappy to have upset him or Noemi, but what he said was "only the truth". After he had made this apology the Letizia family dropped their case against him. It was *Il Giornale*, rather than *La Repubblica* that gave him money, for the purpose of seeking to discredit him.

CHAPTER 7: SEX SCANDALS

Gino's story was supported a few days later by Noemi's aunt. After pre-empting various possible attacks by saying that she had no previous convictions, and that she was on excellent terms with her sister-in-law, she said that, when she read Gino's account "I felt very emotional, because I saw for the first time, in this history of lies, somebody telling how things were, with a courage which nobody in the family has had until now". Asked why she had decided to come forward, she said "I would have liked to stay out of it. But after seeing the violent quarrels on *Ballarò* [a TV programme] I decided to come forward. I saw too many things that aren't right. 'Old friendships' that were born overnight. Fiancés popping up out of nowhere. Sad events that had afflicted the family being used to support new versions of the facts affecting my niece Noemi: like the reference [in Elio's account] to a letter of condolence. It's after a great deal of struggle that I have decided to speak now. I've been in torment these last weeks."

"Why are you doing it?" asks the interviewer. "If I'm honest, I'm doing it for my children, so that they know that there is such a thing as true and false, good and evil. I want to be clear that, as far as I' m concerned, this story has nothing to do with politics or with plots, but just the need to be able to look myself in the mirror without feeling the shame that would follow from swallowing a story that, if it wasn't sad, would be a family joke." Asked when she first heard Berlusconi being mentioned in relation to the family, she says "at the end of 2008, between November and December, was the first time that Noemi picked up her mobile during a family meal, and I heard her saying *Papi*. I didn't have a clue at that time who it could be. I thought it was a joke between girls. I just noticed that everybody around her pretended to be busy to avoid showing curiosity".

"When did you first hear Berlusconi mentioned in the context of the family?"

"I can say for sure. It was on the 11th of January, my son's birthday. I organized a little party. And it was that evening that I got to know that they were preparing great festivities for Noemi's 18th. And that, unless other engagements intervened, Silvio Berlusconi was also going to be there".

"So as long as three months before, they were counting on the prime minister being there?"

"I was told that we had to be 'prepared' for that. Confirmation that he would come was expected only at Easter. I was told that Berlusconi had expressly asked Noemi to invite him, and counted on getting the invitation from her hands. I don't know if Noemi visited him in Rome or how that happened. Anyway, at our Easter family lunch it was confirmed that we had to be prepared, because we were going to get to know the prime minister on April 26th, at the party that had been organised in the restaurant in Casoria."

"What did you make about the fact that Noemi and Berlusconi were acquainted?"

"I only know what my sister-in-law, her mother, told me. Anna said that the prime minister felt a father's love for my niece. I recall the expression "He's taken her to his heart". I didn't doubt it. Noemi has always been a sweet, good girl, with one dream: to be a dancer, actress or showgirl." At the end of the interview, she says that she is worried for her family, and that they have all been dragged into a highly embarrassing situation, thanks to a lack of clarity and honesty.[84]

Further evidence also began to come to light suggesting that the only ones who had been telling the truth were Gino and the aunt. Nobody in the Letizia's circle of acquaintance seemed ever to have heard either the father or the mother mentioning the close relationship which Berlusconi had said he had had with the family for a prolonged period. ("at least ten years" in one of Berlusconi's accounts, "since the time of the Socialist party", that is, more like fifteen years, in another account). Various people were interviewed who one might have expected to know about this long-standing friendship. For example, Elio Letizia's brother-in-law who worked in the family newsagent knew nothing about it; nor did Elio's parents; nor did his lawyer. Gino Flaminio was clear that no such relationship existed: "Noemi's parents have nothing to do with it. The relationship was just with her, between Berlusconi and Noemi. Noemi never told me that he, *Papi* Silvio, ever spoke about politics with her father. I just don't think so. Absolutely never".[85]

In addition, the photographer at the party said "Maybe the prime minister's presence at the party was a surprise for the birthday girl, but not for us in the staff of the restaurant. Some people knew about it, I think, the day before. And then on the Sunday morning people from the prime minister's security guards came to visit the place for security reasons... Even the cleaning ladies knew"[86]

At the end of this long and complex set of stories, we can establish that Berlusconi contradicted his own story on many occasions. First, he said that Elio had been Craxi's chauffeur. Then he said that he had never said that Elio had been Craxi's chauffeur. He said that he always met the girl in the presence of her parents, but later said that she had been to his villa in Sardinia without her parents.

CHAPTER 7: SEX SCANDALS

On other occasions, his assertions seem not to fit the facts. He says that he decided at the last minute to go to the party, because his flight to Naples was brought forward, and yet has a gold necklace ready to give Noemi when he gets there. His last-minute decision to attend the party was known months in advance by the aunt, and well in advance also by the staff at the restaurant and the security guards. There is not a hint in any of the evidence that would lend credence to the idea that Elio Letizia is a man whose opinions about candidacies for the European elections should carry any greater weight than anyone else's – yet this was, in Berlusconi's account, the prime reason for him attending the party. (Asked about this point in a TV programme, Berlusconi's lawyer said that this just showed that Berlusconi was indeed a man of the people, ready to listen to the views of the man in the street. A good try, but it doesn't show why he apparently went to the party to ask for Letizia's views, rather than, say, those of the cook or the cleaning ladies). The story about a long-standing family friendship seems highly implausible, given that none of the family ever mentioned it to anyone.

Knowing all this, it is instructive to go back and listen to Berlusconi's interview on *Porta a Porta*. The calm incisiveness of his story, the way everything is made to appear so simple and straightforward: this is, as Montanelli knew and said, the work of someone who is a real master of the art of lying.

Later again, Berlusconi gave another interview in which he merely said "I have said nothing" about the matter.

It was on May 14th that *La Repubblica* began to publish ten questions to Berlusconi, seeking clarification of the true story behind all these confusing tales. The questions were as follows:

- How and when did you first meet Noemi Letizia's father?
- During the course of this friendship how many times, and where, have you met?
- How would you describe the reasons for your friendship with Benedetto Letizia?
- Why did you discuss candidates with Mr Letizia, who is not even a member of your party?
- When did you get to know Noemi Letizia?
- How many times have you met Noemi Letizia, and where?
- Do you take an interest in Noemi and her future, or support her family economically in any way?
- Is it true that you promised Noemi you would help her career in

show business or in politics?
- Veronica Lario said that you "frequent under-age girls". Do you meet any others or "bring them up"?
- Your wife says that you are not well and that "you need help". What is the state of your health?

The questions were to be modified in the following months in the light of the next set of facts that was to come to light.

The attack on Veronica

Generous rewards for loyalty have always been Berlusconi's way of doing business. His wife's actions could only be perceived as gross disloyalty, and so his media power was unleashed to punish her. Soon after she had announced her intention to divorce him, Berlusconi had given an interview in which he said that she would have to publicly apologise to him, and even that might not be enough to make him want to patch things up. It was the third time, he said "that she has played this kind of joke on me during an election campaign. It's really too much". But a month later, after all the embarrassment he had suffered from the exposure of his mendacity during the Noemi affair, the heat was to be turned up on Veronica.

It was *Libero*, the paper then edited by Vittorio Feltri, which took the lead in this. First, it devoted a front page to an article calling Veronica an "ungrateful *velina*", together with pictures of her with bare breasts, dating from the time when she first came to the notice of Silvio Berlusconi as an actress at the Teatro Manzoni in Milan. Then, at the end of May, it published an interview with the journalist and politician Daniela Santanchè, as follows:

> "Every morning I open the papers and read about Berlusconi here and Berlusconi there. And every morning I hope to find the truth that I know and that would turn everything on its head, every morning I hope that the prime minister will have the strength to say it. But nothing happens. The Country could be in the throes of a phoney scandal, its international image is being compromised. It's unacceptable, unbearable...
>
> "The prime minister hasn't broken up any family, but it is Veronica Lario who has a companion. Gossip? Not at all. Here the future of the country is in play. Veronica Lario has for a long time had a companion at her side. His name is Alberto Orlandi, he is 47 years old, he is head of security at Villa Macherio, and he shares

plans, interests, and holidays with her. Not only does the prime minister know about it, but he's done everything he could to keep the family going. He accepted the absence of his wife by his side, he accepted that Italy wouldn't have a first lady, he put his manly pride to one side. He made a pact with his wife – let's keep going, let's not break it all up. He thought about his children and grandchildren. He's done what few men, especially in his way of life, would have had the courage to do. He has accepted what few men accept. What would it have cost him to divorce her and make another family? The whole thing would be resolved in an instant. But he didn't do it. He kept the secret for years. Then Veronica broke the agreement, presumably advised by someone who wanted to throw mud at her husband. I don't know who, but it seems odd to me that nobody has asked even the simplest question. Journalists, politicians and intellectuals have been busy digging up scandals and commenting on Silvio's private life and nobody, but nobody, has done any investigation into his wife's. Does that seem reasonable? Every cubic centimetre of Berlusconi has been examined, but nobody has glanced into Veronica's garden…The truth is that Veronica is being used by someone who is close to her. They already tried once, with the famous letter to *La Repubblica* [in which Veronica had protested after Berlusconi had said that he would marry Mara Carfagna if he wasn't already married]. Now they've gone on the attack again, they're using her, they're bringing up the Mills case…the timing is perfect for the election. As for the party at Casoria, the New Year party in Sardinia, I'm not an investigator, but I know that the prime minister likes to surround himself with people, including girls, sure. He is a lone man, and I think he needs to feel loved. Years ago I went to one of those parties in Sardinia: fireworks, music, dozens of guests of all ages. I was struck by the high spirits. I didn't see and don't believe there was anything else. I don't know what Berlusconi will say about all this, I hope he forgives me. I hope this will help to show this whole affair in its true light".

Berlusconi had publicly deplored the publication of the bare-breasted pictures of Veronica Lario, and he also publicly deplored the statement by Santanchè (and the accompanying editorial by the editor of Libero, Vittorio Feltri), saying that intrusions into family life were not acceptable and that in publishing the photos, *Libero* had "touched rock bottom". A couple of months later, Feltri was to take over as editor of the Berlusconi family newspaper *Il Giornale*.

Alberto Orlandi denied that there was any liaison of the kind suggested by Santanchè, saying that he was head of security and that was all. Some photos of him accompanying Veronica in the gardens of Villa Macherio were shown, but there was nothing in the photos to lend substance to the notion of an amorous liaison. Nothing more can be said about the matter. Some will notice that, just as it suited Berlusconi's book to provide a specious male partner for Noemi, so it was also in his interest to provide one for Veronica. But whether the similarity in the two cases is significant or misleading is a matter that can only be guessed at.

The photos of Villa Certosa

In a summer that was to keep Italy's newspapers well-supplied with scandal, the next issue to surface related to some pictures of Berlusconi's villa in Sardinia that had been taken with a long-distance telephoto lens by an enterprising photographer named Antonio Zappadu. The news that Noemi and her friend Roberta had been to a New Year's Party at Villa Certosa had given rise to press interest about the kind of parties that were given there, creating a ready market for the photos, which were apparently 700 in number. Some of them were taken in public places, such as the airport at Olbia, showing guests arriving by various methods, including occasionally the presidential jet. Others showed scenes in the park and gardens of Villa Certosa.

At the end of May, Berlusconi's lawyer Niccolò Ghedini sought an injunction to prevent the publication of these photos. *Panorama*, one of Berlusconi's newspapers, had been apparently negotiating to buy some of them, but in the event denounced the photographer and demanded the confiscation of the photos, including the ones of Olbia airport. The use of state flights had been a sensitive matter since two ministers in the preceding Prodi government had been found to have taken with them people who were not on official business. The law was changed as soon as Berlusconi came back into office, to make it more permissive, but some of the pictures had been taken before the new law came into effect. Rome magistrates were obliged to investigate whether the law had been broken, but quickly decided that there was not sufficient evidence of wrongdoing to justify taking the matter further.

Even if they had not been used illegally, there was no doubt that Berlusconi was making more liberal use of state flights than his predecessor. In the period of Berlusconi's first government, the cost of state flights had risen from €23 mn per year to €65 mn. Under Prodi's more austere regime, this fell back to €35mn in 2007, but began to rise again under the more liberal rules which permit them to be used by those who are not part of any official delegation, provided they have been invited by someone else who is part of one.

Some of Zappadu's pictures were eventually shown, first in the Spanish newspaper *El País*, though with all the faces blurred so as to render them unrecognisable. They subsequently made their way around the internet. One of them showed a naked man approaching a young woman beside a swimming pool. In the words of the American TV presenter Jon Stewart, he "seems to be pointing out some interesting features of the park – but not with his finger". Because of a characteristic wristband, this figure was later identified as that of Mirek Topolanek, who until recently had been the Czech Prime Minister. Topolanek said that it was indeed him, but alleged that the photo had been tampered with, and accused "European socialists" of being behind this brutal intrusion into his privacy. Other photos showed armed security guards being used to drive young women around the park in golf carts, and various other scenes, all fairly harmless, though more reminiscent of films such as *Carry on Camping* than what one would expect to find in a place where heads of state congregate. The girls wandering through the grounds didn't seem to be in jeans and trainers, as one might normally expect on holiday, but in velvet boots, or high heels, or miniskirts.[87] There were various pictures of girls kissing each other, in one case while having a shower, in another case in the presence of the prime minister, as well as some pictures in which one girl sits on each of the prime minister's knees.

Escorts and Recordings

However, all of this seemed relatively harmless compared to the next scandal that was to blow up. It emerged as part of an investigation into corruption concerning the health care system in Puglia, where the opposition Democratic Party was in charge. A manufacturer of artificial limbs in Bari, named Gianpaolo Tarantini, was trying by all possible means to ingratiate himself with those in power, both regionally and nationally. He had inherited the business from his father, and was seeking to increase both the volume and the profitability of sales. Various members of the local administration resigned after it appeared that he had supplied them with young women as part of his strategy of ingratiating himself. Massimo D'Alema, who in the late 1990s had been prime minister following Prodi's resignation, was the first to note, with rather obscure hints, that matters that were potentially highly embarrassing to Berlusconi might be about to emerge from the corruption hearings that were going on in Bari.

IMPUNITY BERLUSCONI'S GOAL AND ITS CONSEQUENCES

This immediately led to an outcry about how D'Alema had come to be in possession of any such information, and whether the magistrates had been leaking information which they ought to have kept confidential. In the past, it had been possible for Berlusconi to divert attention away from his actions and towards the subsidiary question of how people had come to hear about his actions, and for a time it appeared that this might be another such case.

The story, however, was not to emerge directly from the investigation into health care, but via another route. Just before the European elections on June 6th, a woman in Bari had approached a journalist from *Oggi*, a magazine that is not part of the Berlusconi group. Berlusconi had recently been visiting Bari, and the woman, Patrizia D'Addario, was upset that she had not been allowed into the reception that was being given for him. She had reason to expect that she might have been invited, since she was a candidate in local elections for the "Puglia First" party, which was allied with Berlusconi's People of Freedom party, and other candidates were allowed in.

Oggi decided to take its time in order to check up on the story – it was anxious not to appear to be spreading rumours specifically in order to influence the outcome of the European elections. However, before it published, it was scooped by an interview in the *Corriere della Sera*, a newspaper belonging to the same group. The interview and the article connected to it were as follows:

> Patrizia D'Addario was a candidate for "Puglia First", a movement allied to the People of Freedom at the local elections in Bari. She took part in the opening weeks of the electoral campaign alongside Raffaele Fitto, Minister for Local Government, and other politicians running for the PDL. But now she has decided not to take part in the local election, because she has another story to tell. She sought out *Il Corriere*, and we recount her story, with great caution and with a pinch of salt. "They made me a candidate", she says, "because I was present at two parties at Palazzo Grazioli [Berlusconi's residence in Rome]. I have proof of what I am saying and I want to talk about what happened before I decided to withdraw from the election. My name is still on the list, but I won't take part".
>
> "Let's start at the beginning. When do you claim to have been at Palazzo Grazioli?"
>
> "The first time was in mid-October".

"Who invited you?"

"A friend of mine in Bari told me that he wanted to have me talk to someone he knew, to take part in a party in Rome. I told him that I would have to be paid, and we agreed on €2,000. Then he introduced me to someone called Gianpaolo."

"What did he suggest?"

"I was to take a plane to Rome and there would be a driver waiting for me there. They told me right away that it was a party organised by Silvio Berlusconi."

"Didn't you think it was a joke?"

"My friend is someone I trust totally. I realised it was true when they gave me the air ticket."

"So you went?"

"Yes, I got to Rome and took a taxi to a hotel in via Margutta, as agreed. A driver came to fetch me and took me to the Hotel de Russie where Gianpaolo was staying. We went to Palazzo Grazioli with him and two other girls in a car with blacked-out windows. They told me to say my name was Alessia."

"And then?"

"We were taken to a big room where there were other girls – there must have been about twenty of them. We were given champagne and bits of pizza, and after a bit Silvio Berlusconi arrived."

"Had you ever met him before?"

"No, never. He greeted us all and then he stopped to talk to me. I realised I had made an impression on him because he asked me what my work was, and right away I told him about a bed-and-breakfast that I want to build on a bit of land belonging to my family. Then he showed us videos of his meeting with Bush and pictures of his country houses, and he sang and told jokes."

"Did you go straight back to Bari?"

"It was night, so I went back to my hotel and Gianpaolo told me that he was only going to give me €1,000 because I hadn't stayed the night."

"Is there anyone who can confirm this story?"

"I've got proof."

"How do you mean?"

"I mean that wasn't the only time. I went back to Palazzo Grazioli a few weeks later, the same night that Barack Obama was elected."

"Are you saying that you were with Berlusconi the night of the US presidential election?"

"Yes. Nobody will be able to deny it. I've got my air tickets. That night too I was in a hotel, the Valadier. There were two other girls with me, one that I knew well. Once again it was Gianpaolo who organised everything."

"And what happened?"

"The driver took us to the prime minister's residence, but that evening there weren't any other guests. We found a buffet with sweets and the usual pianist. When he saw me, Berlusconi immediately remembered about my building project. Then he asked me to stay behind."

"You realise that you are saying that you spent a night at Palazzo Grazioli?"

"I've got recordings of both meetings."

"And how can you prove they're genuine?"

"You can hear his voice, and then there were plenty of witnesses, people who won't be able to deny that they saw me."

"Excuse me, but do you always take a recording device to your meetings?"

"Once I had a serious problem with a man, and since then whenever I go to important meetings I always take it with me."

"And you're asking us to believe that you weren't checked before you went into the prime minister's Rome residence?"

"That's the way it was, maybe I was clever. But I can assure you that that's the way it was."

"And can you also prove it?"

"Berlusconi phoned me that evening, as soon as I got back to Bari. And a few days later Gianpaolo asked me to go back. But I said no."

"Your story doesn't seem very credible to us."

"I'm telling the truth. Berlusconi had promised that he was going to send two people to Bari who would get the go-ahead for my project. He didn't keep his promise and from then on I didn't want to go back to Rome any more, despite repeated invitations from Gianpaolo. They knew that I had proof of the two journeys there I'd made earlier."

"And don't you realise that this is blackmail?"

"You think so? I can tell you that a few days later Gianpaolo asked for my CV because he said they wanted to make me a candidate in the European elections."

"But you weren't a candidate for them?"

"When all the fuss started about the *veline*, Gianpaolo's secretary rang me to say that it wasn't possible anymore."

"So your candidacy in the local elections was to make up for that?"

"At the end of March Tato Greco, the nephew of Materrese whom I've known for a long time, got in contact with me. He asked to meet and suggested me for the "Puglia First" list with his uncle at the head of the list. I accepted right away, but a few days later I realised I'd made a mistake."

"Why?"

"My house was completely ransacked. They took away my CDs, computer, clothes, underwear. It was a very odd theft."

"Really? Did you tell the police?"

"Of course. But I went on with the election campaign. Everything went well up to the day when Berlusconi came to Bari for the presentation of the PDL candidates. I was waiting for him at the Hotel Palace. He looked at me, shook hands and went into the room. As I was a candidate, I followed him. But at the entrance I was stopped by security guards and party officials who stopped me taking part."

"And why are you telling this story now?"

"No, I could have gone on with the electoral campaign and negotiated with them behind the scenes. I am telling you because I realise that I was let down. All I had asked for was help with my project, instead of which they used me."[88]

The President's lawyer, Niccolò Ghedini, immediately said that Berlusconi had never met D'Addario and that there was no recording of the event. He went on to say that even if the story had been true, which it wasn't, the President would only have been the "end-user" (*utilizzatore finale*) of the woman, and hence would not have committed any offence. (A draft law that had been tabled by the new Minister for Equal Opportunities, Mara Carfagna, was to make prostitution a criminal offence for the buyer as well as the seller). The odd phrase that Ghedini had used sounded like some technical legal term, but Enrico Carofiglio (crime novelist, lawyer and politician) quickly pointed out that its legal use only applied to objects, not to people. Ghedini responded by saying that Berlusconi had great respect for women, and had no need to pay for them, since he could get "vast quantities" of them for free.

IMPUNITY BERLUSCONI'S GOAL AND ITS CONSEQUENCES

A couple of days later Vittorio Feltri, editor of *Libero*, stepped in with the following:

> "For some years I have been in contact with urologists. Matters to do with the prostate, given my age. If the prostate is enlarged, you can have a surgical intervention to reduce its volume. Afterwards there is a risk of impotence, but it is by no means a foregone conclusion, far from it. But if you have a tumour there, the prostate gets removed along with the tumour. And it's goodbye sex. At risk of invading privacy I will state that Silvio had an operation for prostate cancer at the San Raffaele hospital in Milan in 1996. Berlusconi is almost 73 years old and he doesn't have a prostate. Science can perform miracles, but not that one. To say that he is a sex maniac is simply ridiculous. If I was Silvio I would be tempted to go on TV waving the doctor's certificate."

This temptation, however, was one that Silvio either didn't experience or was able to resist. Shortly after, Patrizia D'Addario's story was confirmed (and Feltri's at least implicitly belied) by the friend of D'Addario who had shared her hotel room. Barbara Montereale described herself as an "image girl", and said that everyone at the dinner, including the prime minister, knew that D'Addario was an "escort". Her impression was that Tarantini was working for Berlusconi. Tarantini used the formal mode of address when talking to Berlusconi, but Berlusconi called him *tu*.

She said that it had been agreed with Tarantini that they would leave Patrizia with Silvio after the dinner "to work", and that is what happened. "She told me that she had had sex with the prime minister," said Barbara about Patrizia, "and that she had not been paid. She said she wasn't interested in money because she wanted his help with the bed-and-breakfast she wanted to build." Barbara Montereale went on to say that she had been invited to the Villa Certosa in Sardinia in January, where Licia Ronzulli (the European candidate who worked in healthcare, and was one of the three *veline* to be selected) had been in charge of working out the girls' journeys, and who was to sleep where. She said that she called Berlusconi Silvio, but all the other girls there called him *Papi*. He had been very sweet, like a father, and before she left had given her an envelope with a generous amount of cash, though she hadn't done anything because she wasn't an escort. She had also been paid by Tarantini for making the visit. Finally, Barbara said that she would defend Berlusconi to the death.[89]

Patrizia D'Addario gave interviews to various, mainly foreign, journals about all this. To the Sunday Times she said, about her night with Ber-

CHAPTER 7: SEX SCANDALS

lusconi, "I never slept. He was tireless, a bull"[90]. More recently she has also published a detailed account of the night in a book entitled *Gradisca, Presidente*. To judge from that account, the little chap may afterwards have felt pride in his performance, though it seems to have been more than a little tiresome for her.

By July some transcripts of the intimate conversations that Patrizia had recorded on the night of the US elections Berlusconi began to circulate – such as:

> SB: I'm going to have a shower, if you finish first will you wait for me in the big bed?
> PD: Which bed – the one from Putin?
> SB: Yes, the one from Putin.
> ...
> PD: A young man would have come in a second, you know? Young men are under such pressure.
> SB: If you'll allow me to say so, these problems often run in families.
> PD: What problems?
> SB: Having an orgasm.
> PD: Do you know how long it's been since I've had sex like we've had tonight? Many months, since I left my man.
> SB: If you don't mind my saying so, you ought to have sex on your own. You ought to touch yourself quite often.

When Patrizia D'Addario got back to the hotel her room-mate Barbara Montereale asked her if she had had an envelope with €5,000, saying that she, Barbara, had been given an envelope with €10,000 by Berlusconi after she had visited Villa Certosa, though not apparently in exchange for sex. Patrizia then called Tarantini and told him that she hadn't received an envelope. However, Patrizia mentioned to Tarantini that she had been promised help with her construction project. She also mentioned that Berlusconi wanted to see her again with another girlfriend of his, whom he wanted to lick her. However, Tarantini is adamant that Berlusconi must not think he is taking her as an "escort", but as a friend.[91]

Berlusconi's response to all this (which might have been expected to be to retreat into private life and quietly follow the advice he had given to D'Addario) was essentially one of denial. We have admired the audacity and coolness with which he wove implausible stories about the Noemi Letizia affair. But by now he seemed understandably somewhat shell-shocked by the succession of blows to his image, and if Montanelli had been alive, that acute observer of Berlusconi's qualities as a liar would probably have judged the interview that Berlusconi gave to his in-house gossip magazine *Chi* as a below-par performance. In it he said that he could remember neither the name nor the face of Patrizia D'Addario, and that he would have stayed a thousand miles from her if he had known that she was a prostitute. He had never paid a woman for sex, since he had never understood what satisfaction there could be without "the pleasure of conquest". Every day he met thousands of people, and he really couldn't remember all of them. He had met Tarantini in Sardinia [where Tarantini had a villa near the Villa Certosa] but hadn't known that there were any investigations into his dealings.

He thought that someone had given Patrizia D'Addario a very specific and highly paid commission to do what she had done before the elections. (Some months later, the Berlusconi-owned magazine *Panorama* was to allege, ridiculously, that magistrates and journalists had clubbed together to pay D'Addario to entrap him). However, there was nothing in his private life for which he needed to apologise. Instead it was the publishers of Italian newspapers who ought to apologise to him for what they had been writing.

The interviewer – Berlusconi's employee – ends the interviewer with a couple of rather unctuous questions, asking him if it is true that his closest friend call him "Duracell", and whether he often thinks about his mother during these difficult days.

Berlusconi's other public comment about the affair was at a press conference held with the Spanish prime minister Jose Zapatero. A journalist said that he wanted to ask about the presence of *veline* and prostitutes at Berlusconi's dinners - "you're envious" interjected Berlusconi when he paused. In his response, he said that the reference to *veline* was a complete libel, since the young women were highly qualified and had undertaken an intensive training course to qualify them, not to be candidates for the parliament, but to be assistants to the parliamentarians. (We have seen that this was quite untrue, and that a number of the candidates had been told that they were to be candidates for election rather than assistants).

The reference to prostitutes was, he said, also a libel. The reality was that Premier Berlusconi (he referred to himself in the third person) had to have many meetings with members of his party, including the group of fans called "Thank Heavens for Silvio" (*meno male che Silvio c'è*). He referred to an entrepreneur from Bari, called Tarantino or Tarantini, affecting not to be sure of his name, though the telephone calls between the two, intercepted during the investigation of Tarantini, had been so frequent that he can hardly have been in doubt about his friend's surname. He said that Tarantini had brought beautiful women with him, and he thought that most men would agree that it was pleasant to sit round a table with attractive and pleasant women. These women had been presented as friends of Tarantini. One of these women had made allegations which he intended to pursue through the courts. He said that he had behaved as any normal host would behave towards this woman. He repeated that he had never paid for sex, since if you like to conquer, the joy was in the conquest. This was why 68.4% of Italians liked him.

He ended this intervention by recalling an aunt of his who liked to look in the mirror and say "Marina, how lovely you look". When asked why she was saying this, she said "I have to, because nobody else does". In the same sense, he said that he was by far the best prime minister that Italy had had in the 150 years of its existence. This last assertion – outrageous as it is – has often been quoted out of its context. While the statement reveals his overweening egotism, the context conveys his ability to charm a large part of his audience into sympathising with his claims.

Patrizia D'Addario kept a recording of that first evening on her mobile phone. During the dinner, Berlusconi jokes with Tarantini, saying that Tarantini has come to ask him to increase the number of teeth from 36 to 40 so that he can sell more medical supplies, and that he wants to accompany Berlusconi to China so that he can supply geishas to doctors in exchange for contracts for the prosthetic limbs from Tarantini's business. These jokes show very clearly that Berlusconi knew exactly what kind of a person Tarantini was – one who supplied women in the hope of getting business favours in return, and give the lie to the story that he only knew that "Tarantino or Tarantini" was an entrepreneur from Bari.

The Heartstealer

On May 27th 2010 a young model named Caterina Pasquino walked past the "Maminail" beauty salon in Milan. Glancing inside, she recognised a young Moroccan girl named Karima el-Mahroug, but going by the name of "Ruby Rubacuori" or Ruby the heartstealer. Some time earlier, Ruby had stayed in Caterina's flat after a night at a discotheque, and the following morning the other occupants had left the flat before Ruby, who still seemed to be asleep. When they got back, Ruby had disappeared, and so had €3,000 together with three Rolex watches. On spotting Ruby in the beauty salon, Caterina alerted the police, who arrested Ruby on suspicion of theft. She was found not to be in possession of documents, but was identified as having absconded from a youth centre in Messina in Sicily, where her parents lived. The police contacted the magistrate responsible for seeing that her case was handled in accordance with the usual procedures. In line with these procedures, the magistrate suggested that they send her to a youth custodial centre, or, if these were now all shut for the night, keep her in the police station till the morning.

Meanwhile, a young Brazilian escort and friend of Ruby named Michelle Coiceicao had found out about Ruby's arrest, and began to alert those she thought would be interested in knowing this. (Later, the contacts shown on her cellphone were found to contain a number for "Papi Silvio Berluscone" [sic] and one for "Silvio House in Rome"). As a result, Silvio Berlusconi, who was then attending a meeting in Paris, came to know that the Moroccan girl was detained. Soon after 11 pm, the head of the police station, then in bed, received a phone call from someone who said he was putting the prime minister through, because there was a problem. Berlusconi told the policeman that the North-African girl detained at his station had been indicated as being the niece (or granddaughter – the word *nipote* is ambiguous) of Mubarak. "Who is Mubarak?" enquired the policeman, and it was explained that Hosni Mubarak was President of Egypt, and that the release of the girl would help to avoid a diplomatic incident. A "ministerial councillor" was being sent round by the prime minister's office to collect her from the police station. Telephone records show that six calls were made that night from the prime minister's personal phone to the head of the police-station, and one from the phone of the prime minister's chief security guard.

The police were in a difficult position. The magistrate responsible was clear about what ought to be done: whatever anybody said, the ordinary procedures ought to be followed, and the girl should be sent to an appropriate youth care centre, or detained in the police station until one could be found. The magistrate also seems to have been doubtful about the plausibility of the story that this was the niece of Mubarak. But the police did not feel able to ignore the pressure being brought to bear on them. Accordingly they released Ruby into the care of the person who had been represented to them as a "ministerial councillor".

This person was another young woman, Nicole Minetti, daughter of an Italian businessman married to an English teacher of ballroom dancing from Rimini. She had appeared as a dancer on a TV variety show, before retraining as a dental hygienist. In this capacity, she had met Silvio Berlusconi while he was being treated for facial injuries incurred when a mentally ill man had flung a model of Milan cathedral at him. Berlusconi had quickly seen that she had the attributes that, in his eyes, made her suitable for a political career, and she was duly elected as a regional councillor in Lombardy. Her more important function, however, appears to have been helping to arrange parties at Arcore, and managing the young women invited to such parties.

Once the police had handed Ruby over to Nicole Minetti, Nicole then almost immediately handed her back into the care of Ruby's flatmate, the Brazilian escort Michelle. Clearly it was known to all involved that Ruby was under 18 – otherwise there would have been no question of finding an adult into whose care she could be entrusted.

A few days later police were again summoned when a fight broke out between Ruby and Michelle Coiceicao, after which Ruby told the police that Michelle had made off with the necklace given to her by Berlusconi. These incidents, and the statements made by Ruby, alerted the authorities to the involvement of underage girls and others in what appeared to be an organised system under which payments were made, and favours extended, in return for the presence of these girls in revelries at the prime minister's villa at Arcore. Prostitution was suspected, and arrangements were made to intercept the phones of some of those involved (though not of course the prime minister's own phones).

The Meaning of Bunga-Bunga

The investigation pieced together a picture of parties that were frequently held at Arcore. The word "bunga-bunga" soon spread across the media in connection with these parties. The term seems to come from a joke which Berlusconi likes (or used to like) to tell: two men are captured by a savage tribe, whose chief asks them which punishment they prefer, death or bunga-bunga. The first chooses bunga-bunga, and is then raped by all the other men present. The second chooses death, to which the chief responds: "All right, first bunga-bunga and then death".

In the context of the parties at Arcore, bunga-bunga seems to refer to the time after the guests – typically many young women and a few old men – had left the dinner table, and moved to a room where music was playing, and the young women danced. One should regard Ruby's account with a certain scepticism, but here it is, as reported by *La Repubblica*:

"We dined," she recalls, "but I didn't stay overnight. After supper I left. By 2:30am I was already home, with a black and white dress by Valentino and Swarovski glasses, given to me by Silvio. The second time I went to Arcore was the following month. Straightaway Silvio tells me that he would be pleased if I stayed there all night. Lele had already mentioned that he would ask me to. He had reassured me: 'Don't worry, you won't be the object of sexual advances, nobody will embarrass you.' And that's the way it was. We had supper and afterwards I participated for the first time in bunga-bunga.

"All the girls were naked during the bunga-bunga and I had the feeling that they were competing with each other to make Berlusconi notice them by performing more and more daring sexual acts. I was the only one dressed. I watched while I served a drink (a Sanbitter) to Silvio, the only man. Afterwards, they all went for a swim in the covered swimming pool; I wore white shorts and top that Silvio found for me and immersed myself in the hydromassage tub.

"The third time I went to Arcore was for a dinner, which was a much, much calmer event. When I arrived Silvio told me that he would introduce me as Mubarak's niece." At table, she maintains, were Daniela Santanché, George Clooney and Elisabetta Canalis.

The young women attending these parties were shepherded by an ageing impresario called Lele Mora, and by Nicole Minetti, both of whom, along with the broadcaster Emilio Fede, are now charged with procuring women for prostitution. Many of the young women were given flats in Milano 2, Berlusconi's early property development, and much of the telephone material intercepted consists of Minetti discussing the allocation of these flats among the girls. All were handsomely rewarded with gifts and money, and soon began to become fractious if the supply threatened to give out.

Another participant at these parties gave a similar account. This 21-year-old was a friend of a regular attender, Aris Espinoza, who told her that she had been in bed with the Prime Minister on several occasions and had received money. She went along to Arcore on January 6 2011, finding about twenty other young women and girls there along with Berlusconi, Emilio Fede and the Neapolitan singer Apicella. After dinner, Berlusconi said "Now it's time to dance", and mentioned bunga-bunga (a word which the young woman giving this account had not heard before, to the incredulous amusement of the others). They went into another room lit like a discotheque, with a pole for pole-dancing. All the girls were given a bag and some jewels. They danced around, some doing striptease, while Berlusconi and Fede sat and watched. They kissed and caressed, and were caressed in "intimate parts" by, the Prime Minister. The girl giving this account said she felt too shy to join in. Psychologically, she says, she had been prepared to have sex with him in the presence of other women, and Aris had told her she would be given money (it could vary between €1,000 and larger figures, said Aris), but "when I saw him in person, I honestly didn't feel like it".[92]

Similar accounts of these parties emerged from other sources. A belly dancer named Maria Makdoum who had participated spoke of a Brazilian woman dancing the samba in a G-string, after which the De Vivo twins stripped to pants and bra, and were felt up by the Prime Minister and Fede, as were other young women. "If I'd known what was being done at Arcore I'd never have gone", said the belly-dancer. Other accounts, including photos found at the young women's apartments, show the young women dressing up to attend these parties as nurses or as policewomen, with nothing on under their pretend uniforms.

Managing the participants at these entertainments was an arduous task for poor Nicole Minetti. One participant, a Dominican called Marysthelle Polanco, cohabited with a drug dealer, and when Nicole was absent on holiday in the Seychelles, they borrowed her BMW Mini. Marysthelle's boyfriend arrived at the Milano 2 flats in the Mini, and was arrested in possession of 12 kg of cocaine. Another of the young women, Barbara Faggioli, discussed with the Prime Minister the embarrassment caused to Minetti by this event, and relayed to Nicole the Prime Minister's suggestion that she should pretend that her car had been stolen. When she was interviewed by magistrates, she was asked why the Prime Minister had suggested that she commit a crime (falsely denouncing a theft). In response she availed herself of her right to remain silent. During this interview, she said that she had had sex with Silvio Berlusconi. She also had received "loans" from him, and, when asked if she intended to repay them, said "We'll see".[93]

Another participant at these evenings, a young Brazilian woman named Iris Berardi, also seems to have started participating in them before her 18 birthday. She was, however, over 18 when, in one of her telephone conversations that was intercepted, she reads out a letter that she is sending to the Prime Minister, as follows:

> My love, I start this letter with my heartfelt thanks for changing my life, you are a really good person, absolutely unique, and I do

love you, but I really need work because I've always worked and I'm going crazy being at home doing nothing all day, and also because I'm practically keeping three families, my mother and granny, my dad and the other granny, and now my aunt with two children, earning only €600 a month in a temporary job and with rent of €450, I'm so ashamed to be always asking for something, but I don't ever want to go back to going to bed with people I don't like..

Indictment for Abuse of Office and Juvenile Prostitution

On the basis of the material that they had gathered, Milan magistrates brought a case against Silvio Berlusconi for abuse of office, and for juvenile prostitution. It was alleged that Ruby had been paid for sexual acts on 13 occasions. Berlusconi dismissed the charges, saying that, although he hadn't wanted to mention the matter before, ever since he had been separated from his wife he had been in a stable relationship, and that the person concerned was often at these dinners at Arcore. It was, he said, unthinkable that she should have allowed the kind of goings-on which the newspapers had alleged.

For a few days, the press played "hunt-the-fiancée", trying to establish the identity of this person whose existence had never been suspected. Various people said that this relationship had long been known within the inner circle of friends, but nobody was willing or able to identify her. Many suggestions were made, including Daniela Santanché, whom we have seen throwing mud at Veronica a few pages back; Nicole Minetti, who, however, began to resent the difficulties which her friend the prime minister had made for her, and was intercepted on the phone saying that he was a shit whose flaccid arse she didn't want to protect; Roberta Bonasia, a young woman who had been persuaded to attend one of the bunga-bunga parties wearing a pretend nurse's uniform with nothing on underneath; and many other suggestions.

After a few days Berlusconi's own paper began to stop referring to the matter, until in late March Lele Mora provided more details, specifying that the little fiancée (*fidanzatina*, as Berlusconi had referred to her) was beautiful, very intelligent, about 28 years old, studying for a degree, and definitely not Neapolitan. Up to the present, no candidate has yet come forward willing to play the part described by Berlusconi. The most probable hypothesis at the time of writing – though it could still be proved wrong – is that this invention of a fictitious fiancée is yet another example of Silvio Berlusconi's extraordinary mendacity, and his tendency to overestimate the gullibility of the public. Certainly the story jibes oddly with the statements by Nicole Minetti and others about having had sex with the prime minister during the period of his alleged betrothal.

In bringing the case, magistrates also sought to search the offices of Berlusconi's accountant, who was charged with disbursing the funds for making "gifts" to the girls. This search required the consent of Parliament, since the accountant was considered to benefit from the immunity from search accorded to the prime minister. Parliament did not answer this request, but instead replied if that these offences had been committed, it was in the course of carrying out the prime minister's official duties, and therefore could not be tried by the ordinary court in Milan, but would require a special Tribunal which Parliament itself would have to authorise.

The judges had themselves considered these questions of where the competence to investigate should lie. However, they had concluded that, if Berlusconi had genuinely been motivated by a concern to avoid a diplomatic incident with Egypt, it would have been more natural to have arranged to have Mubarak's supposed niece handed into the care of, say, the Egyptian Consulate in via Modena in Milan. The fact that instead the representative whom Berlusconi had sent to collect her immediately passed her over into the hands of a Brazilian prostitute seemed to suggest that he was not in fact acting for reasons of State.

What is surprising, and infinitely depressing, is that a majority of members of the Italian Parliament was willing to swallow this ridiculous story. Their unconditional support for Berlusconi, and his unwillingness to relinquish the impunity which his occupation of high office has until now conferred on him, have unleashed what promises to be a long and distasteful battle. This battle will have two consequences. Firstly, it will further erode the rule of law in Italy. Berlusconi plans to fight back with a host of laws which will make it harder to prosecute criminals. Secondly, Italy's international image will suffer from the ridicule and contempt which – by this point it should be apparent – Berlusconi fully merits, but the country as a whole certainly does not.

Postscript: The Honest Clerk of Fkih ben Salah

The woman responsible for keeping the records of births and deaths in the little Moroccan town of Fkih ben Salah, on the Western slopes of the Atlas mountains south-east of Casablanca, was surprised to receive a visit, on February 7th 2011, from two foreigners, speaking a language she recognised as Italian, and accompanied by an interpreter. They asked her if they could look at the record of the birth of Karima el Mahroug, and, having done so, commented that it seemed to be incorrect. They suggested that the discussion be continued outside her office, and, out in the street, they suggested, according to the clerk, that it be changed to the date that they considered correct – two years earlier, in 1990 instead of 1992.

They offered – the clerk said – a large sum of money if this could be done, but the clerk explained that it was illegal to falsify the register of births, and that she could not do it. After they had left, she tried to find out who they were, and was told that the interpreter worked in the Italian consulate, but nobody knew who the two Italians were. A few weeks later, (but before anyone else had heard of the goings-on in Fkih ben Salah) on March 3rd, the Berlusconi family newspaper *Il Giornale* published an article entitled "The Prime Minister produces the ace: Ruby was not under-age". The article explained that, in private conversations, Berlusconi said he had proof that Karima had been registered two years after her birth. The article spoke of investigations being carried out "on the other side of the Mediterranean". It is unclear whether these investigations had any connection to the two Italians apparently seeking to falsify the birth certificate. It was only a week after this article had been published that the clerk came forward to tell her story. When her story became public, Berlusconi's lawyers professed surprise at it, and said that its purpose might have been to damage the Prime Minister's credibility. They asked Rome magistrates to investigate further. A few days later, a Moroccan lawyer began to cast aspersions on the clerk's professional behaviour.

CHAPTER 8:
IMAGE AND REALITY IN BERLUSCONI'S ITALY

The Dear Leader

Where one finds power, one also finds flattery, servility and obsequiousness. The unrestricted power, both economic and political, which Silvio Berlusconi holds has provided a hot-house in which an exotic variety of this type of flora has blossomed. Most political leaders belong to parties that started before they came to power, and will continue after they have left power – such as the Democratic Party in America, or the CDU in Germany, or the Conservative Party in Britain. However successful they may be, leaders of such parties can never take it for granted that other factions within these parties will not contest their leadership.

Berlusconi is not in that situation. His political party was founded and funded by him; it grew out of his business, and its sole raison d'être is to put him in power. There has never been any threat to his leadership of his party. Grassroots members have little say in policy, or even in the personalities that are chosen to represent them. Forza Italia's constitution at one point made reference to primaries in which local candidates would be chosen, but this provision was never activated. Having started essentially as a wing of the Fininvest company, for the initial years of its existence it was a top-down party, with leaders at all points in the hierarchy being nominated from above rather than elected from below. Moreover, the hierarchy was kept very lean, and the overheads low. (The way in which Forza Italia was formed, and in which it developed, are set out by Emanuela Poli in her book *Forza Italia*).

It is normal, and even desirable, that somebody who founded a business empire should have an absolute say over the way in which that empire is run (though, once there are minority shareholders, their interests must not be jeopardised by manoeuvres such as the one that Berlusconi is alleged to have undertaken with regard to film rights, whereby one part of the profit is appropriated by the majority shareholder only). This is the climate to which Berlusconi is habituated, but it is not the climate in which most political parties operate.

For that reason, it is clear that Berlusconi feels more at home with political leaders whose power is as unrestricted as his. Putin and (until the 2011 uprising) Ghaddafy are among the foreign leaders with whom he appears more comfortable, and significantly he has tended to oppose stricter EU sanctions on other absolute leaders such as Mugabe. He is bewildered in a negotiation in which he is not in a dominant position, and where his fellow-negotiators, despite being heads of government or heads of state, do not have the same unrestricted power to make decisions that he enjoys.

One result of this absolute power is the polarization of public opinion in Italy. On the one hand there are those who subscribe to the view that he himself holds – that he is uniquely qualified to lead Italy, and that any other leader would be bound to lead to disaster. On the other are those who are disturbed by the cult of personality.

An example of the unctuous way in which he is treated by those who support him is provided by an anecdote recounted by Vittorio Sgarbi – himself an admirer of Berlusconi – about the man who until 2011 was Minister of Culture. "Sandro Bondi? The first time I heard him speak I had a shock. It was at a Forza Italia meeting, and Berlusconi's arrival was not expected. Instead, Berlusconi arrived, actually while Bondi was speaking. Bondi stopped, looked at him, and said 'Excuse me, Mr President, if I speak in your presence'".

A further example is provided by a political ally who has also been his long-time personal medical adviser, Mario Scapagnini. In 2004, when Berlusconi was 68, Scapagnini said "Make no mistake: he will outlast us all. His real age is 55. Berlusconi is technically almost immortal...His body and mind show an almost superhuman capacity to ward off disease... Genetically he is exceptional. An excellent neuro-endocrine profile. A truly extraordinary brain. He has foresight, an intelligence beyond the norm, which permits him to foresee what is going to happen. His persistence, his capacity to work and to concentrate are incredible. He never

CHAPTER 8: IMAGE AND REALITY IN BERLUSCONI'S ITALY

gives up". A few of these statements are certainly the simple truth, but others veer over into hyperbole, giving credence to the unrealistically superhuman image that Berlusconi himself appears to hold about his own powers. Although he would have said he was only joking when he described himself as "Superman" in an interview in September 2009, it seems likely that this is not far from what he believes.

Berlusconi himself often tells jokes which play on his exceptional qualities. For example: after his admission to Heaven, he reorganises the management structure there. God congratulates him for his wonderful effort, but then asks why His own office now has a sign outside saying "Deputy Manager".

Scapagnini attributes at least some of Berlusconi's remarkable attributes to his own medical prowess, including the elixir which he administers. (There is much of the comic opera in Berlusconi's Italy, and Scapagnini inevitably brings to mind the quack Dr Dulcamara, "known throughout the universe, and in other places", in Donizetti's Elisir d'Amore. At other times, though, it is Berlusconi himself, claiming to have cures for all Italy's ills, who reminds us of Dulcamara. As fans of this opera will know, its message is that the only love elixir that works is money). These are the secrets of Scapagnini's elixir and of Berlusconi's longevity: "Provitamins, anti-oxidants, immuno-stimulants, enzymes, amino-acids, and above all minerals, magnesium and activated selenium. The same ones that are absorbed by the centenarians that I have met on the Silk Road, to the south of Urumqi and in the oases between the Taklamakhan and Gobi deserts. Then a particular oil, a certain yoghurt".

(The legend of exceptionally longevity in these areas has been widely debunked. Rigorous research into the remarkable number of centenarians in the area that Scapagnini referred to has eventually succeeded in identifying the factor that all of the *soi-disant* centenarians have in common: they are all rather bad at counting).

Mr Scapagnini himself appears to have difficulty in counting, at least as far as money is concerned. In addition to purveying elixirs, he was also Mayor of Catania from 2000 until he had to resign in 2008 because of the deep debts which had overwhelmed the city under his administration. He was sentenced to 2 years and six months in jail in May 2008 for abuse of office and violation of electoral laws, while the candidate whom he had defeated in the 2005 mayoral election was given damages of €50,000.

In the media, and particularly in those parts of it owned by Berlusconi, there is of course a host of lickspittles. Whoever occupies the chair once occupied by Montanelli, as editor of *Il Giornale*, has onerous duties of obsequiousness to perform, which normally take the form of accusing others of whatever crimes Berlusconi himself is currently suspected of having committed. The lack of self-awareness of this newspaper is scarcely believable by those who have not read it. For example, in a recent dispute between Murdoch's Sky TV and the Berlusconi government, *Il Giornale* accused Murdoch of "conflict of interest". There is much to object to in Murdoch's media empire, especially in its US (Fox News) manifestation, but Murdoch never has had, and never will have, a post in any government. That he should have been accused of conflict of interest by a newspaper belonging to the brother of a Prime Minister who also controls the vast majority of private and public television was bewildering.

A further example of the adulation in which some hold Berlusconi is to be found in the campaign to have him awarded the Nobel Peace Prize in 2010. An internet site explained how the recent improvement in relations between the USA and Russia (which the ill-informed believed to be connected to the election of Barack Obama) was actually the fruit of Berlusconi's efforts; also that the 2008 war between Russia and Georgia would not have ended without those same efforts. The site applauded the treaty signed between Italy and Ghaddafy's Libya. (The site has now been taken down).

While there is no reason to suspect that Berlusconi himself was behind this campaign, the tendency to believe himself indispensable to any effort in which he is involved is certainly one of his characteristics. An example of this occurred when the Presidents of Russia and Turkey met in August 2009 to sign an agreement concerning a pipeline to carry natural gas. The Italian oil company ENI was involved in the deal, but the Turkish authorities were baffled when they learnt that Silvio Berlusconi also wished to attend the signing ceremony. A senior Turkish government source told Reuters on August 7th 2009 that Berlusconi's claim of personal success in negotiating the deal was exaggerated. "The deals had already been agreed when the Turkish government received an unexpected last-minute request from Berlusconi to attend the signing ceremony. There was more surprise when it became clear that Berlusconi was claiming the accords as his personal success. 'This is the sort of thing that could be a problem diplomatically. But because it is Berlusconi it just made the two leaders smile', said the source".

CHAPTER 8: IMAGE AND REALITY IN BERLUSCONI'S ITALY

By October 2009, a site – www.Berlusconibeato.com – had appeared on the internet which was calling for Berlusconi's immediate beatification, showing pictures of him in prayer and in the company of bishops, and repeating the claim that Berlusconi himself had made a little earlier, that nobody in 150 years of Italian history had done as much as he had. The site was of course a hoax, but within two days it had received 30,000 visitors, and many had tried to donate money to the campaign (the site helpfully provided an IBAN number for donations). The hoax was dreamt up by a music teacher who, having seen the site promoting Berlusconi for the Nobel peace prize, had decided that there were no limits to people's credulity. And so it proved.

All those Mirrors are Ugly

One result of all this adulation is an inability to contemplate criticism that casts doubt on the miraculous image purveyed by the worshippers. We shall see this reaction above all when we come to consider the reflection in the media of the sex scandals. Any instance in which the image of Berlusconi is reflected in an unflattering way is taken as proving that it is the mirror that is deficient, and in need of correction. For example, Finance Minister Tremonti said, in relation to the interest being shown in Berlusconi's sex-life, that all of this peering through keyholes was damaging Italy's international image. It was not what was being seen that was thought to be damaging this image, it was the act of seeing it. Equally, Berlusconi and his allies consistently decry as unpatriotic those newspapers that report these scandals, claiming that it is their reporting of the facts, rather than the facts being reported, that damages Italy's international prestige.

Again, when suing the newspaper *Unità* for various reports, including those connected with his sex life, Berlusconi's lawyer felt obliged to specify that jokes about the Prime Minister using aids against impotence were "false and harmful to the Prime Minister's honour, presenting Hon. Berlusconi as something that he certainly is not, namely a person with erection problems". We have seen that the then editor of *Libero*, Vittorio Feltri, had himself suggested that, because of an operation on his prostate, Berlusconi's sex life was at an end and the scandals must therefore be baseless. However, rather than being sued for making the same allegation as *Unità*, a different fate awaited Feltri. As he himself recounts, Berlusconi summoned him to a meeting at which he suggested that Feltri return as editor of *Il Giornale*. Feltri took up the post soon after (but relinquished it in 2010). This episode highlights the contempt in which Berlusconi holds the Mammì law which specifies that owners of television channels cannot also own newspapers. Nominal ownership of *Il Giornale* lies with Berlusconi's younger brother Paolo, but Feltri's account makes it clear that this is a mere fig-leaf, and that Berlusconi continues, as he did when he confronted Montanelli, to discharge the functions of the owner.

Berlusconi is always very ready to bring libel cases. In this light, we can see that they are not merely motivated by the need to intimidate and to silence opposition, but also by a real conviction that adverse reports must be mistaken. The other reaction to adverse reports is to smear those who are doing the reporting. For example, the Catholic newspaper *Avvenire* had, for most of 2009, shown a tolerant and even understanding attitude to the sex scandals affecting Berlusconi. But, at a certain point, its editor, Dino Boffo, began to voice concerns about whether the Prime Minister's behaviour was really quite what one would wish for the leader of a predominantly Catholic country.

Once this happened, *Il Giornale*, now directed by the combative Feltri, devoted the first two pages of one of its issues to a case that had occurred five years previously, in which Boffo had agreed to pay €516 in damages to a woman who had alleged that somebody had been harassing her with phone calls. *Il Giornale* produced a document, which it initially claimed was an official document connected with the court hearing, but later turned out to be an anonymous letter that had been sent to various ecclesiastical authorities. In this document, it was alleged that Boffo had been having a homosexual relationship with the woman's husband, and that he was a "known homosexual who was already been watched by the Police on account of this type of relationship". The idea that the Police had nothing better to do than to keep an eye on people who might be homosexuals should perhaps have warned the readers, if not the writers, of *Il Giornale*, that this was unlikely to be any kind of official document.

The journalist Marco Travaglio, discussing this episode, notes an odd statement on the matter by Gabriele Villa who, he says, used to be the golf correspondent of *Il Giornale* in Montanelli's day (when Travaglio also worked on the paper), but had now been promoted to writing about judicial matters, "though he evidently knows a lot more about golf". Villa wrote about the Boffo case in *Il Giornale* that "gossip is not enough to crucify a person, or rather it *is* enough, but only in the case of two people: Jesus Christ and Silvio Berlusconi". Even the most unctuous of hagiographers seldom puts their patron into that particular pairing. However, he was not the first to do so: Berlusconi himself had said "Of course I was joking about Napoleon: I am the Jesus Christ of politics, a victim, patient, I put up with everything, I sacrifice myself for everybody."[94]

CHAPTER 8: IMAGE AND REALITY IN BERLUSCONI'S ITALY

This attempt to smear critics is only one relatively recent example – many more are to be found in the archives. For example, there have been unsuccessful attempts to prove that Romano Prodi acted corruptly in the SME affair (when, as manager of a state holding company he sold a failing food manufacturer for less than what Berlusconi considers to have been a fair price); there have been numerous smear campaigns mounted against Di Pietro, none of which have succeeded in demonstrating any wrongdoing; there were persistent smears against Stefania Ariosto, who first brought to the attention of the police the probability that Previti had acted corruptly. It is part of what any opponent or critic of Berlusconi must learn to expect.

Now that it has been possible to view Berlusconi's record over a fairly long period, a pattern emerges in his technique of smearing: he aims specifically to suggest that the accuser is guilty of the particular offence that Berlusconi himself has committed. Thus, when Berlusconi is at risk of being thought guilty of corruption, he charges his rival Prodi with the same offence.

A similar smear campaign was attempted in the 1990s against the magistrate Antonio Di Pietro, who had spearheaded the Mani Pulite investigations in Milan. Di Pietro enjoyed enormous popularity at the time of the investigations and, given that he was known to be a man of the right, Berlusconi offered him a position in his first government. However, Di Pietro refused, knowing that Berlusconi's own company was one of those that were the subject of corruption investigations. Following his refusal, long and arduous attempts were made to smear Di Pietro, too, with corruption charges – these attempts culminated in an embarrassing climbdown when *Il Giornale* had to devote an issue to a full admission that Di Pietro's career had in fact been blameless, and led to Feltri's resignation from his first stint as editor of the paper. As part of the climbdown, Feltri then wrote "Dear Tonino [Di Pietro], I had a high opinion of you and I have not changed my mind".

A further attack on Di Pietro was mounted in early 2010, just before the regional elections. It had been rumoured that Feltri was again preparing material, this time to allege that Di Pietro had been collaborating with the CIA and associating with Mafiosi at the time of the Mani Pulite investigations. However, it was not *Il Giornale*, but the previously respectable *Corriere* which produced a photograph of Di Pietro at a police dinner in 1992 in the company of a man who was subsequently accused of associating with the Mafia, and of a spy said to be close to the CIA. It was insinuated that the CIA had been in some way responsible for Mani Pulite. What interest the US would have had in arranging the disintegration of the Christian Democrats and the Socialists, its strongest allies in the Italian political galaxy, was never explained.

Similarly, when Dino Boffo criticises Berlusconi's sex life, it is Boffo's own sex life that is trawled in search of material for smears. Equally, when a judge awarded Berlusconi's rival De Benedetti €750 mn in damages after another judge had been bribed to award the Mondadori company to Berlusconi – readers will recall that the judge's sentence had been written for him by Berlusconi's lawyers – Berlusconi alleged that the judge in the damages case had had his sentence written for him by De Benedetti's lawyers. So well established had this habit become, by the end of his career, that one could safely regard any insinuation by Berlusconi that his rivals had committed a particular crime as almost being tantamount to a confession that he had committed that same crime himself.

A further feature of Berlusconi's response to his opponents is to allege that they are all communists. This has led to the legend of the *toghe rosse*, the red magistrates, who have allegedly had Berlusconi in their sights and sought at all costs to subvert the people's will by removing him from government. (More recently, Berlusconi has described magistrates as Taliban – evidently they have been converted from Stalinism to fundamentalist Islam). Many of those who have made the case against Berlusconi most forcefully and persuasively have in fact been of the right. The journalist Montanelli was certainly an ardent anti-Communist, and Marco Travaglio, whose journalistic career began on *Il Giornale* when it was under Montanelli's leadership, is also not a man of the left. We have noted that Antonio Di Pietro, whose political party *Italia dei Valori* provides the most vocal, and sometimes the only, criticism when Berlusconi seeks to undermine the rule of law, is also to the right of the spectrum. The judge Paolo Borsellino, who was assassinated before Berlusconi's ascent to power, but who, as we have seen, was investigating suspected links between Fininvest and organised crime, is believed to have voted for the neo-Fascist MSI.

The idea that the magistrates who have prosecuted Berlusconi have been *toghe rosse* has been thoroughly dismantled by Elio Veltri, in a book of that name. Even Berlusconi's closest and oldest friend Fedele Confalonieri has said that "Berlusconi's mistake is that he thinks all magistrates are reds. He's wrong. And I tell him so."[95] But the continued allegation in the media controlled by Berlusconi that they are animated by bias has undermined the standing of the judiciary, and thus the rule of law, in Italy. It helps to remind oneself that unfavourable judgments in relation

CHAPTER 8: IMAGE AND REALITY IN BERLUSCONI'S ITALY

to Berlusconi's business dealings have been delivered, not just by Italian judges, but also those in the United Kingdom and Switzerland – two countries seldom accused of having a judiciary run by communists.

An important function of calling all opponents "communists" is to divert attention from Berlusconi's own poor record in bringing about market-oriented reforms, which we have already documented. Adam Smith, in his day, poured scorn and invective on the East India Company, which was the largest monopoly at the time, and there is little doubt that, if he were alive today, he would be sharply critical of Fininvest and its monopolistic and subversive doings. But defining all opponents as communists tends to obscure what would otherwise be glaringly obvious: that Berlusconi's economic management has had little objective other than the preservation of his monopoly power, and has had the disastrous results documented in Chapter 5. It also diverts attention from the increasing similarities between Berlusconi's Italy and pre-1989 East Europe, in matters such as dismantling of the rule of law, economic stagnation, monopoly of information and corruption.

The use of *Il Giornale* to attack opponents and potential opponents was also shown up when, in September 2009, the paper launched a vitriolic attack on Berlusconi's oldest political ally, Gianfranco Fini, who had criticised the newspaper's recent treatment of Dino Boffo. In its attack on Fini, *Il Giornale* called on him to "rejoin the ranks" of the party, and in a subsequent article said that "to create a scandal, all that is needed would be enough to dig up a file from 2000 dealing with red-light matters concerning people from Alleanza Nazionale. Better let sleeping dogs lie".[96]

Il Giornale's editor Feltri was thus using a newspaper in a rather different way from what is usual. Normally, if a newspaper knows of a scandal, its interest, and in most cases its duty, lies in making that scandal known to the general public as quickly as possible. In this case *Il Giornale* was stating that it knew of a scandal that was nine years old, but rather than making it public, it was using it as a threat to seek to exercise control over a politician who was acting in a way that it considered damaging to its proprietor (or, strictly speaking, its proprietor's brother), the prime minister. In other words, this was essentially blackmail.

Later, when Fini left the People of Liberty to set up his own party, enormous efforts were made during the latter half of 2010 to smear him in connection with a flat in Monte Carlo, rented by his brother-in-law. No convincing proof of misconduct was revealed, and the efforts eventually ceased when they began to have the effect of re-igniting interest in

IMPUNITY BERLUSCONI'S GOAL AND ITS CONSEQUENCES

Berlusconi's own property dealings, some of which were recounted in the first chapter.

A different approach to blackening the name of opponents came following the judgment in which Fininvest was ordered to pay damages of €750 mn to De Benedetti's group CIR, to compensate for having bribed a judge to deprive CIR of Mondadori (see Chapter 4). A few days after the case, Berlusconi remarked that "we're going to hear some fine things about" the judge, named Mesiano. This was clearly the green light to his journalists to dig dirt. They do not appear to have found any, but a couple of days later one of Berlusconi's TV channels (Canale 5) surreptitiously filmed the judge during his leisure time in Milan. The judge's behaviour during this time was absolutely unexceptional – he had an appointment at the barber, for which he arrived a little early, and paced up and down in the street smoking until it was his turn. He was then filmed having a shave and haircut at the barber, after which he sat on a park bench and smoked another cigarette. Yet the commentary made his behaviour seem odd, saying that he was pacing "up and down, up and down… he's impatient, he can't stand still…he stops, lights a cigarette and then…up and down again. Perhaps he doesn't yet know that he's been promoted….Here's another strange thing, but we're now used to his extravagant behaviour, look at him sitting on the bench. Blue shirt and trousers, white moccasins and purple socks. He's not used to showing *those* off in court". This was followed by an interview with a journalist from *Il Giornale*, the Berlusconi family newspaper, alleging that the judge had been seen in a restaurant raising a toast when a television programme spoke about Berlusconi's resignation.

It is worth stepping back and reviewing what we have here. The television programme is clearly trying to undermine the authority and image of the judiciary, even though it has been unable to find any clear evidence either of wrongdoing or of any odd behaviour. The reason why the television programme is seeking to discredit the judiciary is because the owner of the television company, who escaped punishment despite having corrupted a judge, has been ordered to make amends to the organisation which suffered as a result of his crime. And the owner of the television programme, and the owner (in substance if not in name) of the newspaper whose employee attacks the judge is not only guilty of a severe offence against justice, but is also the prime minister.

Those who wished to show solidarity with Judge Mesiano for a time wore purple socks, and it may be for this reason that purple later became the colour associated with a nationwide movement of protest against the government, organised by individuals unconnected with any political party, using Facebook as a mechanism for organising demonstrations.

The Image of the Sex Scandals on TG1

Having seen how Berlusconi's media attack those who criticise him, we turn to considering how they treat his own behaviour. In October 2009 the newspaper *Il Fatto* usefully summarised the way in which the events, and especially the sex scandals, of the summer had been reflected in the most widely viewed television news programme, and the account that follows draws on this.

On the 17th June 2009, the first news about parties with escorts at Palazzo Grazioli had emerged in the *Corriere della Sera*. In most countries, this would have been the opening story in TV news programmes, but that evening on television, the third headline on TG1, the principal news programme put out by the public television RAI, the evening news was: "Investigation into health contracts in Bari: Berlusconi says 'it's rubbish, and I won't be influenced by it'". Ten minutes into the news programme, the announcer spoke to camera to elaborate on this enigmatic headline: "Once again newspapers are being filled up with rubbish and lies, but I won't be influenced by this aggression and will go on working for the good of the country. These were the words of Berlusconi after the leaks appearing in the *Corriere* concerning suspicions linked to an investigation by Bari magistrates." A reporter then said that "this is one of many investigations into health contracts, a normal matter in Italian life. But this affair in Puglia is linked to the shock revelation by D'Alema … Interceptions talk about parties that are said to have been organised at Villa Certosa and Palazzo Grazioli. All of this has yet to be verified, and could be fantasy or something else. The investigation is headed by Giuseppe Scelsi, a member of Democratic Magistrates. But the explosive thing about it is how Massimo D'Alema came to be in possession of this information".

Some familiar tactics can be seen in this short report. First, the news that the magistrate belongs to a particular grouping of magistrates who are more vocal in their defence of the independence of the judiciary carries an insinuation that the magistrate is biased against Berlusconi. Secondly, the highlight is placed, not on the allegations of libidinous goings-on in the prime minister's residences, but on the secondary matter of how this information came to be in the public domain. But the most striking thing is what is missing altogether, namely exactly what was alleged to have happened at these parties: the use by the prime minister, albeit apparently unknowingly, of escorts paid (by others, not by him) for their sexual services.

On June 19th, the day on which Niccolò Ghedini made his statement about the prime minister being only the "end-user" of the escort, the third headline on the lunchtime news programme was "Political clash after the Bari investigation", and, eleven minutes into the broadcast, the reporter says "it's all political" and refers to the "thread of the investigation concerning girls' participation at some of the prime minister's parties." The report mentioned a statement by an opposition programme to the effect that Berlusconi ought to answer the questions posed in a newspaper, but did not specify what the questions were. The comments about the "end-user" were absent from the report. By the evening news, the story had been dropped from the headlines, but the news carried a reference to "the thread of the investigations concerning the alleged hiring of girls to get close to powerful men by participating in parties, including some at Villa Certosa and Palazzo Grazioli".

By June 22nd, the failure of TG1 to provide any clarification of the scandals was itself becoming an item of news. The editor of the channel, Augusto Minzolini, whose views had changed drastically since the quotation that we placed at the start of the preceding Chapter, appeared in order to say that "our prudent point of view concerning the latest gossip or tittle-tattle is easily explained. In this story, which is full of insinuations, witnesses who are more or less reliable, and personal vendettas, there is as yet no definite news, still less any hint of a crime that concerns the prime minister or his colleagues". The implication that no story concerning the prime minister was worth mentioning unless it contained a hint of a crime was curious, and Minzolini was subsequently to be reproved by his supervisors for suppressing the news to this extent.

On June 25th, the main headline was Berlusconi saying "they only talk rubbish about me, the Italians like me the way I am". However, since the reports had only spoken about the investigations in Bari, and not about the use of escorts, few of the listeners can have been clear about exactly what way Berlusconi was. Later in the programme, it was announced that Nichi Vendola, the governor of Puglia, had been told to appear at the court, as someone in command of the facts. Tarantini was mentioned as someone who organised a merry-go-round of parties and girls, but no mention was made of Berlusconi. During that night, somebody had burnt the car of Barbara Montereale, one of the girls who had accompanied Patrizia D'Addario to the party in Rome, and who had spoken about the

CHAPTER 8: IMAGE AND REALITY IN BERLUSCONI'S ITALY

events. The news programme said this event was "probably linked to her rowdy past, and definitely not to current events".

On July 6th the newsreader starts without any preamble: "'The display of irresponsible and shameless libertinism that we are seeing shouldn't lead us to dismiss it as a merely private matter, especially if juveniles are involved'. These were the words of the head of the bishops' council at a celebration dedicated to Santa Maria Goretti". That was the end of the item, without any elaboration of what the bishop might have been referring to, which was clearly Berlusconi's private life.

On July 20th *L'Espresso* published some of the recordings made by D'Addario on her mobile phone, some of which we transcribed above. There was no mention of this on the news programme.

On July 22nd, Berlusconi is shown saying "I am not a saint, and I hope even *La Repubblica* will understand this", and ministers are shown laughing at the remark. The subtitle reads: "Berlusconi crisis: the worst is over", though the nature of this crisis has never been explained to listeners.

On August 25th TG1 reported Berlusconi's decision to sue *La Repubblica* for repeatedly posing its ten questions, and gave comments by the editor of *La Repubblica*, though at no point had viewers been told what the ten questions were. This was also the day on which *Il Giornale* mounted its attack on Dino Boffo, but this wasn't mentioned. The evening news said that Berlusconi dissociated himself from the article in *Il Giornale*, but didn't say what the article was about.

On September 15th, a prime time slot was given to a lengthy programme about Berlusconi handing over the keys of the first houses that had been reconstructed for victims of the Abruzzo earthquake. Competing shows on other channels were moved to other slots, though this didn't prevent most viewers from choosing whatever else was on offer.

It should be noted that this obfuscation was not on one of the channels directly controlled by Berlusconi, but on the principal public service channel. Some take the view that broadcasters on Berlusconi's own channels know very clearly where the line is drawn between criticism that is permitted and what is not, and therefore can go right up to that line, while those employed by RAI are less certain and therefore more wary of overstepping that mark. Berlusconi himself has always said that his own channels are fearless in their criticism of him, and it is certainly true that an excess of servility on their part would be counterproductive, since it would make the conflict of interest so flagrant that it could not continue to be ignored.

It is not the case that Berlusconi's channels act as a source of pro-Berlusconi propaganda, in any direct way. Opinions on political matters that are opposed to those of Berlusconi can be heard on them, and there is even to a limited extent some satire on Berlusconi himself. However, his power as owner of those channels gives him great clout with advertisers and with those forming public opinion. And his channels will never give space to matters that directly cast doubt on his innocence in any of his legal cases, or show up the conflicts of interest which they symbolise.

A further attempt to put a favourable gloss on Berlusconi's sex scandals was attempted in February 2010, when his magazine *Panorama* published a story alleging that Patrizia D'Addario was part of a plot to destabilise the government, and that she had amassed considerable wealth as a result of taking part in this plot. One cannot improve on Marco Travaglio's comments on this: "Just imagine, they surreptitiously infiltrated her into the big bed donated by Putin, and there was poor old Berlusconi that evening, as always, with his tartan rug on his knees, playing beggar-my-neighbour with Bondi, Cicchitto and Capezzone, who are letting him win to keep the old boy happy, with a cup of camomile tea in front of him, when in she bursts and rapes him in front of everybody while he shouts 'no, I don't want to, I don't do this kind of thing, save me Veronica'. But it's no good, unfortunately the Mata Hari wins out."[97]

After the Ruby affair became public, Berlusconi's response was to flood the media with messages putting his side of the case. The Osservatore di Pavia, a media research institute, measured that in January 2011 he appeared in RAI news programmes for a total of six hours and 40 minutes. The total for all other political leaders put together was just half of this.

Another sex scandal

It is instructive to make a comparison between the impact on public life and public perception of Berlusconi's private life, and that of another scandal that broke a couple of months later. In July 2009 three policemen illegally broke into an apartment belonging to a transvestite called Natalì, and found there the governor of Lazio, Piero Marrazzo, a member of the opposition PD. They took 13 minutes of compromising video. Marrazzo gave them some money and some cheques, pleading with them not to ruin his political career. They didn't cash the cheques, but after leaving

CHAPTER 8: IMAGE AND REALITY IN BERLUSCONI'S ITALY

began to seek a buyer for the video. Their first offer was to Vittorio Feltri, then still in charge of *Libero*. He sent two journalists to look it over, but decided not to buy. However, he of course knew the content of the video, and that it was the result of an illegal break-in.

The burglars then contacted a photo agency, who contacted a weekly magazine called *Oggi*, belonging to the company that also publishes the *Corriere della Sera*. In early September, one of their journalists saw the video, but decided not to publish. By this time rumours had begun to circulate, apparently emanating from sources close to the government, that a compromising video was making the rounds. In early October, the video was sent to Alfonso Signorini, editor of the gossip magazine *Chi* belonging to Berlusconi's group. He immediately declined it, but passed it to his publisher, Marina Berlusconi, head of Mondadori. Unless Feltri had alerted him earlier, it was presumably at this time that Marina's father Silvio first came to know that this illegal video was being sold.

Signorini suggested to the photo agency that was trying to raise money from the video that they might like to try *Libero* again, since it was less compromising if the material was published by someone who was not part of Berlusconi's group. Feltri had by then left *Libero*, and been replaced by Maurizio Belpietro. The photo agency later testified that a deal was reached with *Libero* to sell the video for €100,000. Later, Signorini contacted the agency again, to say that *Panorama*, another of Berlusconi's weeklies, might be interested in buying the video.

On October 19th, Berlusconi telephoned Marrazzo to say that he had seen the video, and to reassure him that it wouldn't be published by any of his journals. He gave Marazzo the phone number of the agency that was selling the video, and seems to have suggested that Marrazzo himself should buy it to take it out of circulation. By this time, the police themselves had got wind of what was going on, and that some corrupt members of their own force had been involved; it is not clear whether at this time Berlusconi knew of this. Signorini then called the agency to say that Marrazzo himself would be in touch with them – presumably Berlusconi had told him of the advice he had given. Marrazzo did indeed try to buy back the video, but by then the police were on the trail, and had arrested their colleagues who had committed the original break-in. They could not allow the evidence to be destroyed, so the existence of the videotape became known. Marrazzo then resigned.

That is the first difference between the Marrazzo affair and the Berlusconi affair. Marrazzo resigned, Berlusconi did not. Of course, there is another difference, which would have struck the public very strongly, and in their view would probably have justified the first difference: Marrazzo was having "deviant" sex, Berlusconi was having normal sex.

A further curiosity is that, although it was apparent that the video was the fruit of an unauthorised break-in, the idea of alerting the police does not seem to have occurred to any of the journals that were contacted, nor to either Marina or Silvio Berlusconi. This contrasts with what had happened when Antonio Zappadu had tried to sell photographs of Berlusconi's villa in Sardinia. On that occasion buyers had led him on, pretending to be interested, but had at the same time denounced him to the authorities for violation of privacy.

The Corruption of Others

A difficult problem of image management occurred in February 2010, when evidence emerged, mainly in the form of intercepted telephone conversations, that seemed to suggest widespread corruption and nepotism centred in the Civil Protection Agency. This was the agency that had dealt with the Abruzzo earthquake the previous year, as well as the Naples rubbish crisis, and was also responsible for preparing events such as the G8 summit of 2009 and the celebration of 150 years of Italian unity in 2011. It had been given widespread powers, and, although its head, Guido Bertolaso, had served under many previous governments, he was held up as an example of Berlusconi's ideal of a *governo del fare* – a government that gets things done. Indeed, a few days before the corruption scandal emerged, Berlusconi had been planning to raise him to the rank of Minister.

Once it did emerge, Berlusconi's immediate reaction was to hold this up as yet another example of magistrates officiously interfering in matters that were none of their concern, probably with the aim of causing personal embarrassment to himself. He said that the magistrates responsible for the investigation should be ashamed of themselves. He rejected the resignations of those concerned – clearly the idea of people resigning when their honesty was called into question would have set a most unwelcome precedent.

As the evidence accumulated, a disturbing possibility emerged: the public's concern about corruption, which had exploded in 1992 and unleashed the wave that he had ridden to power, might once again awaken from the slumbers that he had so carefully induced. It therefore became necessary to announce that the penalties for corruption would be made harsher. At the same time, the law that would have made it much more difficult to authorise telephone interceptions, and an offence to publish them until the court hearings were complete, was put back onto the front burner (from which it had been removed by the need to push forward other legal reforms aimed at securing his impunity). While the penalties for corruption were to be increased, the chances of getting caught at it were to be reduced. In this case, as in so many others, the response was: what must be changed is the image, and not the reality that is being represented.

When the *Corte di Cassazione* confirmed that David Mills had been corrupted, and sentenced him to pay a fine of €250,000, while timing-out the remainder of his punishment, TG1 referred to the matter as his "acquittal", seeking to prevent the growing anti-corruption sentiment from infecting the Berlusconi government.

The Party of Love

The rhetoric coming from Berlusconi and his supporters in the autumn of 2009 was building up to a height of vitriolic intensity, in the aftermath of the public shame of the sex scandals, and of the threat posed by the Constitutional Court to the all-important goal of securing impunity for Berlusconi. In addition to the attacks on Boffo, Fini and the judge Mesiano, the tiny Minister for Public Administration, Renato Brunetta, said at a party conference in September that the "shit elite is preparing a coup d'état...the good part of the left should recover its ideals, and the bad part should be murdered"[98]. A few days earlier he had said that magistrates needed their heads examined. The President of the Senate, Renato Schifani, had said that the Milan courts were "the headquarters of the Italian Taliban fighting against democracy".

This wildly aggressive rhetoric was employed again and again by Berlusconi, and reached a culmination when he made, on November 26th, the ridiculous and irresponsible statement that the legal establishment was "a subversive force which was threatening the life of the government, and had brought the country to the brink of a civil war".[99] The following day, the party machinery sought to deny that he had said this, but the damage had been done.

A few days after this, a man with a long history of mental illness attacked Berlusconi after a public meeting in Milan by throwing a marble model of Milan cathedral at him, causing wounds to the face and teeth (thus bringing him into contact with the dental hygienist Nicole Minetti, who was soon to become an elected politician, and soon afterwards to be indicted on prostitution charges). While there was no evidence that the attacker belonged to any political party, or was attached to any political faction, there were repeated attempts to place the blame for this deed at the feet of those critical of the government. The Berlusconi family newspaper carried an article headed "Who cries 'tyrant' is legitimising tyrannicide", which said that "whoever describes Berlusconi's government as tyrannical or fascist takes on himself the moral responsibility for the aggression inflicted on Berlusconi and for any future such attacks".[100] (It is worth recalling that in 1998 Berlusconi had said "Prodi is a dictator, he is like Mussolini").

These attitudes were widely shared in the press and on television, so that the attack ended up as a public opinion bonus for Berlusconi – all the more so since, a few days later, a Swiss woman jostled the pope and knocked him over, thus enabling the attack on Berlusconi to be seen as part of a general assault on those representing order and decency. Following the attack, Berlusconi said that he represented the "party of love", in opposition to the forces of hatred. The earlier aggressive rhetoric was to be forgotten. Forgotten too, were earlier episodes, such as the occasion during the last Prodi government when a representation of Prodi's coffin had been carried in a demonstration. Berlusconi announced that he had forgiven his attacker, while at the same time making it clear that he felt that magistrates should give him a punitive sentence for his crime.

The Internet

Within the mainstream media, doubts about Berlusconi's fitness for his political tasks are aired only to a limited extent. To some extent this changed in mid-2009, with the launch of a new daily paper, *Il Fatto Quotidiano*, under the aegis of Marco Travaglio, who had started his journalistic career under Montanelli, and Antonio Padellaro, who had been editor of the left-wing *L'Unità*. The paper attracts very little advertising, and is unique in refusing to accept the public money provided by the state to other newspapers. Despite the lack of money, it has attracted sufficient readers to keep it going, and has recently launched a successful website, www.ilfattoquotidiano.it.

Before its launch, much of the opposition to Berlusconi was exiled to the internet, on sites such as Beppe Grillo's (www.beppegrillo.it), one of the most visited of all internet sites, which features a 30-minute webcast by

CHAPTER 8: IMAGE AND REALITY IN BERLUSCONI'S ITALY

Marco Travaglio each Monday. Antonio Di Pietro's website, www.antoniodipietro.it, also normally carries these webcasts, and in addition is unique in covering trials of political interest, such as the Dell'Utri appeal and the Mills trials.

Many internet sites covered Berlusconi's gaffes, and here, too, could be found such gems as Dario Fo's imitation of a Berlusconi speech (search for "Dario Fo imita Berlusconi" and skip the first 45 seconds), and Roberto Benigni's song "When I think of Berlusconi". The former is untranslatable, but the latter deserves translation into English. It can be seen by searching for "Roberto Benigni canta L'Italia".

Ah che bellezza essere Italiano	It's great to be Italian
Ai tempi nostri e quelli di Ben-Hur,	Now, as in the days of Ben-Hur,
Colombo, Dante, Cesare, Tiziano,	Columbus, Dante, Caesar, Titian,
E Camillo Benso Conte di Cavour.	And Camillo Benso Count Cavour.
Sorseggio un cappuccino e ci beo	I sip a cappuccino and as I drink
Pensando a Garibaldi, Galileo,	I think of Garibaldi, Galileo,
E mi sento il corpo turgido, gagliardo,	And I feel my body getting firm and cocky,
Se penso che discendo da Leonardo.	If I think that I'm descended from Leonardo [da Vinci]
Penso a Coppi sul Tonale	I think of Coppi [a cycling hero]
E mi sale su il morale	And my morale rises,
E mi sale una erezione	And up comes an erection
Quando penso a Cicerone...	When I think of Cicero...
Ma poi penso a Berlusconi	But then I think of Berlusconi
E mi si sgonfiano i coglioni	And my genitals deflate,
Mi si sgonfiano le palle	My balls shrivel up
E non so più dove cercarle	And I can't seem to find them any more.
Quando penso a quel biscione	When I think of the serpent [symbol of Mediaset]
Mi s'abbassa la pressione	The pressure falls
E l'apparato genitale	And my genital apparatus
C'ha un colasso verticale...	Collapses vertically...
Ogni cosa mi va giù	Everything goes down
E non si rizza più.	And won't stand up again.

The government's reaction to the internet as a source of news and opinion is doubly hostile, both because it threatens the Berlusconi businesses and because it does not impose the self-censorship which affects most television and press reporting. In 2008, a Sicilian blogger named Carlo Ruta was prosecuted and his site shut down on the grounds that he had not gone through the procedures of registering his website as a newspaper. He was convicted of the crime of "clandestine publication", using legislation that was designed for the pre-internet age.

Later, more specific attempts were made to control the expression of opinion on the internet. A law was drafted obliging any internet site that makes a statement that damages a person's reputation to publish, within 48 hours, any response which that person may choose to make – regardless of whether or not the original statement is true.

Copyright issues relating to the internet are a matter of genuine concern, but it is no surprise that the Berlusconi government has tried to take a very hard line to prevent You-Tube putting up clips taken from Mediaset programmes. Mediaset is suing Google (the owner of You-Tube) for half a billion dollars. In addition the Italian government is the only Western democracy which, from February, will require anyone who regularly wishes to put live streaming transmissions on the internet to seek Ministerial permission. One of the leaked cables from the US Ambassador in Italy expressed concern about Berlusconi's attempts to censor the internet.

The Italian government has also legislated to require internet service providers to prevent their clients visiting sites where files can be illegally copied. Some Google executives were convicted and given a suspended sentence after a tasteless video clip mocking a mentally-ill boy had been put up on You-Tube. Google had taken it down as soon as it had been reported, but was still held responsible. (Google said that this was like suing the Post Office when it delivers an offensive letter). It remains to be seen whether these attempts to tame the internet in ways normally associated with countries like China and Iran will succeed. But what they certainly demonstrate is that, when the internet increases individuals' power of self-expression, Berlusconi's reaction is to seek to use the power of the State to exercise control.

CHAPTER 9:
DEMOCRACY OR THE RULE OF LAW

In his conflicts with the judiciary, Berlusconi poses a fundamental problem about democracy: if the leader of a country has been elected by the will of the people, is it permissible for that leader to be prevented from governing by the judiciary? There are two ways in which the judiciary might prevent him from governing: if he has been found guilty of a crime which demands a prison sentence, then he clearly cannot continue to exercise his functions from within a place of detention. Alternatively – and this is the issue that Berlusconi particularly likes to bring up – the amount of time required to defend himself might prevent him from governing effectively. "It is strange that a leader elected by 11 million votes should have to be bound by the dictates of the courts".[101] This statement was not in fact made by Berlusconi, but by Thaksin Shinawatra, the ex-Prime Minister of Thailand, currently in exile after being convicted of conflicts of interest (in Thailand, in contrast to Italy, they seem to have a functioning law about this). But it expresses very clearly Berlusconi's point of view.

There are two ways of looking at this issue, one that concentrates (perhaps too much) on the formal constitutional position, and one that deals with the fundamental clash of values. To start with the first argument: formally, Italian voters did not elect Silvio Berlusconi to be head of government. Italy is a parliamentary democracy, and is not governed by a President elected directly by the people. What Italians were voting for in 2008, as in any other year, were the individuals who were to represent them in the two houses of parliament. The prime minister, who effectively governs the country, is selected by the President as being an individual able to command a majority in Parliament, and is thus normally the leader of the winning coalition. Should he for some reason – health, for example, or a jail sentence – be unable to continue governing, the President is obliged to invite someone else who can command a majority in Parliament, or, if no such person can be found, to call an election. The President himself is not directly elected, but selected by Parliament. His role is limited to that of guarding the Constitution, holding the ring, and seeing that the rules are adhered to. He is normally a senior politician commanding respect from all major parties. If he considers a bill to be unconstitutional, he may refer it back to Parliament for further consideration.

At this point, it is necessary to make a digression in order to explain how Italy's complicated electoral system works. Those who feel that the formal position is irrelevant, and that the reality is that the Italian people were in practice voting to be governed by Silvio Berlusconi, may wish to skip this section.

Italy's Electoral System

Even before the corruption scandals of the early 1990s, many Italians were unhappy with the fluctuating and unstable coalitions that emerged from the proportional representation system in operation until then. In 1991 Mario Segni, a Christian Democrat who was to be untainted by the corruption scandals, had successfully promoted a referendum that reduced the number of preferences on the ballot from four to one, thus giving the electors more say, and party managers less, in the choice of members of parliament. (Segni himself was for a time considered to be the best candidate to govern after the corruption scandal, and when Berlusconi decided to enter politics, one of the options that he considered was to throw his company's weight behind Segni. In the event Segni effectively disappeared from the scene – some said he was as if he had picked the winning lottery ticket and then lost it).

Further changes were made in 1993, and led to what is known as an Additional Member System. 75% of parliamentary seats were allocated by direct single-member ("first past the post") election, and the remaining 25% by proportional representation, with the proviso that parties with less than 4% of the vote were excluded.

The new system did succeed in providing an incentive for the mass of small political parties in Italy to group themselves together into coalitions, and since 1993 there has been an alteration between a centre-left coalition and a Berlusconi coalition at each election. However, there is no guarantee of the cohesion of the coalition after the election, as Berlusconi found to his cost in 1994, and the centre-left has found to its cost each time it has governed.

The system was revised towards the end of Berlusconi's 2001-2006 term of office – it was becoming clear that he was headed for defeat, and he

CHAPTER 9: DEMOCRACY OR THE RULE OF LAW

sought to modify the system so as to prevent this defeat, or at least to make it harder for the centre-left to govern if it did succeed. In fairness, it must be added that the previous system was not working well, and was in need of revision, even though it would have been better to make that revision on a less partisan basis. The revised system was devised by Roberto Calderoli, a member of the Northern League, who himself described his revision as a *porcata*, or cock-up, and it has since been known as the *porcellum* system.

The new system is a proportional representation system, but with a premium for whichever party or coalition has the plurality of votes. Coalitions have an official status under the law; to qualify as such, a coalition must present a programme that has been signed by all of the parties within it. Electors vote for lists of candidates associated with parties, and seats are allocated proportionally to those parties. The parties may or may not form part of a coalition, and the party or coalition that has the most votes is assured at least 55% of the seats in the lower house of parliament. If the result of the proportional count itself gives it more than 55% of the seats, then no further changes are made. If not, then the number of seats allocated to the ruling coalition in the lower house is automatically increased to 55% of the total, with the parties within the coalition benefiting proportionately. If there are any parties within a coalition that fail to obtain at least 2% of the total vote, then only the one of these parties that gets the most votes (the "top loser") counts in the distribution of the proportional vote. Any parties outside a coalition must reach 4% of the total vote in order to qualify. A similar system applies to the Senate, except that the threshold for small parties in coalitions was 4%, and the apportionment of the "premium" seats is done on a regional, not a national basis.

"First-past-the-post" seats, which existed under the old system, were abolished in 2005, and this gives the parties' central offices a much greater say in deciding who will be a member of parliament, and the regional representatives much less say. The voter is no longer choosing a specific individual to represent him, and therefore has less reason to care about the personal qualities of the members of parliament. Equally, the members of parliament are devalued, since they know that they are there simply to represent the party that chose them, and have no validation from the electorate that is independent of their party (as, for example, an American Senator or Congressman, or a British Member of Parliament has). One member of Parliament, normally a keen Berlusconi supporter, said that "the sense of futility is so great that the work of a parliamentarian is mortifying."[102]

IMPUNITY BERLUSCONI'S GOAL AND ITS CONSEQUENCES

The absence of first-past-the-post seats benefits Forza Italia (now the PDL), since the party still carries the traces of its origins as a "top-down" party, and has less local rooting and organisation than other parties. In addition, the new system penalises coalitions with many small parties, which was characteristic of the centre-left. It has often been observed in Italy that voters tend to prefer the programmes presented by parties of the right, but the individuals nominated by parties of the left. By downplaying the importance of the individual members of parliament, the new system thus benefited the right. The new electoral system also provided for separate representation for Italians resident abroad. All of these factors were thought to favour Berlusconi's coalition, though in practice the results of the 2006 and 2008 elections are unlikely to have been much different under any other system.

While formally Italy remains a parliamentary democracy, the role of parliament has been radically downgraded, both as a result of the electoral system, and of the style of government favoured by Berlusconi. Under the previous Prodi government, Berlusconi had sharply criticised the use of "decree laws" which bypassed parliamentary discussion, as well as criticising the use of votes of confidence to ensure that controversial measures were passed by Parliament. In August 2006, when the Prodi government introduced a decree law with a vote of confidence, Berlusconi had said that this way of governing "introduces a sort of police state...it is a dangerous and alarming development which risks undermining parliament". Under his own government, the techniques that he then criticised so trenchantly have become almost standard. In his first year in office, there were 10 votes of confidence, while in Prodi's first year, when Prodi's majority was much slimmer, there were only 8. Berlusconi introduced 31 decree laws in his first year, Prodi only 17.

It has been left to Gianfranco Fini, as speaker of the lower house, to protest at the increasingly marginal role played by Parliament. Berlusconi himself seldom makes an appearance. The logical conclusion was reached in October 2009, when parliament, having nothing to do, was effectively given a short holiday. On average, the lower house is currently working only 18 hours per week, the Senate less than half that.[103] Despite this, Italian members of parliament are, as David Gilmour notes: "the best-paid in the world, earning over twice as much as their counterparts in France, and three times that of deputies in the Swedish Riksdag. They are driven around in chauffeured cars and often live in suites in Rome's smartest hotels; perks include free haircuts, free cellphones, subsidized meals and life pensions after spending only a few years in Parliament".[104]

CHAPTER 9: DEMOCRACY OR THE RULE OF LAW

The purely decorative function expected of members of parliament was illustrated at one of the few occasions in 2008 when Berlusconi attended a parliamentary session. He passed a note down to two women MPs in his party who who were also there, saying "Gabri, Nunziata, you look great together! Thanks for staying, but there's really no need. If some handsome guy invites you to lunch I authorise you to go. Lots of kisses to both!" They replied "Dear prime minister, you are the only handsome guy we want to accept invitations from. And it's a pleasure for us to be here"[105].

The move to the 2005 electoral system was a step towards a more presidential style of politics, and Berlusconi has made it clear that he would like to reform the constitution so as to formalise this change – in November 2009 he formally advanced this idea[106]. His election campaigns have always put the focus on his own personality – for example, Forza Italia specifies that candidates' publicity material must contain Berlusconi's photograph, and not the photograph of the candidate. Given this, it seems a little pedantic to say that it is parliament, rather than Berlusconi himself as the leader of the winning coalition, that carries the legitimacy of democratic approval.

The Fundamental Issue: Will of People versus Rule of Law

We must therefore confront the fundamental problem: which is more important – the will of the electorate or the rule of law? Is it, as Berlusconi claims, "subversive" for judges to seek to indict him of crimes? Are those judges attempting to carry out a coup d'état, as he has also claimed? This is a venerable debate in political theory. Indeed, before it was accepted that the wishes of the electorate should carry weight, in the days when monarchy was seen as the source of legitimacy, the same debate was carried on in different terms: should the rule of law be allowed to trump the wishes of the monarch?

In his essay "On Liberty" John Stuart Mill rehearses Berlusconi's argument:

> As the struggle proceeded for making the ruling power emanate from the periodical choice of the ruled, some persons began to think that too much importance had been attached to the limitation of the power itself. *That* (it might seem) was a resource against rulers whose interests were habitually opposed to those of the people. What was now wanted was, that the rulers should be identified with the people; that their interest and will should be

the interest and will of the nation. The nation did not need to be protected against its own will. There was no fear of its tyrannizing over itself. Let the rulers be effectually responsible to it, promptly removable by it, and it could afford to trust them with power of which it could itself dictate the use to be made. Their power was but the nation's own power, concentrated, and in a form convenient for exercise. This mode of thought, or rather perhaps of feeling, was common among the last generation of European liberalism, in the Continental section of which it still apparently predominates....

Having rehearsed Berlusconi's argument, Mill then demolishes it:

The notion, that the people have no need to limit their power over themselves might seem axiomatic, when popular government was a thing only dreamed about. [But when it came to be established in practice] it was now perceived that such phrases as 'self-government' and 'the power of the people over themselves' do not express the true state of the case. The 'people' who exercise power are not always the same people with those over whom it is exercised; and the 'self-government' that is spoken of is not the government of each by himself, but of each by all the rest. The will of the people, moreover, practically means the will of the most numerous or more active *part* of the people; the majority, or those who succeed in making themselves accepted as the majority; the people, consequently, *may* desire to oppress a part of their number; and precautions are as much needed against this as against any other abuse of power. The limitation, therefore, of the power of government over individuals loses none of its importance when the holders of power are regularly accountable to the community.

The rule of law requires that people within society should conform to general legislation, rather than to arbitrary or *ad hominem* decrees. The two uses of the word "law", the scientific and the juridical, have this in common: they rule out the arbitrary and require regularity and predictability. The principle that "Be you never so high, the law is above you" is an integral part of what it meant by the rule of law: as Tom Bingham says in his book on the subject, "all must be subject to the same laws administered in the same courts"[107]. In most societies, political development was oriented first to limiting the arbitrary powers of monarchs by instituting the rule of law. Bingham also quotes John Locke: "Wherever law ends, tyranny begins" and Tom Paine: "As in absolute government the King is Law, so in free countries the law ought to be King, and there ought to be no other". Only later did the battle switch from limiting the powers of monarchs to substituting them by the power of elected authorities. Once the second goal had been achieved, as Mill makes clear above, there was no wish to go back and dismantle the rule of law, since elected authorities were seen as being equally prone to govern arbitrarily. The rule of law is about *how* governments should govern; democracy is about *who* should govern.

To grant immunity to democratically elected representatives creates a danger of which Mill was well aware, and which resonates strongly in Italy today:

> The moment a man, or a class of men, find themselves with power in their hands, the man's individual interest, or the class's separate interest, acquires an entirely new degree of importance in their eyes. Finding themselves worshipped by others, they become worshippers of themselves, and think themselves entitled to be counted at a hundred times the value of other people...This is the meaning of the universal tradition, grounded on universal experience, of men's being corrupted by power.[108]

To maintain that the "will of the people" should have priority over the rule of law is a dangerous course, particularly in divided societies where the will of the majority may involve inflicting all kinds of damage on a specific minority (I am not suggesting that this applies to Italy, though the situation of immigrants within Italy is certainly at some risk). If one were to accept that the wishes of the majority should be the sole criterion for the choice of leader, and that no manner of wrongdoing by the chosen person should make that person subject to judicial restraint, then one would have abolished controls not only on *who* governs, but on *how* that person governs. Few would be comfortable with that.

This is not the place to review the mass of political theory that bears on this topic; our only present concern is to suggest that, whatever apparent plausibility there might seem to be in Berlusconi's claim that judges should leave him alone because he was elected by the people, a little thought will show that to accept that claim is to open the floodgates to arbitrary and authoritarian rule, and to throw away the labour of many generations that has been expended in securing those floodgates.

These considerations should also be borne in mind when considering Berlusconi's wish to change the constitution to allow direct election of the President of the Republic. Under the present constitution, the

President is agreed upon by parliament, and his function is essentially to make sure that the rules of the game are upheld. He can refer back legislation which he considers might be unconstitutional, but cannot propose legislation. His function corresponds much more closely with that held by the German President, rather than that of the French, let alone the American President.

There is, of course, nothing wrong with a system in which a President is directly elected. But any such system must have some other body to make sure that the rules and the constitution are upheld – for example the Supreme Court in the USA. A player in the political game cannot at the same time be a referee of the political game. Yet it is apparent that this is exactly what Berlusconi intends. He is intolerant of any third party having a voice, independent of his own, and potentially in opposition to his own, about any matter connected with the rules of political as well as judicial procedures. That is why, in this case, his suggestion that the President be directly elected should be regarded with extreme suspicion.

The President's Tough Decision

A very clear clash between the rule of law and the principles of democracy arose before the regional elections in March 2010. In the central region of Lazio (which includes Rome) Berlusconi's PDL failed to present its electoral list to the authorities before the required deadline. The party organiser, Alfredo Milioni, arrived with the lists shortly before the deadline, but before presenting the lists he left the office. His first story was that he had popped out to buy a sandwich; others have suggested that he may have wanted to make a last-minute change to the list. Later he said that he had gone out to check on his daughter, whom he had left in his car. Later still, he changed his story again to allege that he had been prevented from returning by representatives of the opposing party. Whatever the reason, he failed to return and present the papers within the deadline. His incompetence thus had the effect, if the rules were applied, of depriving all those who wished to vote for the PDL of the right to vote. A similar situation arose in Lombardy, where the list (which incidentally included Nicole Minetti) presented by the PDL's candidate Roberto Formigoni was found to lack the requisite number of valid signatures.

The PDL appealed to the body supervising the elections, but the appeals were rejected: there could be no doubt that the PDL had failed to comply with the qualifications set out in the legislation. It then complained that democracy was being undermined by an overzealously bureaucratic

CHAPTER 9: DEMOCRACY OR THE RULE OF LAW

interpretation of these rules. Representations were made to the President, Giorgio Napolitano, who thus had presented to him in the clearest possible way the dilemma discussed in this chapter: should he enforce the rule of law, or should he return to the voters the right to vote for the PDL, of which they had been deprived by its incompetent failure to comply with electoral rules?

It was a cruel dilemma. The President's role is to see that the rules of the game are adhered to by all parties. He is also the guardian of the Constitution – both of its letter and of its democratic spirit, which might be held to be violated if so many people were deprived of their right to vote, even if the reason for this deprivation lay clearly at the door of the party for which they wished to vote. There was a tense meeting at which Berlusconi threatened Napolitano with dire consequences if he refused to sign a decree that had been drafted by the government to "reinterpret" the electoral law so as to allow the excluded lists.

Napolitano insisted on some changes in the decree – though what these were is unclear. For obvious reasons, the Constitution explicitly forbids government decrees which have the effect of altering electoral procedures. The decree could not change the rules, but could only "interpret" them. The decree thus "interprets" the rule that lists of candidates must be submitted before the deadline as meaning that those who plan to present the list must have arrived at the offices at which they are to be presented before that deadline. In this interpretation the deadline has been met even if the person due to submit the list then pops out for a sandwich before doing so. Similarly, it declared that lists of signatures should be deemed to be valid despite "merely formal" problems, such as the lack of any legible indication (or indeed any indication at all) of the authority who provided the validation that is required.

The President decided to sign this decree, and thus to permit the candidacy of the PDL in both regions, although the decree was worded in such a way that it did not grant similar exemptions to other parties who were disqualified for similar reasons. (However, a closer scrutiny of the law showed that it was regional, not national, legislation that determined qualifications to vote in regional elections, so that the decree that had been rushed through was soon found to be irrelevant). Explaining his decree later, he said that the principle of legality and the principle of the right to vote were "equally valuable". To say that they are of equal value is nonsensical in a context in which the two unavoidably conflicted, and priority had to be given either to one or the other. In practice, his decision showed that he thought the second to be more valuable than the first. He said that it was intolerable that the largest party of government should not be allowed to be a candidate in the largest region in Italy, and in his view this was more important than rigidly respecting the electoral rules.

Napolitano's decision immediately provoked Antonio Di Pietro to call for his impeachment, since it clearly violated the letter of the law. The decision will be argued over by jurists and constitutional experts for years. It would perhaps have been the right decision if it had been taken within the context of an election in which all the parties were equally committed to the rule of law. But instead the context was one in which the party which benefited from Napolitano's decision had proposed many *ad hominem* laws, were continually undermining the magistracy, and were undermining, one by one, the checks and balances that prevent a democracy from becoming an elective dictatorship. In that context, his decision could only be seen as lending his support to this process of degrading the status of the law.

This so-called Save-the-List decree clearly showed its ad hoc nature, designed to save the ruling party from the consequences of its own incompetence, and led Marco Travaglio to propose a list of other decrees that might be passed in the future, including:

> "The Save-Flights decree: Whoever misses a train or plane may secure its immediate return to the boarding gate or station by declaring that he got to the airport or station in time but was delayed by a communist sandwich or a patrol of radicals.
>
> "The Save-Film decree: Anyone arriving at a cinema after the film has started may secure the return to the initial credits by declaring that he got to the neighbourhood in time, but couldn't find a parking space because of communist motorists.
>
> "The Save-the-Goal decree. A footballer scoring a goal while offside in the qualifying round of the Champions League may have the goal confirmed by declaring that he was delayed in the offside position in order to have a quick beer at the end of the field. This shall apply only to AC Milan, as it is intolerable that a team belonging to the leader of the largest political party in the government should be excluded from international competitions."

While the PDL list in Lombardy was eventually allowed by the tribunal, the list in Lazio was not. Although *Il Giornale* had initially protested against the incompetence of the PDL in this matter, it now became intolerable to the thin-skinned Berlusconi that he should suffer a political setback for which none of his opponents was to blame. The past had to be changed,

CHAPTER 9: DEMOCRACY OR THE RULE OF LAW

and he alleged that the whole event was the result of a carefully designed plot by the opposition. To regain the sympathy that he was losing, fears of an assassination plot were spoken of – there was said to be a bomb scare on his official plane, and his friend Gianni Letta said that the atmosphere was the same as it had been before the December 2009 attack with the model of Milan Cathedral.

Foreign Policy

One of the alarming aspects of Berlusconi's Italy is the nature of its alliances. During the Berlusconi years, foreign policy has emphasised improved relationships with countries whose democratic credentials are dubious. Two countries above all have received attention: Putin's Russia and Ghaddafy's Libya. (Their influence is apparent even in the sex scandals: the bed Berlusconi shared with D'Addario was a gift from Putin, while the idea of the "bunga-bunga" party was said to have come from Ghaddafy). The picture below, taken from the Observer newspaper, shows one of Ghaddafy's frequent visits to Rome. Rafael Behr of The Observer commented on the meeting as follows: "The two leaders enjoy, according to Berlusconi, 'a true and profound friendship'. In practical terms, that means, in exchange for billions of Euros of Italian investment, Libya has agreed to scoop migrants out of the Mediterranean before they

get to Europe. Trusting alliance shines through their cordial demeanours. Oh, wait, no. That's nose-wrinkling mutual distaste locked inside steely realpolitik. One of the two men is thinking: 'I'll take this swaggering, sleazy, tinpot clown to the cleaners the first chance I get'. And so is the other one."[109]

IMPUNITY   BERLUSCONI'S GOAL AND ITS CONSEQUENCES

There are two explanations for this choice of friends. The first relates to Italy's lack of energy resources. Perhaps more than any West European country except for Germany, Italy is highly reliant on imported oil, coal and gas. It therefore makes sense for its government to take care to avoid any unnecessary falling out with the countries on which it depends for these resources. Paolo Guzzanti has gone so far as to say that, for Berlusconi, energy has displaced property development and television as his main economic interest. When, in January 2011, Berlusconi announced that he was engaged, there was even speculation that the lady in question might be Ghaddafy's daughter. The Libyan uprising the following month soon put a stop to such speculation, and, despite the considerable amount of time that they had spent together, and the much-heralded friendship treaty that they had signed in 2008, Berlusconi was not slow to join the other political leaders calling on Ghaddafy to resign (receiving the response from Ghaddafy that, since Berlusconi had not resigned in the face of public demonstrations, why should he?)

If it is the hunt for energy resources that explains Berlusconi's choice of friends, this is a respectable pursuit of Italy's national interest, even if it often disturbs other Western democracies (the US, for example, has been very critical of Berlusconi's support for the Southstream gas pipeline, which has threatened to undercut the US' own attempts to develop gas resources which reduce reliance on Russia). However, this pursuit may not be entirely selfless. In a cable leaked by Wikileaks, the US Ambassador in Italy said that his contacts in the Italian government "believe that Berlusconi and his cronies are profiting handsomely from many of the energy deals between Italy and Russia", and adds that "The Georgian ambassador in Rome has told us that the government of Georgia believes Putin has promised Berlusconi a percentage of profits from any pipelines developed by Gazprom [the Russian energy giant]"[110].

The second explanation for the choice of foreign friends relates to the aversion of statesmen in other democratic countries to being seen in the company of Berlusconi. Because he is widely regarded outside Italy as at best a figure of fun, and at worst a criminal, it is difficult for him to entice respectable leaders to state visits.

Chancellor Angela Merkel, for example, is said to have given orders in the run-up to the German elections of 2009 to avoid any situation in which she might be photographed together with Berlusconi, since that would cost her votes[111]. Nicolas Sarkozy's wife Carla Bruni is known to be allergic to Berlusconi. Even Tony Blair, until now the politician who has risked the most (and perhaps paid the price) in terms of being seen with Berlusconi,

CHAPTER 9: DEMOCRACY OR THE RULE OF LAW

took care that his wife was interposed between himself and Berlusconi when they were photographed on holiday together. Barack Obama was one of the few senators who refrained from applauding when Berlusconi addressed the US senate, and when Silvio advanced on Michelle Obama with the apparent intention of folding her in an embrace, she offered instead a frosty handshake. The *Daily Mail* printed the picture below with a caption showing Berlusconi saying "Hey, how you doin'" and Obama saying "Don't even think about it Silvio".

But there is also a third reason, at once simpler and more sinister, for the focus of Berlusconi's international attentions. It is simply a case of like attracting like. Ghaddafy's wish to hang on to power at any price mirrors Berlusconi's. Russia and Italy show increasing similarities. In both, the market economy is heavily distorted by monopolies run by cronies of the ruler (or in the case of Italy, by the ruler himself). In both, opposition is increasingly marginalised by the mainstream media, though Italian critics mercifully do not yet run the risks taken by Russian journalists. The centralisation of power and the marginalisation of the rule of law in Russia correspond, if not to the realities of Italy, at least to the desires of its prime minister and to recent trends. When, on a recent visit to Russia, Berlusconi jokingly made the gesture of machine-gunning a journalist who asked a difficult question, the joke must have seemed to be in rather poor taste to anyone who had been a friend or admirer of the murdered journalist Anna Politkovskaya. What the slant of Italian foreign policy emphasises is how far Berlusconi's Italy is drifting away from the mainstream of democratic societies.

In early 2011, many of the assessments by US diplomats in Italy came to light as a result of the Wikileaks affair. It is worth quoting at length from Ambassador Spogli's final dispatch:

> Italian leaders' unwillingness and inability to address many of the chronic problems that plague their society - a non-competitive economic system, decaying infrastructure, rising debt, and endemic corruption - have caused concern among Italy's partners and given the impression of feckless and inefficient governance. PM Silvio Berlusconi has inadvertently come to symbolize this image. His frequent verbal gaffes and poor choice of words have offended nearly every demographic in Italy and many EU leaders. His perceived willingness to put personal interests above those of the state, his preference for short-term solutions over long-term investment, and his frequent use of public institutions and resources to gain electoral advantage over his political adversaries has harmed Italy's reputation in Europe and has provided an unfortunately comic tone to Italy's reputation in many quarters of the U.S. government.

This judgment is realistic, though it must be said that a thorough reading of the cables shows a much more positive assessment of Berlusconi's usefulness as an ally, along with a readiness to believe some of the myths that he propagates (for example, that his interventions in the rubbish crisis in Naples or the earthquake in L'Aquila were effective, or that Italian judges are often communists).

The deal with the Vatican

Berlusconi, like many people, would be shocked by the item that features third on Shelley's list of society's evils:

> Fear, Hatred, Faith, and Tyranny, who spread
> Those subtle nets which snare the living and the dead.[112]

The approval of the faithful and of the clergy is a powerful source of votes, and throughout his political career, Berlusconi has assiduously

CHAPTER 9: DEMOCRACY OR THE RULE OF LAW

wooed the Vatican. It is a source of personal distress to him that, because of his divorce from his first wife, he is ineligible to receive communion in church, and he has often sought to obtain a special dispensation against this provision. The thought of Silvio Berlusconi in church calls to mind the pious Beppa in Nietzsche's poem:

> Man lispelt mit dem Mündchen,   You murmur a little and then
> Man knixt und geht hinaus,   Bob your knee and quit the scene,
> Und mit dem neuen Sündchen   And with the next little sin
> Löscht man das alte aus.[113]   You wipe the last one clean.

If any pretentions to economic liberalism are constrained by the need to protect his businesses, any pretentions to social liberalism are constrained by the need to retain the approval of the Vatican. One of Berlusconi's closest friends and colleagues, Gianni Letta, has the particular task of fostering Berlusconi's relations with the Vatican (rather as his other close friend, Marcello Dell'Utri, has done in respect of another power group). Berlusconi's personal relations with John Paul II were never close, and Letta's mediation was important. However, it appears that things changed with the election of Cardinal Ratzinger. According to the priest Gianni Baget Bozzo, who was close to both Berlusconi and Ratzinger, "there is now a direct relationship between Berlusconi and the Pope: Ratzinger appreciates Berlusconi because he is not a Christian Democrat of the old style".[114] Berlusconi has tried to disarm Vatican criticism of his private life by openly declaring himself a "sinner".

When he was in opposition in 2006-2008, Berlusconi opposed legislation to extend some of the rights of married couples (in matters such as pensions and inheritance for example) to other civil unions, including those between homosexuals, in accordance with the Vatican's wishes. Following the juvenile prostitution scandal, Berlusconi was quick to reiterate that he would never permit gay marriages, in the hope of getting back some of the goodwill he might have lost with the Vatican.

On his return to power in 2008, the case of Eluana Englaro came up for a decision. This was a young woman who had entered a persistent vegetative state after a car accident in 1992, and whose family sought permission to have her feeding tube removed. After previous unsuccessful attempts, the Milan Court of Appeal finally gave its permission in July 2008. This decision was of course counter to the wishes of the Vatican, and in February 2009 Berlusconi issued a decree that would have forced her to continue to be treated. The President of the Republic, however, refused to sign the decree, and she died soon afterwards[115].

Berlusconi's government had another opportunity to come to the defence of the Vatican in April 2010. Pietro Forno, the Milan magistrate dealing with sexual crimes, gave an interview in *Il Giornale*[116] in which he said that, while the Church had never obstructed any investigation into sexual crimes such as paedophilia committed by priests, he had also noticed that, in the many years in which he had been investigating such cases, they had never been brought to his attention by bishops or priests. Instead it was usually family members who had raised concerns. Angelino Alfano, the Minister of Justice, immediately retaliated by saying that Forno's comments had been defamatory, and unleashing a formal investigation of Forno's office.

Important as these matters of policy are in securing the approval of the Vatican, the most efficacious Elixir of Love – money – has also been generously administered by Berlusconi's governments. In 2005, Berlusconi had a law passed which exempted all ecclesiastical buildings – whether places of worship, of residence, of administration, or of business (such as church-owned shops) – from paying any property tax. This exemption to the Church imposed an annual cost on other taxpayers of some €2.4 billion.[117]

A Not-so-Glaring Absence

No recent leader has polarised opinion to the extent that Berlusconi has. A recent programme on BBC television by Mark Franchetti, named "The Berlusconi Show", illustrated this well. A participant in an anti-Berlusconi demonstration told the interviewer that he came from a very poor and unprivileged background, yet all his relations voted for Berlusconi. When the interviewer asked why this was, he replied "Because they're all shits".

Yet this polarisation obscures the one thing that is missing in Italy – a party that reflects the concerns that are shared by most centre-right parties in Europe and beyond. The three over-riding concerns of such parties – the CDU in Germany for example, or the Conservative Party in Britain – are the rule of law, a well-functioning market economy, and a relatively low share of taxes and government spending in the economy.[xii] None of these figure in Berlusconi's priorities. After many years in which he has loudly complained that the legal system is unfairly biased

---

[xii] In 2010 Gianfranco Fini broke away from the PDL to attempt to found such a party, but has so far had little success, hampered both by his neo-fascist background and by the venality of the members of parliament who initially joined him, and then were later persuaded back into Berlusconi's fold.

against him, that magistrates who disagree with him are *toghe rosse*, that the constitutional court is packed with left-wingers, the rule of law is, for Berlusconi, not a dream but a threatening nightmare. He has said that he does not know of any right-wing magistrates – he distinguishes only two categories: "true" magistrates and "left-wing" magistrates[118], the former being those who take decisions that please him, the latter those who don't. In his rhetoric, "liberty" and "democracy" stand on one side, and "communism" on the other side. But it is increasingly clear that his real enemy is not communism, but legality, and it is that that he is seeking to dismantle, paradoxically in the name of liberty.

As for the market economy, certainly Berlusconi's rhetoric gives this an importance that matches the priority that other conservative parties accord to this goal. But the reality, as we have seen, is different. For Berlusconi, competition is not a desideratum that the government should seek to maximise, but a threat that his businesses must seek to contain, if necessary with help from the State. While there is much debate about conflict of interest, there has in reality been no such conflict – the needs of Fininvest have always been given priority. We have seen this clearly in the measures that the government has taken to try to put obstacles in the way of Sky TV, in the way that the threat to Rete Quattro was dealt with, in the gift of radio frequencies by the government to the prime minister's business, and in the way that, under the current Berlusconi government, advertising contracts for public service advertisements put out by the government have been switched away from other media (and particularly from newspapers) and towards Berlusconi's own TV channels.

Antitrust legislation and, what is more important, the way such legislation is implemented, have not promoted a well-functioning market economy – this is shown, for example, in the way the Alitalia affair was handled. It was not only taxpayers' money that was spent in support of a rash election pledge; it was also the interests of passengers, damaged by the government's decision to turn a blind eye to the malfunctioning of the market that was bound to occur when Alitalia and Air One ceased to compete.

A well-functioning market economy also requires clear and binding rules concerning financial reporting. The laxer attitude taken by the Italian government to false accounting – an attitude that was required by the imperative need to preserve Berlusconi's impunity – goes in exactly the opposite direction. A direct result of these rules has been the diminishing attraction of Italy for foreign investors. In its 2010 survey of investment, entitled "Doing Business", the World Bank ranked Italy 78th out of 183, far the lowest ranking for any developed market economy except

Greece, and well below, for example, Turkey, Romania, Outer Mongolia or Kazakhstan. Similar surveys, such as the Global Competitiveness Index published by the World Economic Forum, have similar results – for example Italy fares worse than any other Western European country on Transparency International's Bribe Payers Index.

We showed in Chapter 5 that the share of public spending in the Italian economy has steadily increased under Berlusconi governments, though it had fallen sharply in the years before he came to power in 2001. The third item on our list of conservative policies, keeping government spending and taxes low, is in Berlusconi's case clearly rhetoric, not reality.

The US government's survey of the Investment Climate in Italy starts with a quote from the "Financial Times": "Doing business in Italy is like driving with the brakes on", and goes on to say that "Italy's poor investment climate explains much of its low growth rate". There is little to choose between the attitudes of the two large political groupings in Italy when it comes to foreign investment – the right is unenthusiastic because of its nationalism, the left because it is less enthusiastic about private investment generally. This, too, is a part of what is lacking in Italy, and would normally be expected from a right-of-centre party: a programme devoted to improving the country's international competitiveness and its appeal to investors, whether foreign or domestic.

In the face of these disincentives for foreigners to invest in Italy, the counter-argument advanced by Berlusconi during a visit to the New York Stock Exchange in 2003 carries little weight. He said: "Italy is now a great country to invest in…Today we have fewer communists and those who are still there deny having been one. Another reason to invest in Italy is that we have beautiful secretaries."[119]

Small businesses are a vital part of the Italian economy, and they keenly desire all of the measures that were discussed above: lower taxes, simpler and more transparent regulations, measures to increase competitiveness. Ivan Palasgo, the President of the Association of Small and Medium Businesses in the Venice region recently said: "Here we need an economic and cultural revolution. It's time to make ourselves heard. Our businesses are at risk. We're still waiting for the promised reduction of taxes on businesses, which are currently at 57%." In the same vein, Diego Travan, representing the furniture industry in Udine – one of the local concentrations of small businesses which are the heartbeat of Italy's economy – said "We are still waiting for the liberal revolution which Berlusconi promised 15 years ago when he entered politics, and repeats at every election. In the rest of Europe centre-right governments undertake liberalising reforms, while Berlusconi goes in the opposite direction. He promised us three income tax bands, with the highest at 33%, and 15 years later it's more than 50%. Without mentioning the feudal, abstruse and complicated tax system". Mr Travan went on to say that he planned to start producing in France, where things were simpler.[120]

It appears that these Northern businessmen, feeling let down by Berlusconi, are looking instead to the Northern League to promote the liberalising policies that they want. Presumably they have nowhere else to turn, but as long as it remains a junior partner in a coalition with Berlusconi's party, its influence must remain limited, and in any event its attitude to foreign investment is even more xenophobic than that of its allies in government. Moreover, as Berlusconi's partner in government, the Northern League has been complicit in the recent economic failures

Not all readers may share the priorities expressed by these businessmen. But in most democratic countries there is a major national political party that does share them. One of the major tragedies of the Berlusconi era is that this is no longer the case in Italy. The assumption that because Berlusconi is a man of the right, he must favour business-friendly policies, is incorrect. As has often been remarked, the policies that he follows are specifically those that are friendly to *his* businesses. The polarisation of Italian politics into pro-Berlusconi and anti-Berlusconi camps (considered by the former to be "Communists") has deflected attention from the sad absence of any major party that advocates liberal economic policies. In his 2010 book "Forza, Italia" (available only in Italian translation), Bill Emmott, an ex-editor of The Economist, surveys a wide range of dynamic and competitive Italian businesses whose welfare would be actively promoted by most European governments, but which are left to flounder in Italy, where the government's energies are instead dominated by the attempt to secure its leader's impunity.

The question of whether one opposes or favours Berlusconi is in no way an issue about economic policy, nor about any of the issues which divide left from right in most democratic countries. Although he constantly invokes the values of liberty and democracy, these values are being insidiously undermined by the attack on legality and on plurality of information sources being mounted by Berlusconi's paradoxically named People of Freedom (PDL). Rightly seen, regardless of where one stands on a left-right spectrum, *alle Menschen werden Brüder* where this matter is concerned.

Farewell, Silvio

As of Spring 2011, it seems likely that Berlusconi will use his indictment for juvenile prostitution and abuse of office as a launching-pad for an even more ambitious and damaging attack on the justice system than anything yet seen. He retains a majority in Parliament. Gianfranco Fini has definitively broken with him, but many of the politicians who originally left Berlusconi's party at the same time as Fini have now drifted back, after a close-run vote of confidence in December 2010 left Berlusconi with a small majority. Berlusconi undertook a shopping spree among those parliamentarians who are willing to trade support for some tangible advantage that he is willing to offer – the promise of office, a bypass in a constituency, the fear of losing the pensions available to members of parliament and so forth.

We saw in Chapter 7 how he appeared to try to secure Senate votes by persuading his friends in RAI to offer jobs to young women favoured by Senators. There is no evidence that this particular technique was used this time round, but plenty of other inducements have been offered. In early 2011, an opposition member of parliament named Bucchino complained that one of Berlusconi's henchmen had offered him €150,000 in exchange for his joining the group of so-called "responsible" members who can be relied upon to vote for Berlusconi in any confidence vote. On hearing of this, another old hand commented that "we must be at the end-of-season sales. Three months ago [at the time of the close-run confidence vote in December 2010] the going rate was €750,000. It's clear that he's now got all the votes he needs".

Berlusconi's fate is in the hands of the Northern League, whose willingness to collude in his attempts to evade punishment remains strictly conditional, and whose power and influence have never been so great. Although they, as much as Berlusconi, must bear responsibility for the mismanagement of the Italian economy – Finance Minister Tremonti is close to the League, though not a member – they remain popular in the North. They will support Berlusconi for as long as he promises to deliver the greater regional autonomy that they demand. There may be a limit to the extent to which they are willing to be seen to undermine the rule of law in his cause, but they have yet to make clear where that limit lies.

The changes which Berlusconi plans to introduce to the justice system will require modifying the constitution, and as such will require a larger majority than he commands, as well as a referendum which he would be unlikely to win. For as long as Berlusconi remains in power, his battle to

CHAPTER 9: DEMOCRACY OR THE RULE OF LAW

ensure his impunity will continue to absorb the government's energies. In this battle, he shares clear interests with many others who wish to remain unpunished. The resurgence of corruption and organised crime since 2001 is the prime reason for the economic failures that were documented in Chapter 5, and nothing will change while he survives politically. His electoral appeal has been severely eroded, but his control of the media – and hence, perhaps, his ability subsequently to regain public approval – remains unimpaired.

As Italy passes its 150th birthday as a nation – a low-key affair, since the Northern League does not regard it as a matter for celebration – the dangers that threaten Italian democracy seem as threatening as at any time since 1945. The spell that has been cast over the country since 1994 is as strong as ever. Yet it will eventually be broken; when it is, the revolt against corruption that started in 1992 and was then subverted may yet be brought to its rightful conclusion; and liberty and democracy may be re-established on their only durable foundations – the rule of law and freedom of information from a plurality of sources.

What is important in all this, for those observing Italy from outside, is what it teaches about the way in which similar episodes can be avoided in other countries. There are three clear lessons:

- Conflicts of interest must be taken seriously. Those who are active players in the world of business cannot at the same time be permitted to have a role in setting the rules of the game.
- Plurality of information sources must be rigorously guarded.
- If a choice has to be made between the will of the people and the rule of law, it is the rule of law that must be given priority.

The story that this book tells is unfinished, but its outcome matters less than these lessons. The only forecast that can be ventured is the one made by Jim Morrison of The Doors:

The old get old and the
Young get stronger.
May take a week and it
May take longer.

INDEX

AC Milan, 48, 96, 99, 146
Accardi, Salvatore, 42, 43, 44
Agrama, Frank, 46, 109
Air France, 132-136
Air One, 134, 135, 143, 239
Aitken, Jonathan, 94
Aktiengesellschaft für Immobilienanlagen, 34
Alfano, Angelino, 91, 111, 113, 118
Alitalia, 132-145, 239
All Iberian, 100, 103-108
Alleanza Nazionale, 58, 76, 143, 166, 211
Almirante, Giorgio, 59
Amato, Giuliano, 52, 137
Ambrosoli, Giorgio, 31
Andreotti, Giulio, 30, 45, 48, 55, 97
Arcore, 17, 19, 36, 37, 55, 64, 69, 70, 112
Ariosto, Stefania, 96, 209
Armati, Federico, 163, 164
Attanasio, Diego, 111
Azzaretto family, 30, 32
Bacigalupo Football Club, 37, 68, 69
Balzac, Honoré de, 48
Banco Ambrosiano, 31, 93
Barber, Tony, 121, 132, 143
Batliner, Herbert, 30
Ben Ammar, Tariq, 105, 106
Benigni, Roberto, 56, 221
Bergamasco, Giorgio, 36
Berlusconi, Luigi, 29, 30, 31

Berlusconi, Paolo, 47, 63, 64, 102
Bernasconi, Carlo, 111
Berruti, Massimo Maria, 38, 92, 99, 102
Biagi, Marco, 126
Bingham, Tom, 228
Boffo, Dino, 208, 210, 211, 215, 219
Bondi, Sandro, 204, 216
Bonincontro, Giuseppe, 43, 44
Bontate, Stefano, 68, 69,-744
Borsellino, Paolo, 41, 76, 77, 140, 210
Bossi, Umberto, 31, 54, 60, 64, 141, 164
Brancher, Aldo, 53, 95
Brugherio, 32, 33, 35, 58
Brunetta, Renato, 168, 219
Cagliari, Gabriele, 53
Calderoli, Roberto, 225
Calvi, Roberto, 31, 93
Cancemi, Salvatore, 77, 78, 96
Cantieri Riuniti Milanesi, 37
Carfagna, Mara, 167, 185, 191
Cartotto, Ezio, 16, 30, 56, 57, 59, 84
Casati Stampa, Annamaria, 36, 40
Cecchi Gori, Mario, 61, 145
Century One, 100, 108
Chiesa, Mario, 51
Ciampi, Carlo Azeglio, 117, 147
Ciancimino, Massimo, 83, 84
Ciancimino, Vito, 38
Cinà, Gaetano, 37, 67-75
Cirami Law, 115

INDEX

Cito, Ferdinando, 17, 18, 37
Codignoni, Angelo, 16
Colannino, Roberto, 134, 145, 146
Confalonieri, Fedele, 17, 19, 32, 57, 62, 93, 210
Constitutional Court, 45, 114, 147, 219
Corte di Cassazione, 91, 98, 112, 116
Cozzolino, Domenico, 175
Craxi, Bettino, 45-53, 77, 92, 95, 100-107, 172, 173, 176, 182
Cucuzza, Salvatore, 78
D'Addario, Patrizia, 141, 188, 191, 192, 193, 194, 195, 214-216
D'Alema, Massimo, 65, 187, 188, 213
Dal Santo, Giovanni, 43
Daley, Arthur, 20
De Benedetti, Carlo, 47, 53, 97, 98, 107, 210, 212
Dell'Oglio, Carla, 33
Dell'Utri, Marcello, 12, 19, 24, 32, 37, 38, 42, 56, 57, 67-84, 92, 95, 96, 158-159, 220, 237
Di Carlo, Francesco, 69, 70, 73
Di Pietro, Antonio, 51-54, 64, 95, 141, 148, 209, 210, 220
Diakron, 58, 59
Dini, Lamberto, 64
Doris, Ennio, 48
Dragoni, Gianni, 136
Dulcamara, Dr, 205
Edilnord, 32, 34, 38, 39, 92, 99, 102, 146
el-Mahroug, Karima ("Ruby Rubacuori"), 161, 195, 196, 197
Emmott, Bill, 241
Englaro, Eluana, 237
Europa 7, 147, 148, 151
ex-Ciriello Law, 114
Falcone, Giovanni, 77, 140
Farefuturo, 166, 168
Fauci, Jimmy, 72, 73
Fede, Emilio, 177, 178

Feltri, Vittorio, 166, 184, 185, 191, 192, 207, 208, 209, 211, 216, 217
Finanzierungsgesellschaft für Residenzen, 33, 34
Fine, Cordelia, 17
Fini, Gianfranco, 54, 60, 77, 166, 169, 211, 219, 226
Fininvest, 16, 17, 32, 38-48, 53-58, 62, 92-95, 98-108, 203, 210-212, 239
Flaminio, Gino, 177, 182
Forlani, Arnaldo, 45, 55
Forza Italia, 16, 56, 58, 60, 64, 77, 84, 166, 204, 226, 227
Foscale, Giancarlo, 103
Galliano, Antonio, 69
Gardini, Raul, 53, 145
Gasparri, Maurizio, 147, 148
Gelli, Licio, 31, 93
Ghaddafy, Muammar, 204, 206, 233, 234
Ghedini, Niccolò, 174, 175, 186, 191, 214
Giannini, Silva-Maria, 138
Gilmour, David, 19, 226
Giuffrida, Francesco, 39, 40, 41, 42
Grado, Nino, 72
Graviano Brothers 79, 80, 81
Guarino, Mario, 93
Guerra, Maria Cecilia, 138
Guzzanti, Paolo, 70, 234
Guzzanti, Sabina, 168
Hill, Benny, 20
Il Giornale, 47, 53, 63, 157, 166, 180, 185, 206-215
Inzaranto, Antonio, 43
Johnson, Boris, 116
La 7, 61, 145, 146, 153
La discesa in campo, 55
La Repubblica, 45, 47, 48, 97, 138, 170, 180, 183, 185, 215
Lane, David, 23, 55
Lario, Veronica, 23, 49, 169, 170, 183, 184, 185

Lentini, 96, 98, 99, 100
Letizia, Elio, 172, 173, 176, 177, 179, 182, 183
Letizia, Noemi, 121, 169-186, 193
Lufthansa, 135
Lunardi, Pietro, 141
Mafia, 24, 31, 38, 41, 42, 67-84, 96, 141, 209
Malpensa, 133, 135
Mammì law, 45, 47, 48, 100, 102, 103, 207
Mangano, Vittorio, 31, 37, 68-81, 96
Mani Pulite, 20, 52, 53, 63, 64, 115, 145, 209
Maranelli, Adriana, 40
Marcinkus, Paul, 31
Marrazzo, Piero, 216, 217
Matera, Barbara, 166, 170
Mediaset, 46, 61, 64, 107, 108, 138, 145-157, 164, 165, 166, 177, 222
Mediatrade, 46
Mediolanum, 48, 102
Medvedev, Dmitri, 19
Merkel, Angela, 18, 30, 234
Mesiano, Raimondo, 212, 219
Metta, Vittorio, 47, 48, 96, 97, 98
Milan 2, 34, 35, 38
Milano 3, 40
Mill, John Stuart, 13, 227
Mills, David, 30, 90, 99-112, 185, 220
Minetti, Nicole, 196, 197, 198, 200, 219, 230
Minzolini, Augusto, 158, 162, 214
Mondadori, 45, 47, 48, 53, 90, 96, 97, 98, 102, 106, 116, 147, 149, 150, 175, 210, 212, 217
Montanelli, Indro, 23, 37, 46, 47, 53, 55, 63, 65, 91, 95, 183, 193, 206, 208, 210, 220
Montereale, Barbara, 192, 193, 214
Moroni, Sergio, 52
Mubarak, Hosni, 196, 198, 201

Mussolini, Benito, 41, 47, 54, 59, 60, 143, 220
Napolitano, Giorgio, 231
Northern League, 51, 53, 54, 57, 60, 64, 133, 135, 141, 143, 164, 170, 225, 241
Obama, Barack, 18, 19, 139, 189, 206, 235
P2, 31, 64, 93, 94
Palina, 40
Pecorella Law, 117
Pirelli, 134, 145
Porrà, Enrico, 40
Previti, Cesare, 34, 36, 37, 48, 92, 96, 97, 107, 115, 116, 209
Previti, Umberto, 37
Prodi, Romano, 107, 116, 124, 137, 144, 165, 179, 186, 187, 209, 220, 226
Prostate, 192, 207
Provenzano, Bernardo, 78, 84
Publitalia, 38, 58
Putin, Vladimir, 16, 193, 204, 216, 233
Queen Elizabeth II, 19
RAI, 45, 56, 145, 148, 151-157, 163-166, 213, 215
Rapisarda, Filippo Alberto, 38, 73
Rasini, Banca, 29, 30, 31, 32, 34, 39, 41
Rete 4, 45, 147, 148
Rete Sicilia, 42
Reteitalia, 99
Riina, Totò, 74, 75, 77, 78, 96, 141
Ruggeri, Giovanni, 35, 93
Saccà, Agostino, 164, 165
Sanjust, Virginia, 163, 166
Santanchè, Daniela, 184, 185
Sargent, John, 18
Saviano, Roberto, 32
Scapagnini, Mario, 204, 205
Sciascia, Salvatore, 40, 102
Segni, Mario, 224

INDEX

Segrate, 34, 35
Sgarbi, Vittorio, 204
Shelley, Percy Bysshe, 236
Shinawatra, Thaksin, 223
Sindona, Michele, 31, 93
Sky, 22, 151, 152, 153, 154, 155, 164, 206, 239
Smith, Adam, 22, 211
Spatuzza, Gaspare, 79- 81, 158
Squillante, Renato, 92
Standa, 56
Stille, Alexander, 23, 55, 146
Sucato, Vicenzo, 42, 43, 44
Sylos Labini, Paolo, 13, 21, 37
Tangentopoli, 51, 53, 57, 95, 157
Tarantini, Gianpaolo, 187, 192, 193, 194, 195, 214
Telepiù, 100, 102, 103, 152
Teresi, Girolamo ("Mimmo"), 68, 73, 74
Teresi, Mimmo, 69, 72, 73
Thatcher, Margaret, 48, 57, 131, 143
The Economist, 34, 38, 39
Travaglio, Marco, 39, 48, 63, 140, 144, 208, 210, 216, 220
Tremonti, Giulio, 64, 138, 139, 207
Treu, Tiziano, 127
Trotter, Derek, 20
Universal One, 100
Urbani, Giuliano, 57, 59

Vatican, 29, 30, 31, 55, 236, 237, 238
Velinismo, 168
Veltri, Elio, 39, 210
Ventura, Sofia, 168, 169, 170
Verzé, Don Luigi, 35
Villa Certosa, 167, 178, 186, 192, 193, 194, 213, 214
Wagner, Richard, 60
Zapatero, Jose, 194
Zappadu, Antonio, 186, 187, 218
Žižek, Slavoj, 18

ACKNOWLEDGMENTS...

To Tony Davies, Jane Hope and Prue de Vere Cole, who very kindly read the text and provided helpful suggestions.

To David Ellwood, of the University of Bologna, who over many years has gradually dispelled some of my ignorance of Italian politics.

To Anne-Sophie and the late Professor Michael Grant, without whom I would not have the relationship that I have to Italy.

To the Bigotti and De Santi families for helping to make that relationship enjoyable.

To Emily and Juliet for helpful suggestions about the cover.

To Wiltrud for everything else.

ABOUT THE AUTHOR

Charles Young has a bachelor's degrees in politics, philosophy and economics (Oxford) and a master's degree in economics (LSE). He worked as an economist for the Zambian government for four years before joining, and becoming a Senior Economic Adviser in, the UK Government Economic Service. He resigned to co-found LMC International, now the acknowledged source of global economic analysis of soft commodity markets. His work on the rubber and tyre industries led him later to found another company – also successful, but now part of a larger grouping – specialising in analysing and forecasting global motor vehicle production and sales. He acquired a life-long love of Italy after spending some of his childhood in Rome (where his father worked in the British Embassy) and continues to spend several months of each year there.

NOTES

1. J.S. Mill, Considerations on Representative Government, p.4
2. Il Fatto, 24/20/2009
3. Pinotti and Gümpel, L'Unto del Signore, p 94
4. La Stampa, 2/11/2009
5. A Mind of Its Own, p.23
6. Berlusconi in Tehran, Slavoj Zizek, London Review of Books, July 23rd 2009
7. Pinotti and Gümpel, L'Unto del Signore, p.98
8. David Gilmour, The Pursuit of Italy, p. 380
9. See http://www.youtube.com/watch?gl=IT&hl=it&v=WiYppEt5QSY
10. La Repubblica, 17/3/2003
11. ANSA, 11/1/2002
12. See, for example, Paolo Guzzanti, Guzzanti vs Berlusconi, p.40 and practically any book in English on the subject.
13. Paolo Sylos Labini, Berlusconi e gli Anticorpi, p.13
14. Adam Smith, The Wealth of Nations, p.377.
15. Marc Lazar, L'Italia sul filo del Rasoio, p. 93
16. Pinotti and Gümpel, L'Unto del Signore, p.23
17. Ibid, pp 40-43
18. Corriere della Sera, 20/4/1995, quoted in Travaglio and Gomez, Se li conosci, li eviti.
19. Roberto Saviano, Gomorrah, p. 216
20. David Lane, Berlusconi's Shadow, p. 47
21. Pinotti and Gümpel, L'Unto del Signore,p. 61
22. Alexander Stille, The Sack of Rome, p. 30
23. Ibid, p. 30
24. Paolo Guzzanti, Guzzanti vs Berlusconi, p.91
25. See the judgment in the 2004 Dell'Utri trial, pp. 700-850. It can be downloaded at http://www.narcomafie.it/sentenza_dellutri.pdf
26. 2004 Dell'Utri trial judgment, p. 897
27. Marco Travaglio and Elio Veltri, L'Odore dei Soldi, p. 153
28. ibid, p. 163
29. 2004 Dell'Utri trial judgment, p. 876.
30. Interview with Oscar Mammì, "Vanity Fair", 7/7/2005
31. Ezio Cartotto, reported in Marco Travaglio and Elio Veltri, L'Odore dei Soldi, p. 105
32. Dell'Utri appeal verdict, pp. 239-240
33. 2004 Dell'Utri trial judgment, pp 143-170.
34. Paolo Guzzanti, Guzzanti vs Berlusconi, p.43
35. 2004 Dell'Utri trial judgment, p. 389
36. Marco Travaglio and Elio Veltri L'Odore dei Soldi, p.40
37. Dell'Utri appeal verdict p.124

38 Dell'Utri appeal verdict p.243
39 Dell'Utri appeal verdict p.244
40 Dell'Utri appeal verdict p.262
41 Dell'Utri appeal verdict p.220
42 Dell'Utri appeal verdict p.273
43 Dell'Utri appeal verdict p.320
44 2004 Dell'Utri trial judgment, p. 1107, p.1110
45 Testimony reported in Marco Travaglio and Elio Veltri *L'Odore dei Soldi*, p.84
46 Archiviazione no. 1370/98, Tribunale di Caltanissetta, p. 16
47 Ibid, p. 20
48 Dell'Utri appeal verdict pp. 453-454
49 Dell'Utri appeal verdict pp. 493
50 *Il Giornale*, 21/12/2009
51 *Il Fatto Quotidiano*, 09/03/2011
52 *Repubblica*, 12/7/1998
53 *Repubblica*, 23/11/2009
54 *Il Fatto*, 22/10/2009
55 Sentence on the first round of Mills case, quoted in P. Gomez and A. Mascali, "*Il Regalo di Berlusconi*", p. 218
56 Sentence on the first round of Mills case, quoted in P. Gomez and A. Mascali, "*Il Regalo di Berlusconi*", p. 158
57 Sentence on the first round of Mills case, quoted in P. Gomez and A. Mascali, "*Il Regalo di Berlusconi*", p. 187
58 P. Scognamiglio, Unversity of Padua, *La Prescrizione dei Reati dopo la Legge ex Cirielli*, available at http://appinter.csm.it/incontri/relaz/12889.pdf
59 This point was argued by an ex-President of the Constitutional Court, Valerio Onida – see *Il Fatto Quotidiano* 3/3/2011.
60 OECD, Tax Policy Development in Italy
61 Report on Crime in Italy, Ministry of Internal Affairs, 20/6/2007
62 Martin Schindler, "The Italian Labour Market", IMF Working Paper, March 2009
63 *La Repubblica*, 13/3/2008
64 http://www.lavoce.info/articoli/-fisco/pagina1000965.html
65 Financial Times, 21/5/2008
66 Quoted in Marco Travaglio and Beatrice Borromeo, *Annozero*, p.60
67 Marco Travaglio, *Passaparola*, 13/7/2009
68 Alexander Stille, The Sack of Rome, p. 280-84
69 *L'Espresso*, 12/3/2009
70 BusinessWeek, 4/2/2010
71 *La Repubblica*, 29/10/1994
72 Betjeman, Collected Poems, "In a Bath Tea-Shop"
73 *Corriere della Sera*, 21/12/2007

NOTES

74 *El Claron*, 5/7/2008
75 *Il Giornale*, 24/4/2009
76 *Corriere della Sera*, 29/4/2009
77 Peter Gomez, Marco Lillo, Marco Travaglio, *Papi*, p.130
78 ibid, p.133
79 *La Repubblica*, 3/5/2009
80 Peter Gomez, Marco Lillo, Marco Travaglio, *Papi*, p.209
81 *Il Mattino*, 25/5/2009
82 ANSA, 21/10/2006
83 *La Repubblica*, 24/5/2009
84 *La Repubblica*, 28/5/2009
85 *La Repubblica*, 24/5/2009
86 Peter Gomez, Marco Lillo, Marco Travaglio, *Papi* p. 189
87 ibid p. 241
88 *Corriere della Sera*, 17/6/2009
89 *The Observer*, 21/6/2009
90 *Sunday Times*, 28/6/2009
91 *Unità*, 21/7/2009
92 Interview with T.N., born in Milan on 07/05/1990, reported by Milan magistrates and reproduced in various newspapers, including *Il Fatto Quotidiano* 01/03/2011
93 Transcript of Minetti interview with magistrates, 30/1/2011
94 http://corrispondenti.net/external_link.html?http://www.rainews24.it/Notizia.asp?NewsID=59833
95 *La Stampa*, 2/11/2009
96 *Il Giornale*, 14/9/2009
97 Marco Travaglio, *Passaparola*, 8/2/2010
98 *Corriere della Sera*, 20/9/2009
99 *Corriere della Sera*, 27/11/2009
100 *Il Giornale*, 16/12/2009
101 Elio Veltri, *Toghe Rosse*, p. 154
102 *Il Fatto*, 7/11/2009
103 *La Repubblica*, 10/11/2009
104 David Gilmour, *The Pursuit of Italy*, p.390
105 *Corriere della Sera*, 13/5/2008
106 *La Repubblica*, 4/11/2009
107 Tom Bingham, *The Rule of Law*, p. 4
108 John Stuart Mill, "On Representative Government", p 297
109 *The Observer*, 21/6/2009
110 *The Daily Telegraph*, 29/11/2010
111 Paolo Guzzanti, *Guzzanti vs Berlusconi*, p. 297
112 Shelley, *The Revolt of Islam*, Canto 1, Verse 29
113 Friedrich Nietzsche, "*Die fromme Beppa*", in "*Die fröhliche Wissenschaft*"

IMPUNITY BERLUSCONI'S GOAL AND ITS CONSEQUENCES

114 Pinotti and Gümpel, *L'Unto del Signore*, p. 184
115 The Times, 10/2/2009
116 *Il Giornale* 1/4/2010
117 Pinotti and Gümpel *L'Unto del Signore*, p. 141
118 *La Repubblica*, 20/3/2010
119 Time Magazine, Berlusconi's worst gaffes
120 *Il Fatto*, 17/10/2009
121 La Stampa, 25/2/2011

NOTES

IMPUNITY BERLUSCONI'S GOAL AND ITS CONSEQUENCES

NOTES